RSAC

DEC ▩▩ 1993

D0022623

PLEASE RETURN THIS ITEM
BY THE DUE DATE TO ANY
TULSA CITY-COUNTY LIBRARY.

FINES ARE 5¢ PER DAY; A
MAXIMUM OF $1.00 PER ITEM.

DATE DUE		
FEB 15 1994		
MAR 0 1 1994		
MAY 1 1995		
JUL 3 1 1995		
DEC 08 1995		
APR 1 6 1997		
JUL 1 2 1999		

Printed
in USA

AMERICAN POLICY AND AFRICAN FAMINE

Recent Titles in
Contributions in Afro-American and African Studies

Visible Now: Blacks in Private Schools
Diana T. Slaughter and Deborah J. Johnson, editors

Feel the Spirit: Studies in Nineteenth-Century Afro-American Music
George R. Keck and Sherrill V. Martin, editors

From a Caste to a Minority: Changing Attitudes of American Sociologists
Toward Afro-Americans, 1896-1945
Vernon J. Williams, Jr.

African–American Principals: School Leadership and Success
Kofi Lomotey

Class and Consciousness: The Black Petty Bourgeoisie in South Africa,
1924 to 1950
Alan Gregor Cobley

Black Novelist as White Racist: The Myth of Black Inferiority
in the Novels of Oscar Micheaux
Joseph A. Young

Capital and the State in Nigeria
John F. E. Ohiorhenuan

Famine in East Africa: Food Production and Food Policies
Ronald E. Seavoy

Archetypes, Imprecators, and Victims of Fate: Origins and Developments
of Satire in Black Drama
Femi Euba

Black and White Racial Identity: Theory, Research, and Practice
Janet E. Helms, editor

Black Students and School Failure: Policies, Practices, and Prescriptions
Jacqueline Jordan Irvine

Anne, the White Woman in Contemporary African-American Fiction:
Archetypes, Stereotypes, and Characterizations
Anna Maria Chupa

AMERICAN POLICY AND AFRICAN FAMINE

The Nigeria–Biafra War, 1966–1970

Joseph E. Thompson

Contributions in Afro–American and African Studies,
Number 130

GREENWOOD PRESS
NEW YORK • WESTPORT, CONNECTICUT • LONDON

Library of Congress Cataloging-in-Publication Data

Thompson, Joseph E., 1938-
    American policy and African famine : the Nigeria-Biafra War,
1966-1970 / Joseph E. Thompson.
        p. cm. — (Contributions in Afro-American and African
studies, ISSN 0069-9624 ; no. 130)
    Includes bibliographical references.
    ISBN 0-313-27218-2 (lib. bdg. : alk. paper)
    1. Nigeria—History—Civil War, 1967-1970—Civilian relief.
2. Food relief, American—Nigeria, Eastern. 3. United States—
Foreign relations—Nigeria. 4. Nigeria—Foreign relations—United
States. I. Title. II. Series.
DT515.836.T46 1990
966.905′2—dc20   89-23353

British Library Cataloguing in Publication Data is available.

Copyright © 1990 by Joseph E. Thompson

All rights reserved. No portion of this book may be
reproduced, by any process or technique, without the
express written consent of the publisher.

Library of Congress Catalog Card Number: 89-23353
ISBN: 0-313-27218-2
ISSN: 0069-9624

First published in 1990

Greenwood Press, 88 Post Road West, Westport, CT 06881
An imprint of Greenwood Publishing Group, Inc.

Printed in the United States of America

The paper used in this book complies with the
Permanent Paper Standard issued by the National
Information Standards Organization (Z39.48-1984).

10 9 8 7 6 5 4 3 2 1

966.9052 T374am 1990
Thompson, Joseph E.,
American policy and African

For Susanne

TULSA CITY-COUNTY LIBRARY

Contents

Illustrations

Maps

Figures

Tables

"The Good Samaritan was the man who stopped and helped. The others in the parable just passed by. They did not injure the man--they just passed by. For us who believe in the unity of mankind...it is unthinkable to pass by. We must stop and help. Indecision and inaction mean social and moral irresponsibility."

Thomas Melady

Preface

When the killing and starvation in Biafra became front-page material in the daily press during the summer of 1968, U.S. officials felt pressured by growing domestic demands to have America become more involved with the civil war in Nigeria. The sudden increase in U.S. private and public contributions to the relief need of the secessionist territory initially confused the government bureaucrats. As a result of their specific decisions to become more embroiled in this West African conflict that was using famine as a weapon of war, official U.S. neutrality toward Nigeria was stretched to eventually allow for a very activist policy of humanitarian assistance for Biafra.

This book describes the events and decisions that led to the increased American involvement in the conflict, while the United States was trying to extricate itself from the Vietnam conflict. Those domestic and international pressures that brought about the eventual dichotomous U.S. policies are examined along with the reasons why they were sustained for such an extended period. The conflict of policies was more than a question of semantics because America had become so deeply involved in relief and humanitarian programs in Biafra that the United States was the chief supporter of those groups pressing for Biafran self-determination.

The Epilogue reflects on the plight of famine victims in Africa today and the question of American involvement. At the root of these political and bureaucratic struggles are the different conceptions about the requisites for international peace and security on the one hand, and international justice on the other hand.

AMERICAN POLICY
AND
AFRICAN FAMINE

Map 1. Nigerian Ethnic Groups, 1966

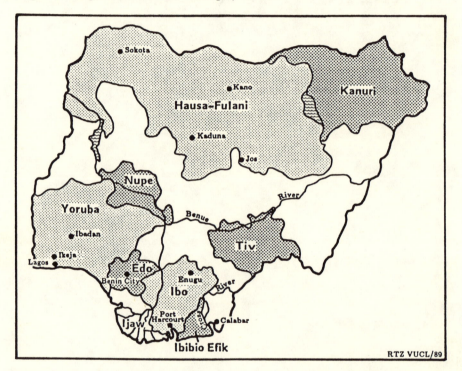

Source: Adapted by Villanova University Cartographic Laboratory, Villanova, Pennsylvania, from
John de St. Jorre, The Brothers' War (Boston: Houghton Mifflin, 1977), front endpaper.

Introduction

On October 1, 1960, Nigeria received its independence from the United Kingdom of Great Britain and Northern Ireland. It emerged as the largest and most populous Commonwealth state in West Africa. In retrospect, Nigeria's internal ethnic fragmentation, held together by a fragile parliamentary federation, was destined to be resolved by civil war because Nigerian and British politicians failed to develop a bridge between their citizens and their government.

The British-style structure of "indirect rule" (governmental rule through established indigenous authority[1]) in Nigeria was organized before and after independence around a loose federation of regional territories. An extraordinary complex of ethnic groups totaling approximately 55 million Nigerians were governed within these administrative regions, and each region was dominated by one of the country's three major ethnic groups. The Northern Region was ruled for centuries by the politically conservative Muslim emirates. Largest in territorial size and population, Nigeria's northern tropical grassland and savanna region was governed by the Hausa-Fulani people. Premier Sir Ahmadu Bello was their religious and dynastic political leader. The other northern peoples, most of whom share the Islamic faith, are minority groups, such as the Kanuri, Nupe, and Tiv.

Second in population but first in natural wealth, the Eastern Region was governed by the Ibo people. Traditionally ruled by democratic councils, the Ibos, who quickly accepted western education with its mobility and Christianity, always resented and opposed the country's national domination by the north. However, the eastern rain forest region, which is peopled by minority groups such as the Efik, Ibibio and Ijaw, were not united by either religion or politics.

The national capital of Nigeria is Lagos, located in the western grassland region. The Western Region, governed by the Yoruba people, had been the first to be exposed to European culture but lacked the natural resources and population to challenge the other groups for national domination. The three-way political (north, east, west) and ethnic (Hausa-Fulani, Ibo, Yoruba) split prevented a direct confrontation between the north and south to control Nigeria.

The American University Foreign Area Studies group were correct when they wrote: "In 1962 the plan to create the new Mid-Western Region from the eastern provinces of the Western Region further complicated the country's internal administrative situation and prepared the way for unprecedented political agitation."[2]   The creation of this fourth region, embracing other diverse minority groups such as the Edo people who almost always supported policies similar to those of the Eastern Region, was to reopen the discussion of a general reorganization of Nigeria. The Premier of the Eastern Region, Michael Okpara, was the most vocal advocate of moving beyond Nigeria's four regions to a larger number of smaller states in a federal system similar to that of the United States. This would accommodate the growing ethnic expressions in Nigeria. It is also possible to suggest that behind the Ibo plan was a wish to break up northern control.

Attempts to change or shift the existing regional ethnic coalitions were never successful, and so Nigeria's tenuous framework continued to be governed on the colonial foundation of northern political hegemony. But hegemony had its price. The ethnic and regional identities became the basis for separate Nigerian political parties. Even before the nationalist movements brought independence, the adversarial competition among the country's leaders had divided the political system into the Northern Peoples Congress party (NPC) controlled by Bello, who was the traditional leader of the Hausa-Fulani; the Yoruba Action Group party lead by Chief Obafemi Awolowo; and the Ibo National Council of Nigerian Citizens party (NCNC) led by Dr. Nnamdi Azikiwe.

The first federal election in 1959 resulted in no clear majority ruling party for Nigeria, although the NPC held more seats than either the Action Group or the NCNC. The most likely coalition government based on party issues would have been between the Action Group and the NCNC. But the fact that Awolowo and Azikiwe were personally incompatible only added to the already existing Yoruba-Ibo rivalry. Their personal struggle for power made it impossible for any cooperative action between these two parties. Therefore, the NCNC struck a deal with the NPC to create a coalition government with Sir Abubakar Tafawa Balewa (north) as the country's first Prime Minister, Azikiwe (east) as Nigeria's Head of State, and Awolowo (west) as leader of the government's parliamentary loyal opposition. But Awolowo and 18 other Action Group leaders were soon linked to a conspiracy to overthrow the government and summarily imprisoned at the end of 1962.

The NPC formed another uneasy coalition government with the NCNC when Nigeria became a republic on October 1, 1963. It followed as no surprise to anyone that Balewa was elected as the republic's Prime Minister and Samuel Akintola, who was staunchly allied with Premier Bello of the north, was made Premier of the Western Region. The political scene became more complicated in early 1964 when Akintola formed a new party--the Nigerian National Democratic party (NNDP)-- that attempted to unite all the former members of the Western Region government. But the NCNC leaders denounced the new party as a tool of the NPC and allied itself (NCNC) with the remnants of the Action Group in the Western Region to oppose the NNDP administration. This unstable regional power structure was maintained until the violence and political corruption of the Western Region's 1964 and 1965 elections challenged the legitimacy of Nigeria's government. These election and corruption events also called into question America's fossilized perception of Nigeria.

The origin of the U.S. government policy toward Nigeria is to be found in the post-World War II period. Sanford Unger wrote for many who believed that America was slow to recognize or admit its participation in the racist attitude of the European colonizers.[3] However, such attitudes toward Africa began to change during the Eisenhower administration when it reluctantly agreed to move America and Americans toward a more positive approach in domestic civil rights. The 1960 International Year of Africa movement augmented this evolution in U.S. policy toward Africa and consequently toward Nigeria.

These changes in perception were not readily accepted by many in the American bureaucracy. They often waited until there was no other alternative. For example, official U.S. recognition of Nigeria occurred only one month before its independence. But, Vice President Richard M. Nixon, who attended the Ghanaian independence ceremonies in 1957, very proudly recalled becoming aware of Africa's growing importance "to the strength and stability of the free world" during his trips to Liberia, Ethiopia, and Sudan. This unique White House public expression of African awareness became the political touchstone Secretary of State John Foster Dulles used to encourage the creation of a separate African Bureau within the restructured State Department.

This momentum to recognize Africa's legitimate role in American foreign policy was temporarily suspended the following year with the loss of Dulles in 1959. Because the new African Bureau was now without its champion, the "old guard" State Department bureaucrats were relieved when the African policy formation process was restored to their former European sections. When President Dwight D. Eisenhower became his own Secretary of State, the Assistant Secretary of State for African Affairs Joseph Satterthwaite and Deputy Assistant Secretary Joseph Palmer also felt more comfortable with these restorations of policy-making priorities and policy leadership.[4] Eisenhower had always agreed with the European foreign policies toward their African colonies and, similarly, these beliefs permeated the attitudes of established Foreign Service Officers (FSOs). Palmer, whose job it was to express the government's conservative approach toward Africa, often cited the period's familiar phrases concerning the dangers of any "premature independence" in Africa without some "orderly transition."[5]

If the administration's hesitancy toward recognizing any African states was well known, Congress was also marginally interested in this new field. The Senate created the Subcommittee on Africa in 1958 in response to Dulles's request for a new Bureau of African Affairs. Senator John F. Kennedy (D-MA) accepted the position as the first subcommittee chairman because it was neither active nor burdensome.

Compared to the Senate, the House of Representatives Subcommittee on Africa, which was created in 1945, was more interested in the African continent.   Congressman Barrett O'Hara (D-IL), the first subcommittee chairman, was known to be personally interested in Africa as were other subcommittee members such as Charles Diggs (D-MI) and Frances Bolton (R-OH). But even these congressional interests were dealt with on an informational and personal level for many years.

It remained for the 1960 presidential election to make an issue of the extent of U.S. support for European colonial policies vis-à-vis African demands for self-determination. Satterthwaite was often at pains to explain why Eisenhower's administration had not extended formal diplomatic recognition and official representatives to several African states that had already been granted independence by the fall of 1960.   This was no oversight by the administration but a deliberate decision; a decision reflected in the last two years of the Eisenhower administration wherein the United States had reduced diplomatic representation in Africa by nearly 40 percent.   It was during the last months in office that the administration tried to catch up with events. Their most blatant political vulnerability was covered by the president's speech before the United Nations General Assembly.   A public about-face in American foreign policy, Eisenhower now asked the international community to respect the African peoples right to choose their own way of life and to determine for themselves the course they choose to follow.

Beyond this rhetoric it remained for President Kennedy and his administration to implement and solidify the U.S. policy change toward Africa with increased loans and grants, the "Food for Peace" program, Peace Corps volunteers, military aid, and other such programs.   George Mennon "Soapy" Williams, with his strong record in support of domestic civil rights issues, was appointed to be the new Assistant Secretary of State for African Affairs. This appointment was in all probability intended to be a direct signal to the State Department policymakers--they were to abandon their over-sensitivity to European interests in Africa and U.S. cautiousness toward African states in favor of the idealism of "Africa for the Africans."   However well meaning the Kennedy administration intended their demand for an innovative policy approach to be toward Africa, it did not totally eradicate the belief of many old guard bureaucrats who decided to continue their European perceptions by past training.   Although muted, a definite dichotomy began to develop between the FSOs who believed in the new approach toward African states and those who persisted in the traditional metropoles approach.

This dichotomy, which was to become one of the basic elements of confused U.S. entanglement in the Nigerian conflict, began in the field with Eisenhower's appointment of Palmer as the first American Ambassador to the newly independent state of Nigeria.   Palmer had the ideal qualifications for a traditional ambassador.[6]   His first official contact with Africa was an assignment to the British East African colony of Kenya in June 1941.   After six years of successful field service in the capital Nairobi, Palmer returned to Washington as the Acting Assistant Chief of the Division of African Affairs, and within one year was made the Acting Chief.   These contacts and understanding of Britain's African and Commonwealth politics were further broadened by his four and a half years in London.

In October 1953 Palmer returned to Washington as the Deputy Director of the Office of European Regional Affairs, and three years later he was appointed for one and a half years as Satterhwaite's Deputy Assistant Secretary for African Affairs.   Palmer's service in this position and, more importantly, his often expressed desire to return to field operations was rewarded with an appointment as Consul General to Salisbury, South Africa.   After serving only two years with the personal rank of Minister in Salisbury, Palmer was suddenly informed by the Eisenhower White House that they intended to have him installed, one month before its scheduled independence, as the first American Ambassador to Nigeria.

Palmer's four years as ambassador allowed him the time to become the principal field architect of American policy toward Nigeria.   He eagerly facilitated the desires of the new political leaders of both Nigeria and America.   "They became highly conscious of their mutual desire to cultivate a more intensive relationship, each wishing to promote their own interests in the evolving postcolonial regional setting. The pace and extent of the developing links between the two countries was so rapid that by 1965 it was possible for Nigeria to diversity its foreign economic and political ties from exclusive dependence on Great Britain to a multilateral interrelationship embracing both the United Kingdom and the U.S."[7]

Another important aspect of this policy entailed strong U.S. support of the British notion that there must always be a united and "One Nigeria."   The British policy toward a geographically united Nigeria complemented the existing American attitude that bigger is better, that is, it is better to have one large viable country than three small struggling "regional" countries.   Needless to say, the British did have their unique perception of Nigeria that was based on a deep sense of paternalism.   In more concrete political terms Britain had always formulated policies in Nigeria with an eye to the effect of events on the influence it had and hoped to maintain in West Africa.   In this manner, Nigeria became the British showcase in West Africa to which American officials traditionally deferred during periods of policy formulation.

Even at the end of Palmer's ambassadorial assignment in early 1964, when Nigeria's political, economic, and ethnic fabric began to demonstrate visible signs of stress and disorder, he adamantly demanded that the U.S. Embassy stand behind the One Nigeria policy. Palmer recalled these remarks from his last official private conversation as ambassador with Nigeria's Prime Minister Balewa:

> I asked him if I could talk with him frankly.
> He said, "Yes, I certainly wish you would." So
> I told him I was extremely concerned about the
> future, about the regional polarization of the

> country.   I told him the State gave me the
> impression of being a parliamentary democracy,
> but it wasn't.   It was an alliance of two
> regions against a third region, and at that
> time it was the North and the East against the
> West, which accounts for all the troubles they
> were having in the West.   I told him I was
> really very fearful that this was polarizing
> more and more. Some way had to be found for
> keeping the Nigerian system together.[8]

When the Nigerian hope of challenging the political domination of the NPC was diminished by the "fixed" results of the
country's 1963 census and the 1964-1965 elections, many
leaders of the southern political parties began to turn
their attention away from the ballot box to other methods of
change. Palmer recognized these growing forces of disunity
--regional ethnocentrism reinforcing political cleavages--
but he refused, as did the British and northern Nigerian
leaders, to accept them as inevitable.

The commitment to preserve the One Nigeria policy was
well established by the time Palmer was reassigned in February 1964 to Washington as the Deputy Director General of the
Foreign Service. President Lyndon B. Johnson, who initially
tolerated the Kennedy team's activist interest in Africa but
himself believed in the State Department's traditional
metropole policies, approved the new appointment of Elbert
Mathews[9] as the second American Ambassador to Nigeria.

Palmer felt that the structured American policy toward
Nigeria was secure when Mathews arrived in Lagos on April 1,
1964. This confidence was based on the assumption that this
appointment was just another standard operating procedure
for a soon to be retired FSO. It was intended to be just
simply an easy farewell between a faithful bureaucrat and
the foreign service. Mathews, a career minister since his
ambassadorial position in Liberia (1959-1962), accepted
without question the embassy's policy precepts. He reaffirmed it in his 1964 political and economic objectives in
the official document, "Country Assistance Strategy for
Nigeria."

> Nigeria is one of those foci of United States
> policy in Africa, and the United States assis-
> tance program is the central instrument in
> achieving United States foreign policy goals in
> Nigeria. The U.S. objective is the development
> of Nigeria as a strong united democratic, and
> generally independent nation that will encour-
> age emulation by other African states in exer-
> cising pro-Western influence on their policies
> --both bilaterally and through such organiza-
> tions as the Organizations for African Unity
> and the United Nations.[10]

Despite the feeling of a national crisis, which increased as
the time for the first national elections drew closer (it
was scheduled for December 1964), the newly arrived Mathews
was encouraged by the senior American embassy staff to sup-

port the <u>status</u> <u>quo</u> policy of One Nigeria.

When the results of Nigeria's December elections were announced in January 1965 it supported the continuation of northern control.   The following special eastern elections confirmed these results of political coalition, and Balewa formed another government wherein all executive power was held by the three ethnic parties ruling in each region. That, once again, had the effect of reinforcing regionalism and ethnocentric concentration of power (and its concomitant corruption) at the expense of national unity.

The U.S. Embassy reports, however, ignored the growing public and private dissatisfaction with Nigeria's political and economic drift away from democracy and tradition.   The Americans continued to blindly support the policy of a united Nigeria.   For example, when Mathews returned to the United States for some brief official business in May, the chargé d'affaires <u>ad</u> <u>interim</u> in Lagos, William Scott, sent several classified reports to the African Bureau under his own authorship in which he summarized the embassy approach in the following terms: "In recognition of Nigeria's strong commitment to Western values, United States policy has been directed at maximizing Nigerian independence by encouraging national unity, assisting economic development, and advising of Bloc dangers."[11]   Scott not only believed that the United States must continue to support and encourage Nigerian national unity but he went further in his reports than Mathews or Palmer had allowed themselves in official assessments of Nigeria events.   Scott formalized in his written report what had been up to that point a verbal assessment by the embassy staff, that is, a major threat to Nigeria's domestic system should be assigned to external forces.   In what was probably his reaction to the Congo (now Zaire) crisis,[12] Scott believed that Washington would give more attention and support to the One Nigeria policy if a verifiable link could be established between Nigeria's unrest and an increase in Soviet influence.

> The Embassy believes that progress in the achievement of U.S. objectives such as strengthening Nigerian unity and obtaining a satisfactory rate of economic growth will have a strong pre-emptive effect on any significant penetration of Nigeria by the Bloc.   There is need, however, to improve and to speed up the implementation of our programs, and to present a more forthcoming attitude toward international commodity problems.   Higher priority should also be given in the allocation of US aid to projects benefiting large elements of the population and particularly the welfare of the urban proletariat.
>
> As outlined in the Embassy's annual assessment (A-568), we should press the Government to carry out social and economic measures improving urban living and working standards and render all possible assistance in this regard; [U.S. covert support to a Nigerian trade move-

ment is deleted here;] be prepared to respond
quickly to Nigerian requests for military or
police assistance both in terms of training and
material; seek increased use in educational
institutions of materials building resistance
to Communism [; and, a U.S. covert support to
Nigerian education efforts deleted here].[13]

As orchestrated, Scott sent this document to Washington
while Mathews was there so that Mathews could use these
official testimonials from the field as reinforcements in
his argument to strengthen U.S. support for a One Nigeria
program. The embassy staff had also convinced Mathews that
a major cause of the early 1965 riots and government crisis
should be laid at the door of Communist-supported organizations in Nigeria. To prevent any additional "significant
penetration," Scott requested that the State Department
express total support for the existing Nigerian regime.
    At this point in time, the U.S. Embassy staff should be
classified as "clientele" field officers. This term, often
used in a derogatory manner, refers to those FSOs who put
the existing host regime policies first in their consideration rather than those of Washington. But this clientele
problem was more serious than Williams suspected because the
embassy staff were also losing touch with actual events as
they were happening throughout Nigeria. An examination of
the embassy airgram A-693 to Washington makes precisely this
point when it plays down Nigeria's rising intraethnic fears
and political corruption with the following analysis:

    While the Embassy and other observers felt late
    in 1964 that it was quite possible that another
    general strike, offering further opportunities
    for the labor leftists to exploit workers
    grievances, would take place in 1965...the pro-
    spects for another such strike in the immediate
    future have diminished. In part this is due
    to the distractions of the election crisis, the
    involvement of some sectors of the union lead-
    ership in political contests yet to be decided
    (as in the Western Region), and a seeming mood
    of general curiosity in the ranks of the public
    about how well the new Government established
    following the elections will perform in meeting
    social and economic problems. It is more
    likely that strikes will take place in given
    companies, industries or public and quasi-
    public sections (i.e., among teachers) rather
    than on an overall basis for the present. (End
    CONFIDENTIAL Begin UNCLASSIFIED [material])[14]

There is no indication of any impending crisis mentioned in
this report, nor any cause for serious reevaluation of the
Nigerian system.
    Hindsight, however, places the October 1965 elections in
the Western Region of Nigeria as the catalytic event for the
undoing of Britain's showcase. While one section of the
Western Region's electorate wanted the policies of the

incumbent government headed by Akintola to continue, another section of the Yoruba electorate continued to support the weakened Action Group and the imprisoned Awolowo. These elections were of considerable importance because the Western Region was considered the only political arena where opposition groups had any real potential for bringing about some change in the government. For this reason the western election campaign was ruthless and violent. Reportedly, thousands were killed in local violence, which continued beyond the campaign's conclusion. Force won the day, and Akintola's victory ensured the continued dominance of the northern party in Nigerian politics.

The perceived brutal fraudulence of Akintola's campaign sharply divided the Yoruba party. The NCNC party in the Eastern Region, which had become very dissatisfied with the ruling coalition government in Lagos, decided to support Akintola's opposition members during the election period. Now that the campaign was over, Premier Okpara summoned the British Deputy High Commissioner James Parker and the U.S. Consul General Robert J. Barnard to his office in Enugu (the capital of the Eastern Region). Okpara informed the two officials that Nigeria's national politics had taken a very dangerous turn, from the Ibo's viewpoint, that, if pursued further, might destroy the nation. He ardently suggested that the American and British officials do everything in their power to inform their respective countries so that developments leading to the break up of Nigeria would be prevented. Barnard and Parker did not hesitate to report this information.

Although the Western Region was soon pitched into bloody chaos, which rapidly assumed alarming proportions, Nigerian officials did not take any immediate corrective action. The government's false sense of security must be attributed to the belief that the domestic status quo could be maintained and to the belief that the British and the Americans would blindly support the ruling government. This support was so unquestioning that both the British and U.S. ambassadors let it be known that they would not accept any reports from their field officers that might be interpreted in any manner as undermining or contrary to the policies of the existing Nigerian regime. George Sherry, the U.S. Consul in Ibadan, drew Mathews's wrath in late 1965 for reporting "antigovernment" trends in local unrest. The British High Commissioner in Lagos also officially derided Parker, its resident diplomat, for his reporting of local disgust with the Nigerian government.[15] These field evaluations were more accurate than those of their respective embassies as testified to by the many indigenous public appeals for justice to Balewa. But Balewa himself was carefully abstaining from any action that would go against his party or the decisions of his superiors.

Balewa eventually recognized the gravity of Nigeria's disturbances, and he ordered the army to protect the new regional government of the West. But the self-imposed "clientism" belief in the security of the Nigerian government allowed the U.S. Embassy to put forward the best face on even these events in its reports to Washington. Although the country's unity was threatened, Mathews did not envision any necessary action by the Nigerian government beyond the denying of further involvement by external forces. These pedantic opinions of Nigerian events were initially stated seven months after his arrival in Nigeria and never altered. They were also part of his official report, "Country Assistance Strategy for Nigeria," sent to Washington.

> E. Support Action
> 3) The present army and civil police force are considered to be only marginal to adequately maintain internal security in light of the possibility of: 1) increasing unrest of labor and urban unemployment; 2) division of forces within the Nation--an outgrowth of the election and North-South tension; 3) hightened efforts by the CHICOMS, Soviet bloc or disaffected African countries to capitalize on any internal problems which might arise inside Nigeria.[16]

Barnard, who did not agree with his embassy's analysis concerning these events, held the opinion that the internal problems which might arise in Nigeria were far beyond the host government's control. His reports to Washington from Enugu were in direct opposition to the embassy's reports that Nigeria's present military police forces are quite capable of maintaining internal security. Barnard stressed that these forces were at minimal levels necessary in the event of a large scale challenge to law and order.

Mathews awoke in the early hours of January 15, 1966, to the news of Nigeria's first military coup. He soon learned that five army majors had convinced a small contingent of the Nigerian armed forces to rid their system of corruption by killing several important political and military leaders.[17] After the confusion of the night's killing, Major-General John Aguyi-Ironsi emerged as the Supreme Commander of the Nigerian Armed Forces by virtue of his being the ranking military survivor of the coup. He was given the position of Head of the Nigerian government by the surviving politicians in Lagos who had not fled the revolt.

This chaotic period posed numerous problems for Mathews and his staff. First, there was concern for the physical safety of American citizens in the country--businesspeople, religious leaders, social workers, visitors, and U.S. government personnel--who had to be accounted for and aided if necessary. Second, there was the need to know what had actually happened during the revolt. Third and most difficult, there was the problem of how to report this coup so that Washington's analysis of this sudden event would not expose the embassy's inability to adequately read Nigerian affairs.

Chagrined at being caught totally unaware by the revolt, American officials had to relearn a new bureaucracy. The decimation and flight of so many Nigerian politicians, appointed ministers and elected parliamentarians, precipitated a rush by all the embassies in Lagos for new contacts in Ironsi's military government. The new regime presented an unusual and awkward position for Mathews. Because Ironsi proved extremely self-effacing and difficult for senior embassy personnel to meet, Mathews had initially to direct his attention to lesser bureaucrats. In the meanwhile, U.S. Military Attaché Lt. Col. Arthur J. Halligan became the best situated American diplomat among the embassy staff because of his past normal and regular contacts with the Nigerian armed forces.

Imbued with the usual military belief in a unitary and hierarchical structure of command and supported by the British and American Ambassadors who accepted the advice of their military attachés, the Ironsi government issued "The Unification Decree: No. 34" on May 24. The stated intention was to transform the new Nigerian government into a unitary One Nigeria structure. It is very plausible that Ironsi's advisers believed that by replacing the four semiautonomous regions with provinces under the direct authority of a national military governor the corrupt political, regional, and ethnic causes of the Nigerian problem would be eliminated.[18]

What followed for Nigeria was a series of incredibly naive political miscalculations that hardened the northern suspicions that Ironsi sought to impose Ibo domination over the country. The Nigerians did not bury their ethnic or regional suspicions and fears that Ironsi, the British and the American officials had hoped would happen. Instead, the Nigerian people read the Unification Decree and the new military promotions (18 of the 21 officers promoted were Ibo) as Ironsi's ethnic and regional grasp for political power. In response to these government actions, northern Nigerians emerged from their state of shock and insecurity after the January assassinations believing that Ironsi was filling all positions of power with eastern bureaucrats and Ibo military personnel. Demonstrations began throughout the Northern Province against Ironsi's government and against all non-northern Nigerians. These gatherings quickly turned into violent and wholesale riots, especially against anyone from the Eastern Region/Province.

This sudden violence intensified the existing different perceptions of Nigeria that existed between the American Consulate in Enugu and the U.S. Embassy in Lagos. It also initiating a dysfunctional competition between the embassy's senior and junior staff members. The latter were being edged entirely out of circulation among Nigerian officialdom except to the extent that they competed with their embassy superiors. Senior diplomats, especially Mathews and Deputy Chief Clinton Olson,[19] attempted to meet as many senior Nigerian military officials as they could manage through the contacts that Halligan had developed, and the U.S. junior embassy staff struggled to meet with any lesser Nigerian civil servant they could find. Senior American FSOs found that their new xenophobic military counterparts, either by training or personal caution, provided nothing but brusque authorized, official information to foreigners. As a result of these sterile contacts Mathews and Olson became more and more isolated from independent viewpoints and speculative political thought that were available to the junior embassy staff and members of the different American consulates in the field. Eventually a clear schism developed between the different levels of information within the U.S. Embassy in

Lagos and between the embassy and its consulates.

These different perspectives of Nigerian events were now beyond the normal official differences that State Department analysts were accustomed to receiving. These differences between embassy reports and consulate reports became evident as the U.S. Consulate officials sent their reports directly to Washington. Significant regional differences in Nigeria had historically allowed the American consulates to report simultaneously to both their embassy in Lagos and the State Department's African Bureau in Washington.[20] Unlike U.S. Consul General Sherry in Ibadan, who was easily within the geographic controlling reach of his embassy, Barnard in the Enugu Consulate was at a good distance from the embassy-- inside the Eastern Region/Province, which was soon to become the secessionist territory of Biafra. Because of the embassy's refusal to consider Barnard's reports or attach his minority report to their official reports and the increasing pressure Barnard received from Mathews and Olson to conform to embassy guideline reporting, Barnard began to sidestep their approval by reporting first to Washington, then to Lagos.

Barnard's activities received the most punitive of the U.S. Embassy's wrath on its wayward consulate. The embassy tried throughout the Nigerian conflict with intermittent success to technically forbid the consulates to communicate directly with Washington. Although Barnard tactfully tried to cooperate with these embassy requests, he "forgot" when dramatic or important events occurred in the Eastern Region/ Province. Lacking the power of censorship that it exercised over its immediate staff, the U.S. Embassy fell back often to countering reports from its own consulates--Barnard would send information from the eastern point of view and Olson would supplement.

The African Bureau could no longer disguise the growing disparity from Palmer, Williams, or the secretary of state when the embassy and consulate reports contained significant conflicting information on the riots and killing in the northern regions of Nigeria. Barnard passed along the report of David Loshak, a <u>Daily Telegraph</u> reporter from London, that over 600 Ibos were killed by northern mobs that were demanding secession from Ironsi's Ibo-controlled government. Mathews sent along another report that agreed with the British report that officially only 92 deaths occurred in the Northern Region/Province. What could not be cosmetically altered by Washington or the U.S. Embassy were the larger subsequent waves of massacres four months later, which were to be markedly less discriminate.

Barnard's reported rumors of another possible military counter-coup was also discounted by Mathews because Ironsi and his military staff discounted such a possibility.   Not surprisingly, therefore, Mathews and Olson were again caught by the confusion of the Friday morning news of the night's counter-coup rebellion.   Northern soldiers mutinied, killed Ironsi and his aide in Ibadan, and went on to slaughter many of their Ibo officers.[21]

Brigadier Babafemi Ogundipe, a Yoruba, arrived at the pinnacle of military power by the accident of being the top senior officer to survive the July 28-29 coup. Ogundipe

tried to rally the mutinous troops to himself by sending
senior officer Lt. Col. Yakubu Gowon, who was a member of a
minority northern group, to their headquarters at Ikeja.
Gowon, however, was detained under housearrest in Ikeja by
the ill-tempered soldiers led by Lt. Col. Murtala Mohammed.
In the meantime, strong action came from another sector when
Ogundipe "was asked by two junior Northern officers to
resign and he complied."[22]

For three days, July 29 to August 1, Nigeria had no visible national leadership. The northern Nigerians, faced with
Ironsi's (east) death and Ogundipe's (west) withdrawal,
eventually convinced Gowon (north) to assume authority as
their military leader. As John de St. Jorre observed, "Thus,
somewhat in the way the British Tory party used to choose
its leaders, Jack Gowon 'emerged' by an arcane and tortuous
process: selection being based on political necessity and
personal background rather than egalitarian and democratic
principles."[23]   Despite their ethnic pride in having a
national leader once again from the north, the northern
Nigerians expressed a deeper distrust with the recent course
of Nigerian events.   The military leaders in Ikeja debated
the country's future with an eye toward possible northern
secession.

Several senior Nigerian civil servants in Lagos,
appalled at the rumors of secession, were somehow able to
convince the military leaders at Ikeja to convene an emergency meeting.   These civil servants believed that the
military's commitment to their new leader was wellgrounded
and that Gowon was open to influence.   Gowon, who had no
previous indication that he would eventually be the Head of
State nor any preconceived notion of what he would do if
chosen as the leader, was respected as a reasonable and honest Nigerian.   These civil servants vividly described to the
military leaders the most immediate threat to all Nigerians
--the breakup of the country.   Only after many hours with
Gowon and the other military leaders discussing the difficult problems of domestic political stability through unity
did Nigeria's "Oxford A's" (Philip Asiodu, Abdul Atta, and
Allison Ayida had attended Oxford University in England)
bring up the issue of the British and American government
support for One Nigeria.[24]

When British High Commissioner Sir Francis Cumming-Bruce
was encouraged by the Oxford A's to visit the new Nigerian
leader at Ikeja, he immediately paid a visit to Mathews.
Their discussion inevitably turned to the strong rumor of a
possible disintegration of the country.   Mathews agreed with
Cumming-Bruce that Nigeria must be kept together as a united
country at all costs and that this message be conveyed clear
and strong to Gowon.   "They told me," Gowon later recalled,
"that not another dime in foreign assistance would come to
Nigeria" if the regions were allowed to separate.[25]

A charming personality, northern heritage, backing by
influential antisecessionists civil servants, and public
support by the British and American governments--these factors allowed Gowon to emerge from Ikeja as Nigeria's strong
new Head of State.   The only unresolved dark cloud was the
challenge to Gowon's leadership by Lt. Col. Odumegwu Ojukwu,
the Military Governor of the Eastern Province.   Ojukwu, who

had   telephoned Gowon during the Ikeja negotiations from his eastern headquarters, agreed to help restore order but refused to recognize Gowon's position as supreme commander inasmuch as Ojukwu had military seniority by a few months.

Aside from the question of military rank, Barnard did convey to Ojukwu and the leaders of the Eastern Province that the United States supported an immediate constitutional conference to be convened in Lagos. The agreed conference agenda was to allow discussion of the four possible choices for the country's future political structure: (1) a federal system with a strong central government, (2) a federal system with a weak central government, (3) a confederate system of regions or provinces, or (4) some unique arrangement other than secession. Both the northern and the eastern participants initially favored the confederate arrangement, although for different reasons. But outside the conference meetings the Nigerian civil servants, the British High Commissioner and Ambassador Mathews lobbied intensively for the first option of a One Nigeria.

On Monday, September 19, as the north-east agreement was being formed at the conference, reports of another wave of violence in the north began to surface. "The Northern massacres were not fortuitous," commented one American FSO years later. In his opinion they were linked to the ad hoc conference and were caused by the northern leaders, and those who opposed any proposal other than a return to the status quo ante. News of the bloody anti-Ibo riots in the north ended the constitutional discussions by the end of the week. The positive lobbying for a united Nigeria and the negative reports of violence were reflected in the northern participants' final decision to have a federal system with strong central authority under the newly constituted Federal Military Government (FMG).

Despite the FMG's attempt to maintain peace, law and order broke down in the northern sectors of the country. It was virtually impossible to guarantee the safety or security to any eastern Nigerian living or working in the north. The reported slaughter of 10,000 Ibos and other eastern minority groups in the north during September and October remains unconfirmed. However, the impact of the violence spurred a massive exodus of eastern Nigerians to their homeland. "Terrified Ibos deserted their jobs in Lagos and elsewhere in the country and fled for their lives. Almost a million [new] Ibo refugees jammed the Eastern Region."[26]

The Yoruba trauma of the violent western elections and the Hausa-Fulani trauma of loosing their religious leaders and political hegemony by military coups were sadly balanced by the Ibo trauma of the pogrom directed against them in the Northern and Western Regions. "From these pogroms stems the Ibo fear, which persists even now, of genocide," wrote an American FSO four years later.[27]

Mistrust between the Nigerian ethnic groups increased steadily throughout November and December. The United States was not exempt from this mistrust, especially when Hank Wharton, an American mercenary who was known to be an international gun-runner, caused quite a stir when one of his DC-4 aircraft crashed on its way to the eastern sector scattering "a large load of rifles and ammunition supplied

by the French arms dealer, Paul Favier" near Garoua in northern Cameroon.[28] The State Department decided it was now imperative for all Americans to be engaged in efforts to bring the Nigerian groups together in hopes of averting an impending disaster.

Notes

1. James S. Coleman, <u>Nigeria: Background to Nationalism</u> (Berkeley: University of California Press, 1958).

2. Harold D. Nelson, James McLaughlin, Barbara Marvin, Philip Moeller, and Donald Whitaker, <u>Area Handbook for Nigeria</u> (Washington, D.C.: U.S. Government Printing, 1972), 71.

3. Sanford Unger, <u>Africa: The People and Politics of an Emerging Continent</u> (New York: Simon and Schuster, 1985). "Prejudice toward Africa was just as strong in the United States as in Europe, and was related to the virulent racism in American society toward its own black citizens, especially in the South" (p. 28).

4. U.S. Congress, Senate Committee on Foreign Relations, <u>United States in the United Nations, 1960: A Turning Point</u>, Vol. 3, 87th Cong., 1st sess., 1961. It was not difficult for Senator Wayne Morse (D-OR) to comment on the State Department's African Bureau as "largely staffed by persons who have spent many years of assignment in European countries and have well in mind the European point of view" (p. 29).

5. U.S. State Department, Bureau of Public Relations, Press release, Oct. 16, 1957.

6. U.S. State Department, <u>Biographic Record, 1972</u>, "Palmer, Joseph, II."

7. Bassey E. Ate, <u>Decolonization and Dependence: The Development of Nigerian-U.S. Relations, 1960-1984</u> (Boulder, Colo.: Westview Press, 1987), 1-2.

8. Ambassador Joseph Palmer, interview with author, Chevy Chase, Maryland, July 23, 1975.

9. U.S. State Department, <u>Biographic Record, 1972</u>, "Mathews, Elbert George."

10. U.S. State Department, Agency for International Development (U.S.A.I.D.), "Country Field Submission FY 1966--Nigeria," Nov. 1964, p. 2.

11. U.S. State Department, Airgram A-708, May 21, 1965, p. 1.

12. Stephen R. Weissman, <u>American Foreign Policy in the Congo, 1960-1964</u> (Ithaca, N.Y.: Cornell University Press, 1974).

13. Airgram A-708, p. 8.

14. U.S. State Department, Airgram A-693, May 14, 1965, p. 19.

15. John de St. Jorre, <u>The Brothers' War: Biafra and Nigeria</u> (Boston: Houghton Mifflin, 1972), 295.

16. U.S.A.I.D., "Country Field Submission FY 1966--Nigeria.

17. An excellent history of the January 15, 1966, coup is found in St. Jorre's first chapter, "The Soldiers Take Over," in <u>The Brothers' War</u>, 27-41.

18. A.H.M. Kirk-Greene, "The Regions Are Abolished," in <u>Crisis and Conflict in Nigeria: A Documentary Sourcebook 1966-1970</u>, Vol. 1 (London: Oxford University Press, 1971), 175. The four regional Military Governors established were in the Eastern Province--Odumegwa Ojukwu; in the Northern Province--Hassan Katsina; in the Western Province--Adekunle Fajuyi; in the Mid-Western Province--David Ejoor. John Aguyi-Ironsi was the Chairman of the Supreme Military Council, which also included the Chiefs of Staff of the army--Yakubu Gowon, the navy--Akinivale Wey, and air force--George Kurobo; and Inspector-General of Police--Kam Selem.

19. U.S. State Department, <u>Biographic Record, 1972</u>, "Olson, Clinton." He was first assigned to the U.S. Embassy in Lagos in April 1966 as the Economic General Counsul and in June of that same year promoted to the Deputy Chief of Mission with personal rank of Minister. Olson was made Ambassador to Sierra Leone in 1972.

20. St. Jorre, <u>The Brothers' War</u>, 67-80. U.S. Consulates throughout the world have individual links to their embassies, for example, the U.S. Consulate in Belfast, Northern Ireland, reports simultaneously to London and Dublin.

21. The Northern Nigerian's concept of an Ibo regime is reflected by the following list of those killed in the July 28-29 coup:

Officers	Eastern	Mid-Western	Western
Major-General	1	-	-
Lieutenant Colonels	1	1	1
Majors	9	2	-
Captains	11	-	-
Lieutenants	8	2	-
Second Lieutenants	3	2	2
Warrant Officers	11	1	1
Sargents	42	10	2
Corporals	47	3	-
Privates	<u>53</u>	<u>-</u>	<u>-</u>
Total	186	21	6

The formal distribution of military power in Ironsi's government according to the tables in <u>January 15: Before and After</u>, Vol. 7 (Enugu: Biafra Ministry of Information, 1967), 28, 73, were as follows:

Major-General	Eastern	(Ironsi)
Brigadiers	Northern	1
	Western	2
Battalions	Eastern	3
	Northern	2
	Western	1
	Mid-Western	1
Headquarters	Eastern	2
	Northern	2
	Mid-Western	1
Special Branches	Western	3
	Northern	2
	Eastern	1

22. St. Jorre, <u>The Brothers' War</u>, 70.
23. Ibid., 73.
24.   The Nigerian Permanent Secretaries Philip Asiodu (Trade and Industry), Abdul Atta (Finance), and Alison Ayida (Economic Development) went on to become after the civil war the Permanent Secretary of Mines and Power (oil), Secretary to the FMG, and Permanent Secretary of Finance, respectively. They were also the architects of Nigeria's 1970-74 Development Plan.
25.   John J. Stremlau, <u>The International Politics of the Nigerian Civil War, 1967-1970</u> (Princeton, N.J.: Princeton University Press, 1977), 35.
26.   Robert Smith, "U.S. Policy Toward the Nigerian Civil War" (paper for the National War College, Mar. 1970), 13.
27.   Ibid., 14.
28.   St. Jorre, <u>The Brothers' War</u>, 321.

1

Two Views of Nigeria

Two distinct American perceptions of what was happening in
Nigeria were being transmitted to Washington by the outset
of 1967. On the one hand, the private and public U.S.
Embassy reports from Lagos supported the newly formed FMG
under the leadership of Yakubu Gowon. Ambassador Elbert
Mathews and British officials acted as though there were no
issue except the perpetuation of the existing geopolitical
unity of Nigeria. These foreign representatives were only
too willing to do business with Nigeria's fledgling leaders
because they controlled the capital. On the other hand,
confidential reports sent directly to Washington from the
U.S. Consulate in Enugu and from the U.S. Embassy in Ghana
presented the Nigerian system in chaos. Their reports
appraised the situation as unstable inasmuch as the FMG had
no more claim to legitimacy than Ironsi's regime. In fact,
Nigerian politicians were also questioning who had the legitimate authority to rule.

State Department "Africanists," especially those who had
experience in Nigeria, were not perplexed by these initial
contradictory reports from their embassies and consulates.
Washington bureaucrats ascribed such conflicting accounts to
field officers who had "gone native," that is, identified
too personally with local events for any clear and objective
analysis. But as the Nigerian reports became more unequivo-
cally dichotomous, the State Department Intelligence and
Research Bureau (INR) analysts began to rely more and more
on advice and assistance from Joseph Palmer and Robert Smith
who were stationed in Washington. Smith had worked for three
years as the principal officer in the U.S. Consulate in
Enugu when Palmer was ambassador in Lagos. Although Smith
had returned to Washington in 1965 as the Officer-in-Charge
of the African Bureau's Ghanaian Office, he was quickly
reassigned as the Officer-in-Charge of the Nigerian Office
in July 1966 because of the growing Nigerian crisis. These
two "Nigerian Experts," Palmer and Smith, assured everyone
at the State Department who expressed any concern about the
crisis that things were still manageable: "The conviction
persistent among many Nigerians that their leaders, with a
long Nigerian tradition of brinkmanship and political

compromise at the last minute, might yet be able to avert a showdown if only the young colonels involved could meet face to face."[1]

Robert Barnard's telegrams and reports to Washington did recount several of the major items of unrest that portrayed Gowon's initial control of the government as far from firm. His reports also described the north's ugly mood and the NPC leaders' inclination that would welcomed the secession of the Eastern or the entire Southern regions from Nigeria, for the Yorubas continued to be restless and unaccepting of the recent FMG regime. Barnard observed, however, that despite the high level of violence in the north and the tackless attitude of the FMG toward the Eastern Province, the eastern leaders did not seek a break in the existing political structure. Instead, in his opinion, the view of a confederation of Nigeria's several regional provinces under a central government with sharply limited powers, often suggested by leading Nigerians in the past, was being pressed by eastern leaders as the only basis for a peaceful future.[2] This position was eventually refined and presented by Odumegwu Ojukwu at the peace conference held at Aburi, Ghana, in January 1967.

It was not easy getting the Nigerian military leaders to agree to meet and discuss their differences. Since Ojukwu would not go to Lagos because of northern control and Gowon would not go to the east, a convenient neutral site was offered by General Joseph Ankrah of Ghana. U.S. Ambassador David Williams in Accra, Ghana, had supported Ankrah as a mediator because it was well known that Ankrah had the respect of both Gowon and Ojukwu. When the two Nigerian military factions did eventually meet in Aburi, their conference was congenial. Nonetheless, these January meetings were reported by the different factions as though there were two different simultaneous events.[3] In like manner, there were two different American viewpoints of the Aburi Conference. Mathews reported the conference was dominated by the shrewd and well-prepared Ojukwu; as opposed to the Gowon approach to the meeting as an informal friendly get-together of brother officers to sort things out. Barnard reported that the Eastern negotiators were astonished to have their package accepted virtually intact at the meetings, presumably because Gowon and the FMG negotiators had no comprehension that the real intent of the meeting was to implement either the political structure of confederation or a loose federation discussed by Ojukwu and Gowon over the phone during the "lost weekend" at Ikeja.

Ojukwu, believing that his points were accepted by Gowon and the FMG leaders, understandably was the first to publish the proceedings of the Aburi Conference. But the civil servants in Lagos, once they received and analyzed the agreements, wrote a detailed memorandum to Gowon explaining the consequences of his actions. According to their memorandum the Aburi Agreements provided for virtually autonomous regions in Nigeria, with each region in control of their own revenues. These bureaucrats argued convincingly that the FMG, which needed these regional funds to keep their government solvent and united, would have to reject the Aburi Agreements as unacceptable.

Mathews supported the civil servants' interpretation and made it known that the United States rejected the results of Aburi. The logical implication that Gowon had not been capable of understanding or managing the conference was rejected by Olson, who insisted in his reports to Washington that Gowon continued to be in control of the Nigerian government. These embassy cables also presented Ojukwu as intransigent, uncooperative, and difficult and provoking the FMG; whereas Gowon was presented as cooperative and restrained and seeking peaceful solutions to the country's problems. Mathews reinforced this official perception by submitting to Washington the verbatim substance of private talks between Ankrah and the British High Commissioner Sir Francis Cumming-Bruce, who had previously served in Accra, wherein Ankrah expressed his belief that Gowon was in control of the Nigerian situation.[4] Later, in compliance with his embassy orders, Barnard cabled Washington that he had informed the eastern officials that the U.S. government believed that Nigeria should stay united under the FMG administration.[5]

Then Mathews joined Cumming-Bruce in publicly calling for continued efforts by the United States and the U.K. to assist in arranging future mediation between Gowon and Ojukwu. Dispute the factual one-sided support for Gowon and the FMG, Mathews believed that an impartial American role was possible and workable. As stated in his February 1967 annual policy assessment of Nigeria, "in the time of their greatest need, Nigerian leaders listened to advice given in confidence by representatives of the U.K. and U.S. governments."[6] Mathews firmly believed that if Gowon did not lead Nigeria and keep it strong and together, then that responsibility would be assumed eventually and willingly by Ojukwu. He suspected Ojukwu to be "a bright, very pleasant and able sort of guy and a very ambitious fellow who was not about to settle for part of the country if he could get it all."[7] So, one way or another, the embassy believed the Nigerians were going to come out with a united Nigeria. "Now, if violence is avoided, there is a chance for lasting unity."[8]

A flurry of British and America diplomatic negotiations ensued during February and March in an attempt to mollify the widening Nigerian differences. In mid-February Palmer sent a special message to Williams in Ghana, encouraging him to support Ankrah's further attempts to bring the Nigerians to another negotiation meeting. The State Department continued to count on Ankrah as the key to any possible compromise among the Nigerian contestants.[9] Ankrah, pleased for personal and political reasons with this American support, willingly accepted to carry on this mediator role. Consequently, he instructed all Ghanaian Ambassadors to visit all parties concerned with the Nigerian crisis in an effort to arrange new meetings.[10]

During this period of heavy telegram traffic between the State Department and the cautious U.S. Embassy in Lagos, Mathews cabled Washington that Williams should be very careful in how and why Ankrah might bring together the Nigerian leaders because this "situation is delicate." Smith sent a reply that Mathews would do better to express more concern to Gowon over allowing the erosion of Aburi to occur so quickly.[11] Mathews immediately shot back that Washington should make a greater effort to "dissuade Ojukwu from provoking the FMG" and give more support to the U.S. Embassy in "encouraging Gowon to seek peaceful solutions."[12] The terse return telegram retorted, "We deplore use of force by either side. Can others mediate?"[13]

Mathews and Olson were now concerned that their analysis of the Nigerian situation was somehow being misunderstood or thwarted by some individual or group in Washington. Affirming once again that their position was the only plausible policy, the embassy undertook to send a series of informative communications to Washington during the first weekend in March. In response to the bureau's inquiry regarding mediation possibilities, the initial embassy cable reiterated that "Gowon says he will try to settle the problem peacefully." This was immediately followed by the statement that "Gowon unenthusiastic about other approaches than Ankrah's." The next day rounded out the embassy's perception of the Nigerian situation when they filed a copy of their cable to Enugu requesting Barnard to personally inform Ojukwu that "we appeal to him [Ojukwu] to avoid force or provocative actions." This phase of the embassy-consulate struggle to influence U.S. policy ended with a direct cable from Barnard to Washington reporting that the embassy's request was communicated to Ojukwu and that his response was simply to accept the message because "Barnard was told to lecture him." This lecture had also included Washington's feelings on the need for peaceful negotiations and the real dangers of a universal declaration of independence by the east, as well as the embassy's request "to point out that the East's economic proposals would break up Nigeria."[14]

Attempts to have Gowon and Ojukwu settle their differences peacefully were complicated by several other factors. Immediately following Ojukwu's "Revenue Collection Edict" of March 31, 1967, whereby all revenues derived from the east were to go to the Regional Treasury and not to Lagos, the FMG retaliated by stopping all postal services to and from the east and suspended all Nigerian Airways flights to the Eastern Region. These events convinced Ankrah that a stronger force than Ghana was needed in the situation. He notified the British High Commissioner in Ghana and Ambassador Williams that he had done his best, "but Ojukwu, under the influence of civilians, is being unreasonable" and "Gowon is playing games with us."[15] Barnard reported the same conclusion after talks with the eastern leaders, i.e., a stronger force, either the U.K. or the United States must intervene at this point to avert a rapid deterioration of Nigeria's domestic relations. Only a respected power like the U.S. could bring the Nigerian soldiers to their senses and stave off disaster, warned a prominent eastern Nigerian. In an effort to find another alternative thread for some future mediation the INR staff held a brainstorming session in Washington. They did arrive at a consensus report of what the United States could do to force the FMG and Ojukwu to negotiate, and their conclusion was simple--"we can't."[16]

Mathews did not agree with the INR evaluation. Encouraged by his staff, the ambassador followed the initiative of the FMG with its economic restrictions against the rebellious

eastern leaders. Barnard was ordered by Mathews to inform
Ojukwu that unless the Eastern administration came to terms
with the FMG an American travel ban would be imposed against
the region. On April 12 Mathews informed Washington that he
had flown to Enugu to personally inform Ojukwu of the U.S.
travel ban and its consequences.[17]   U.S. employees, especially A.I.D., Peace Corps, and government contractors,
would no longer be permitted to return to their posts once
they left the Eastern Region. Sir David Hunt, the British
Commonwealth Secretary General who had frequent discussions
with Mathews about possible new initiatives, also traveled
to Enugu to warn the Eastern leaders of the consequences of
such decisions on the region's economy.

Ojukwu seized this opportunity to demand that all oil
royalties derived from the Eastern Region's operating oil
companies, including Shell-British Petroleum (Shell/BP) and
the Nigerian Gulf Oil Company, which was owned by American
Gulf Oil, be deposited in the banks of the Eastern Region
government.   Shell/BP feebly tried to convince the eastern
government that the company was not involved in taking sides
in the Nigerian leadership crisis. On the question of royalties, Shell/BP insisted that they could not sign over the
large sum of petroleum royalties until the question of who
was the legal recipient was settled. The Nigerian Gulf Oil
Company agreed to comply with a similar U.S. request, i.e.,
the American-owned company would refrain from any royalty
payments until after the British had decided which way to go
politically.

As businesspeople, politicians, and diplomats danced
away from the growing domestic configuration, the field was
relegated to the military by default. The inevitable war
was rapidly approaching. Barnard reported weeks before the
actual May 30 secession that the Eastern leaders were desig-
ning a flag and composing a national anthem for their new
"Biafra."[18]   The image of a multiethnic Biafra, which was
not controlled solely by Ibos, was cultivated by several
minority appointments. When the Consultative Assembly of
the Eastern Region, on May 27, mandated Ojukwu to secede
from Nigeria, Gowon declared a state of emergency that same
evening, reimposed the FMG's ineffective blockade of the
east, and announced officially that Nigeria was now divided
into 12 states.(These 12 states were later divided into 19.)

Gowon, not to be outdone by the Eastern concessions to
minority groups, created the long-desired restructuring of
Nigeria into 12 states on the basis of the nation's minorities.[19] This action divided the former Eastern Region into
three states: the oil-rich, Ijaw-ruled Rivers State; the
Ibibio-Efik South-Eastern State on the Cameroon border; and
the minuscule enclave of the East-Central State for the
Ibos. The FMG leaders also agreed with Gowon that the most
prominent politicians, denied access to power during the
past military governments, were to be brought back into the
Nigerian government.

The division of Nigeria in a dozen states, once supported by the Ibo NCNC leaders, was now perceived by the
Eastern government as an extension of the former pogroms to
the emasculation of their homeland and their wealth.

Map 2. Nigerian Regions, 1966

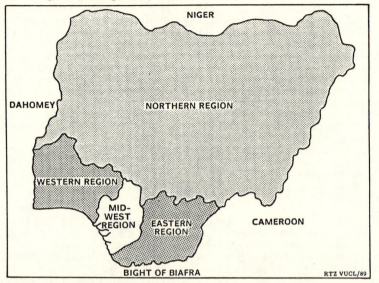

Source: Adapted by Villanova University Cartographic Laboratory from John de St. Jorre, The Brothers' War (Boston: Houghton Mifflin, 1977), front endpaper.

Map 3. Nigerian States, 1967

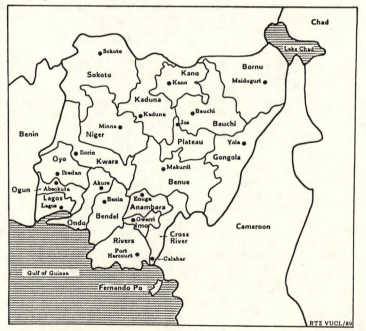

Source: Adapted by Villanova University Cartographic Laboratory from Guy Arnold, Modern Nigeria (London: Longman Group, 1977), Appendix 4.

Table 1.1.   Nigerian Regions and New States

Region	(1967) 12 States	(1976) 19 States	Sq. Kms.	(1963) Population
Northern	North Western	Niger	73,555	1,194,508
		Sokoto	94,588	4,538,787
	North Central	Kaduna	70,293	4,098,306
	Kano	Kano	42,123	5,774,840
	North Eastern	Bauchi	61,814	2,431,296
		Borno	116,589	2,997,498
		Gongola	102,067	2,605,263
	Kwara	Kwara	73,404	1,714,485
	Benue Plateau	Benue	69,740	2,427,017
		Plateau	56,245	2,026,657
Percent of Total			**79**	**54**
Eastern	East Central	Anambra	15,770	3,596,618
		Imo	13,032	3,672,654
	South Eastern	Cross River	29,164	3,478,131
	Rivers	Rivers	21,172	1,719,925
Percent of Total			**8**	**22**
Western	Western	Ogun	20,241	1,550,966
		Ondo	18,165	2,729,690
		Oyo	42,862	5,208,884
	Lagos	Lagos	3,535	1,443,568
Mid-Western	Mid-West	Bendel	38,061	2,460,962
Percent of Total			**13**	**24**
Total			**962,420**	**55,670,055**

Source: Statistical   information from "Nigeria," <u>Africa South of the Sahara 1987</u> (London: Europa, 1986), 782.

In addition to political territorial integrity, Gowon and Ojukwu's struggle for control had always tacitly included the new oil resources recently discovered in the southeastern part of Nigeria. From the Shell/BP discovery in 1958, oil was rapidly becoming the revenue which the country planned to build its modernization schemes. If the FMG laid claim to the oil royalties, so too did the Eastern Region. However, no one took the opportunity before the civil war to publicly acclaim that the precise area of the large reserves was actually among the minority groups of the southern Eastern and southern Mid-Western regions. Nearly two-thirds of the Nigerian high-grade, low sulfur, "sweet" crude petroleum were pumped from these marshy streams and ebb-tide areas, and half of the other remaining production crossed through eastern pipelines to the refinery at Bonny. A channel island near the city of Port Harcourt, Bonny was Nigeria's major export terminal for all this oil as well as the major refinery.

Map 4.   Nigerian Oil and Gas Fields

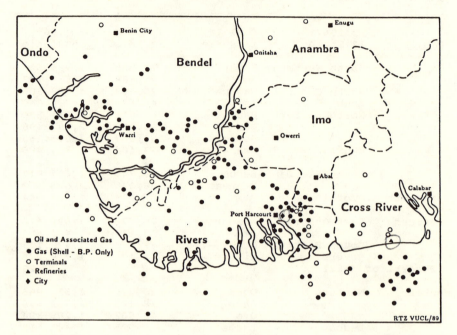

Source: Adapted by Villanova University Cartographic Laboratory from Harold Nelson, McLaughlin,
Marvin, Moeller, and Whitaker, Area Handbook for Nigeria (Washington, D.C.: U.S. Government Printing, 1972), 352, and Keith Panter-Brick, Soldiers and Oil (London: Frank Cass, 1978), 355.

Table 1.2.   Nigerian Petroleum Value, 1958-1968 (millions,
            Nigerian Ł)

Year	Value Production	Exports	Contribution to GNP Value	Percent of GNP
1958	0.9	0.9		
1958	2.6	2.6		
1960	4.2	4.2		
1961	11.3	11.3		
1962	17.2	17.2		
1963	20.1	20.1	8	0.6
1964	32.0	32.0	16	1.2
1965	69.1	68.1	18	1.3
1966	99.7	92.0	24	1.7
1967	76.6	72.4	32	2.2
1968	36.6	36.6	18	1.2

Source: Scott Pearson, Petroleum and the Nigerian Economy (Stanford, Calif.: Stanford University
Press, 1970), 56-58.

Early in 1967, the U.S. Embassy's A.I.D. officer in Lagos, anticipating the need to know more about the actual and potential prospects of Nigerian oil, had convinced Olson and Mathews to send a priority request to Washington for further research analysis. Palmer and Smith agreed with their embassy's request. A.I.D., therefore, went ahead and secured the services of two American economic consultants, Walter Schmidt and Scott Pearson, to conduct a thorough field research on the possible petroleum impact on Nigeria. Their oil report is important because it gives an insight into what the American officials knew and what they admitted to both Nigerian officials and the public.

Schmidt and Pearson also recognized that their sensitive information would "have extremely explosive results if its contents were made known directly or indirectly to the government of Nigeria."[20] The two Americans had discovered that the official Nigerian government statements concerning anticipated Nigerian oil revenues were substantially lower than what the oil company officials knew could be forecasted and that both these projections were lower than the figures estimated by the field operators.[21] Their classified report concerning Nigeria's positive economic future was kept from the host country because they believed it would only aggravate an already "delicate" situation between Gowon and Ojukwu. There may have also been a self-serving motive in this silence--it would avoid any Nigerian pressure on the oil companies to increase production levels that might sour the company's attitude toward producing in a conflict zone.

Although these reasons were stated in their classified report, the authors did not mention another possible reason, which was given by verbal communication--silence would avoid a British confrontation with the American findings. The finding of a future major increase in oil production far above the official prediction was calculated by Schmidt and Pearson even after they accepted only those figures provided by the British government. Needless to say, the American oil consultants also conformed to the U.S. Embassy request for a pro-British, pro-FMG One Nigeria policy by publishing that "as best as we can foresee, and for some time thereafter, Nigeria will not be in a category of oil-producing countries which no longer require Congressional aid."[22] This analysis was proven wrong within two years even though the disruption of the conflict did not allow for optimum production.

Despite these tactics and secrecy, both Gowon and Ojukwu believed in a future oil boom. This made the southeastern parts of Nigeria psychologically important to the political future of the Eastern Region and Nigeria. The FMG was very careful, therefore, when it imposed sanctions on the east because the oil-producing and -exporting areas were under the immediate control of Ojukwu. An economic crisis was initially avoided when the FMG's economic sanctions against the Eastern Region exempted oil and oil shipments as part of their "phony war."[23] The intervening period of 37 days, between Biafra's "Declaration of Secession" and the FMG's first military encounter, was utilized by both sides to mobilize support behind their legitimate right to the oil revenues and to mobilize their military volunteers and officers into a semblance of a fighting force.

Every stall tactic that the oil companies and their supporting governments could use failed when the oil royalty payment deadline arrived. All the oil companies quietly acquiesced to Ojukwu's demands, and Shell/BP is reported to have paid Biafra a token $700,000. These payments brought about the expected results, for on Tuesday, July 4, 1967, the FMG extended their existing economic blockade to oil. This Nigerian energy source suddenly became vital to Britain because of their experience when the Suez Canal closed during the Six Day Middle East War (June 5-11, 1967). Without hesitation Britain initiated a flurry of talks and asked the United States to assist in opening the Nigerian shipping lanes as quickly as possible.

If Britain needed the guarantee of access to petroleum, Nigeria needed military arms for its suddenly expanding armed forces. The need for military supplies became the sword's edge that defined the degree of U.S. deference to U.K. policy. Just prior to the Eastern Region secession, several Nigerian ministers approached Mathews with an unofficial request for additional military assistance. Mathews informed them, unofficially, that he was not able to give any assurances but he would seek additional clarification of the U.S. attitude. In any event, Mathews sent word informally to the FMG Defense Minister that any sudden formal request for the United States to rush new arms and armaments would, in all likelihood, be received with less enthusiasm than had been shown in past experiences.

Nigerians found this concept difficult to accept because Britain and the United States had been the bulwark behind their system. Besides, Britain was publicly denouncing the conflict but sending military arms "surreptitiously," and America knew that the FMG Armed Forces were ill equipped to conduct a successful military campaign against the east. "The Nigerian army of seven thousand men was only slightly bigger and better equipped than the rebel militia....Of the fifty-seven senior officers who had been commissioned prior to Independence, only five were available for duty on the federal side. Eighteen of the original fifty-seven served Ojukwu, and the rest had either left the service or had been killed in the two coups."[24]

The FMG was desperate. Therefore, their defense minister did submit a formal request for U.S. military shipments on a cash purchase basis. Mathews informally encouraged such action by attaching a personal embassy memo to this Nigerian request, in which he reminded the United States to honor past contracts. Nigeria did have a legal contract, signed in previous years, for U.S. military assistance programs. These armament contracts were for parts and ammunition that matched arms sold by the United States to Nigeria since 1964. The original amount of sale was Ł 2,859 and another Ł 14,437 had been contracted the following year through the U.S. Defense Department.[25]

Mathews agreed to test Washington's commitment to Nigeria by submitting the FMG arms request directly to the African Bureau, rather than have these requests go through regular channels to the department's Munitions Control Bureau. Smith, who was still the Nigerian Desk Officer, was disturbed by these military assistance requests. Basing his decision on personal experience and that of Barnard's reports from Enugu, Smith staked his diplomatic career on the need to prevent further U.S. arms from going to either combatant. He proposed a compromise plan in which all parties would be partially satisfied. It was possible to subdivide the original package sent by Mathews into two sections. The 1964 and 1965 contracts had "old" request forms that could be honored and delivered by the U.S. Defense Department before any public statement by the State Department. This action would give the FMG token proof of American support for their regime. It would also encourage the British and American One Nigeria policy supporters who were now threatened by several African states that were "suggesting the U.S. recognize Biafra in order to prevent bloodshed."[26]

Nigeria's request for military arms on the "new" forms, necessary for its growing armed forces, was judged by Smith as a definite future problem for the U.S. administration. Smith strongly advised against any additional military involvement with a country on the verge of civil war because it would again cast the United States as a "merchant of death." On July 6, two days after the fighting erupted, Palmer agreed to support Smith's memo to ban any new arms shipment to Nigeria. Another two days of bureaucratic bargaining ensued before Smith's package of an arms embargo was accepted by Secretary of State Dean Rusk. Although initially critical of an arms embargo and in favor of some limited military supply to the FMG, Rusk was finally persuaded to support American military neutrality.[27]

Rusk's knowledge of a secret British arms commitment to the FMG surely eased his decision to have a public policy of an arms embargo: "The surreptitious nature of Britain's first arms shipments to Nigeria, via Malta, may have been an attempt to protect British subjects in Biafra against hostility. But the secrecy was doubtless also due to the fact that the British Government was not anxious to be seen taking sides in a civil war."[28] Therefore, any statement that the official American policy toward Nigeria was one of neutrality would be a gross oversimplification. The July 10 announcement by Rusk that the United States could not honor the Nigerian request for new military contracts, a full week after the outbreak of fighting, was to gain precious time to deliver those arms already contracted.

America's declaration of military nonintervention was used by the State Department as evidence that the United States was not taking sides in the Nigerian conflict. When the British did eventually admit their covert support of the FMG, the State Department was quick to point out that the U.S. military nonintervention continued to be required because the U.K. was Nigeria's traditional arms supplier. The military British-Nigeria myth was a ruse that worked because substance and data played second to public media reports. "According to the journal West Africa, there are several factors which are said to have influenced the British decision: (1) Britain is the traditional supplier of arms to Nigeria."[29]

But, according to the Nigerian Trade Summary, Britain

was anything but a traditional arms supplier for Nigeria. Since Nigerian independence, Britain had become less and less involved in the supply of arms and ammunition. The 1967 increase in arms value was due to two ferret armored cars, at Ł 14,487 each. Pre-1967 assistance was insignificant, therefore, when compared to the millions of British sterling soon to be contracted and delivered during the war.

After an initial period of hesitation, the U.K. decided to change its covert policy to an official public policy of military arms supply limited to the sale of small arms, ammunition, and armored cars, plus some antiaircraft weapons to combat the two World War II vintage B-26 bombers Ojukwu eventually acquired in Europe. Britain, however, refused to sell aircraft or other military offensive weapons to the FMG despite repeated requests by Gowon. This did not prevent the U.K. from supplying active-duty military personnel to advise and direct FMG operations, both military and adminis-trative.[30] Beyond any question, the sale of British arms and ammunition, and the presence of their military advisers were of more importance to the Nigerian war effort than those of the Soviet Union or other foreign governments, including the United States.

The decision to declare an arms embargo became a fortu-nate policy decision for America. The same day Rusk announced the American arms embargo toward the Nigerian cri-sis, a squabble broke out in Congress over President Lyndon Johnson's decision to become involved in the Congo (Zaire) revolt. U.S. involvement in the Congo, which was "small-scale and clandestine at first, soon escalated and became public" when Americans learned that Johnson had sent over three C-130 transport aircraft and 150 support personnel.[31] This U.S. military involvement in the Congo was considered a failure, and for most of Johnson's remaining five years, preoccupation with the Vietnam War caused Nigeria, like the rest of Africa, to be remanded to the willing leadership of Palmer and the African Bureau. By refusing to supply mili-tary arms initially to the FMG, there was no subsequent pressure on the United States to cut military aid when the killing and starvation in Biafra and Nigeria became an international issue.

Table 1.3. Value of British Arms Imported into Nigeria, 1963-1969 (₦ = new Nigerian currency)

Year	U.K. Imported Value	Total Imported	U.K. Percent of Total
1963	Ł 177,754	Ł 213,499	83
1964	60,918	617,091[a]	36
1965	159,185	435,852	37
1966	76,846	203,557[b]	38
1967	171,391	385,226	48
1968	₦ 2,817,560	₦ 3,558,100	80
1969	10,255,089	10,533,036	97

[a]Sweden was first this year with 39 percent.
[b]Netherlands was first this year with 39 percent.

Source: Suzanne Cronjé, The World and Nigeria: The Diplomatic History of the Biafran War, 1967-1970 (London: Sidwick and Jackson, 1972), 393.

Notes

1. Smith, "U.S. Policy Toward the Nigerian Civil War," 15.
2. Suzanne Cronjé, The World and Nigeria: The Diplomatic History of the Biafran War 1967-1970 (London: Sidgwick and Jackson, 1972), 225. One of Ojukwu's recollections expressed during his interview with Cronje.
3. Kirk-Greene, Crisis and Conflict in Nigeria, Vol. 1, 312-340.
4. U.S. Embassy in Lagos, Telegram 5958, Feb. 8, 1967.
5. U.S. Consulate in Enugu, Telegram 351, Feb. 11, 1967.
6. U.S. Embassy in Lagos, Airgram A-407, "Nigeria: Annual U.S. Policy Assessment", Feb. 12, 1967, 12. Mathews made special note of Britain's Malcolm MacDonald's role in getting Gowon and Ojukwu to meet at Aburi.
7. Elbert Mathews, interview with author, Washington, D.C., June 19, 1975.
8. Airgram A-407, 16.
9. U.S. State Department, State Department Telegram (Deptel) 142128 to Accra, Feb. 22, 1967. Deptel 115922 to Accra, Jan. 10, 1967, also expresses the State Department's appreciation to Ankrah for his efforts to help Nigeria.
10. U.S. Embassy in Lagos, Telegram 6368, Feb. 22, 1967.
11. U.S. Embassy in Lagos, Telegram 6490, Feb. 27, 1967, and Deptel 145337 to Lagos, Feb. 28, 1967.
12. U.S. Embassy in Lagos, Telegram 6620, Mar. 1, 1967.
13. Deptel 148032 to Lagos, Mar. 3, 1967.
14. U.S. Embassy in Lagos, Telegram 6739, Mar. 4, 1967; Lagos, Telegram 6753, Mar. 6, 1967; Enugu, Telegram 445, Mar. 10, 1967; Deptel 161782 to Lagos, Mar. 24, 1967; and Lagos, Telegram 7470, Mar. 29, 1967.
15. U.S. Embassy in Accra, Telegram 2661, Mar. 22, 1967 and Accra, Telegram 3285, May 8, 1967. Ankrah would temporally wash his hands of the whole mess, reportedly "disgusted with both Gowon and Ojukwu who have fallen into the grip of politicians," Accra, Telegram 3663, June 20, 1967.
16. U.S. State Department, Intelligence and Research Bureau, Report, April 12, 1967.
17. Lagos, Telegram 8014, "Report on Meeting" and Telegram 8039, "Comments on Meeting," April 12, 1967.
18. Smith, "U.S. Policy Toward the Nigerian Civil War," 18.
19. "Gowon's Broadcast to the Nation, dividing Nigeria into Twelve States: Lagos, 27 May 1967," Kirk-Greene, Crisis and Conflict in Nigeria, Vol. 1, 444-449. See also Map 3. and Table 1.1.
20. U.S.A.I.D., "Country Field Submission FY 1969--Nigeria, Technical Appendix," "The Petroleum Industry's Impact on Nigeria--Analysis by Schmidt SPHSID, and Pearson, USAID Economic Consultants," 56.
21. Ibid. Schmidt and Pearson gave one example of a forecasted maximum Shell/BP "1970 production at 500,00 barrels per day instead of the official projection of 400,000 barrels per day," whereas the actual "document upon which he (Shell/BP official) was basing the estimate and found, much to his surprize, that the figure, as far as his estimate, was a minimum of 530,00 barrels per day by 1970."
22. Ibid., 2.
23. St. Jorre, "The Phoney War," in The Brothers' War, Chapt. 5.
24. John Stremlau, The International Politics of the Nigerian Civil War, 72.
25. Cronjé, The World and Nigeria, 393.
26. Lagos, Telegram 121, July 5, 1967. Mathews referred specifically to the comments of the Zambian High Commissioner.
27. The United States government always considered Nigeria to be Britain's responsibility. Only Secretary of State Dean Rusk, at the beginning of the Nigerian conflict, let such a notion become an official statement. He is reported to have said, "We regard Nigeria as part of Britain's sphere of influence." West Africa (July 22, 1967), 970.
28. Cronjé, The World and Nigeria, 46.
29. Carolyn Colwell, "Biafra: A Chronology of Developments Attending the Secession of the Eastern Region of Nigeria, January 15--November 15, 1968," Library of Congress, Nov. 22, 1968, 14.
30. American field officers reported to Washington that in 1969 RAF officers toured Nigerian air bases incognito, providing guidance and recommendations on air war operations. Among other things, the British officers were able to point out missing electronic equipment that Nigerian air force officers did not know of and could not have requested without assistance.
31. Unger, Africa, 66-67.

Map 5. Biafra

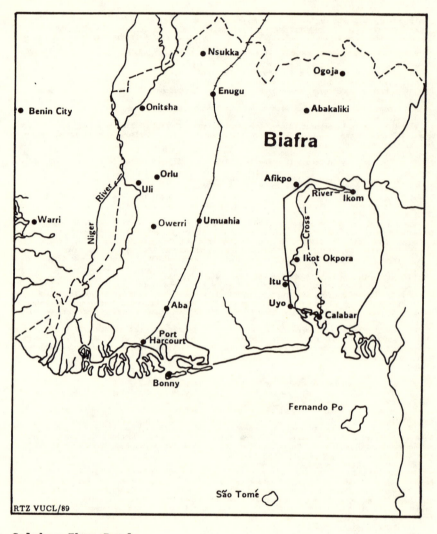

Calabar-Ikom Road:
           original plan   – – – – –
           altered plan   ——————

Source: Adapted by Villanova University Cartographic Laboratory from Odumegwu Ojukwu, <u>Biafra</u> (New York: Harper & Row, 1969), xxii-xxiii, C. B. Beal, "Memoranum: The Calabar-Ikom Road, An A.I.D. Project in Nigeria with Serious Military Implications," and U.S. Army Map Service, series 1301, map NB32, "Douala, West Africa," Nigeria/Biafra Clearing House Papers, Swarthmore College Peace Collection, Swarthmore, Pennsylvania.

2

The Broken Showcase

The Nigerian Civil War was a military reality 37 days after the Eastern Region's declaration of secession. The FMG's First Division forces, led by Col. Mohammed Shuwa, crossed the northern border of Biafra on July 6, 1967. Ogoja, a town in the northeastern corner of Biafra, fell easily to the advancing Nigerian forces. Nsukka, a town in the north-western corner of Biafra, was a different story. A heavily populated university area, Nsukka was captured on July 15 only after several days of stiff fighting. Shuwa requested, therefore, that the Biafran capital of Enugu, his next tar-get, be sufficiently "softened" by the Nigerian Air Force before his attack. The ensuing indiscriminate sortie bomb-ings of Enugu cost many innocent lives.

Reporting from Enugu, Robert Barnard not only described this senseless loss of civilian lives in detail, but he explained to Washington that the initial seemingly effort-less FMG victories were due more to the actual number of Ibos in the area of a particular military skirmish rather than to FMG military tactics and firepower as the U.S. Embassy in Lagos reported. Nsukka offered more resistance because it was a core part of the "fanatical 'Ibo national-ists' area," whereas Ogoja had a large number of non-Ibo people in the war zone.[1]

Barnard also reported that as the Nigerian federal troops pushed victoriously into the northern part of the Eastern Region, the Biafran troops and the surrounding Ibo population trekked deeper into their heartland, especially to Enugu. This behavioral pattern was confirmed by Red Cross medical teams working on both sides of the conflict. "The population of the conquered regions provided the following welcome to the Nigerian soldiers: upon their arrival the population flees. These people [Ibo] move toward the inte-rior and pose a very sharp problem of resettlement."[2] A similar pattern was repeated in Biafra's south. Unfortu-nately, FMG leaders and the U.S. Embassy were more concerned with visible troop movements during this initial period of military conflict than with any possibility of a long-term potential humanitarian impact from the fighting.

To its credit, the State Department did react immediately to Barnard's evaluation of the conflict, especially
the FMG air raids on Enugu. Joseph Palmer and Robert Smith
believed there would soon be an urgent need for medical
assistance around these areas of fighting.[3] Palmer told his
bureau staff to initiate contact with the traditional humanitarian groups in Washington. Matthew Lorimer, a State
Department officer who was temporarily assigned to assist
the Nigerian Desk officer Smith, arranged a meeting with
National American Red Cross (ARC) International Director
Samuel Krakow to discuss possible medical assistance that
might be offered to Nigeria by the ARC and the International
Committee of the Red Cross (ICRC). Krakow left a Wednesday,
July 19, meeting with Lorimer under the impression that
State Department officials were "most anxious that we [ARC]
support the ICRC appeal if and when it comes forth, with the
clear assurance that if government finances are desired they
could be secured as well."[4]
When the ARC asked their overseas posts for an evaluation of the projected dimension of Nigerian and Biafran
requirements in light of the U.S. offer, an emergency cable
arrived from Switzerland. The ARC Geneva Mission Office
telegram described the medical teams the ICRC intended to
sent to each side of the Nigerian battlefield, and it went
on to predict that the conflict in Nigeria would "be long,
involved, and will certainly result in considerable suffering."[5] This last section of their report confused the
American ARC officials because a previous meeting between
Krakow and Lorimer had not given Krakow any impression of
panic or deep concern by the State Department, especially
when some 1,200 Americans still remained in the secessionist
territory of Biafra.[6] When Krakow called and confronted
Lorimer with the ARC Geneva evaluation and asked for a clarification of this unique ARC analysis, Palmer dashed off a
written reply to the ARC that admitted that the State
Department would only go as far as expressing concern for
those caught in the Nigerian conflict. What Palmer was not
prepared to accept was the suggestion that this would be a
large-scale humanitarian problem. He also rejected the
implied notion that the United States offer would involve
America as a leading principal in whatever humanitarian
action might be needed in a possible "fratricidal" war. The
rejection of the ARC mission report by Palmer was based on
the U.S. Embassy's evaluation that Yakubu Gowon's "police
action" would be successful in bringing about a quick military solution.
Elbert Mathews had convinced Washington that the British
support of the FMG's military action in the secessionist
Eastern Region would limit the conflict activity to a brief
period. Besides, wrote Mathews, any question of mass killings incurred in the conflict would be quickly repudiated by
circumstances as testified to by moderate Eastern civilians
who were already urging a cease-fire because the Biafran
forces could not win against the FMG.[7] This field analysis
seemed to be verified the following day, July 26, when Bonny
Island and the offshore oil installations were captured by
the FMG forces. James Rawe, a retired British naval officer
who had joined the FMG's Third Marine Commando Division, had

directed the successful landing of Nigerian troops on the island. In one stroke the Nigerians had captured the region's oil installations, the only sea approach to Port Harcourt, and all major export and import shipment lanes connected with Biafra.

These early military victories on land and at sea reinforced U.S. Embassy expectations that the Nigerian "police action" would soon snuff out the secession. The day after Bonny was captured, Palmer, calculating that the Eastern leaders might now be more inclined to a diplomatic resolution of the conflict, sent a telegram to Mathews suggesting that he begin discussion with British officials "on how best to discreetly stimulate African or Commonwealth efforts" for mediation.[8] During the two-week military lull that followed the FMG victory at Bonny, Washington cautiously explored with Commonwealth Secretary General Arnold Smith and with Joseph Ankrah through U.S. Ambassador Williams, the possibility of encouraging other African mediation. A renewed flurry of diplomatic negotiations behind closed doors attempted to bring about some new peace proposal for the Nigerian conflict.

It is difficult to gage the degree to which the U.S. Embassy in Lagos supported these intensive negotiations. On one hand, official U.S. records display an impressive field effort to arrange a meeting between the two contestants. The American embassy in Accra reported "Ankrah in almost daily contact with Ojukwu and Gowon, trying to get them to come to Accra to discuss differences." The embassy in Lagos also reported "Eastern Civilians concerned about war, want meeting to discuss whether should continue or seek negotiations with FMG." The U.S. Consulate in Ibadan reported, "if West, Mid-West leaders came out against the war, FMG would have to call cease fire," and the U.S. Consulate in Kaduna reported the "New Nigerian editorial call for a door open to peace-- just get rid of Ojukwu."[9]

On the other hand, innuendos of the embassy aversion to mediating with Biafra surfaced throughout these records. When Mathews called for a cease-fire "as a face-saving device for both sides," he felt compelled to add that the "U.S. must help FMG to get war over quickly."[10] These interpretations, reported by Mathews as also representing British and African Commonwealth opinions, were passed along to Washington by an embassy anxious to show the FMG's strength and legitimacy. The U.S. Consulate in Kaduna, within the control of its embassy, was requested to cable Washington the entire text of the New Nigerian Sunday editorial, which "ridicules the idea of cease fire unless East recognized FMG." More important to these American efforts was the news that the Nigerians "may have gotten wind of such a peace proposal, and they are trying to quash it."[11] Someone had deliberately leaked the news of America's secret lobbying to the Nigerian press, and the Nigerian extremists were trying to end such activity.

The problem of dichotomous reporting from Lagos and Enugu was compounded by the embassy's failure to report important information concerning military activity that was public knowledge in Nigeria. A rational assumption for not reporting all vital details to Washington would be to assume that there was a fixed commitment by the embassy staff to support the FMG at all costs, along with the embassy's lack of important contacts with other than FMG officials in Lagos. For example, a "public" secret that everyone knew in Nigeria at the time, even though it was never reported to Washington by the embassy, concerned the planned Biafran invasion of Nigeria. One foreign diplomat "received a commercial cable through Nigeria's telegraph system which reported that the Mid-West would be invaded after August 8th." The Americans in Lagos were not the only professionals who overlooked such important details, as testified to by the Ghanaian Desk officer in Washington who missed the deliberate, but obscure quotation marks in routine cables from Accra--"Ankrah been trying to reach Ojukwu, who is unavailable,'" and another reference just before the invasion that stated "Ojukwu refused contact absolutely' after July 29."[12]

Any suggestion that this war would be a quick federal victory was forgotten during the dramatic "Operation 04" Biafran invasion of the Mid-Western Region, which began on August 9, 1967. Brigadier Victor Banjo, a Yoruba leader in the Biafran military force, gained control over the Mid-Western Region in one day without firing a shot. His troops drove their "mammy" wagons to Agbor and then fanned out; some to Auchi in the northern sector, some southeasterly to the city of Warri, and some straight west to the Mid-Western capital of Benin. Barnard again credited this rapid military success to the help of the region's Ibo leaders. The U.S. Embassy in Lagos, having been out of touch with anyone pro-Biafran, was again caught by "surprise" with the Mid-Western invasion. In fact, Mathews cabled Washington that Clinton Olson had discussions that morning with the British High Commissioner David Hunt about the possibility of a military stalemate producing the right opportunity for peace talks.[13]

After accepting the Mid-Western government's surrender, Banjo really surprised everyone when he took it on himself to declare the secession of the Mid-Western Region from Nigeria and Biafra on August 11. Instead of pushing on to capture Ikeja, and then Lagos as Gen. Odumegwu Ojukwu had ordered, the forward movement of Banjo's forces stopped in Ore. Biafra, at the high water mark of its power--being within 135 miles from the Nigerian capital of Lagos--forced a readjustment of all expectations concerning the duration and intensity of the conflict. The U.S. Embassy in London began to send a series of cables to Washington describing how the escalation of the Nigerian fighting and the success of the Biafran military in the Mid-Western Region had prompted the British press to call for negotiations or other initiatives to get the peace talks underway.[14]

Banjo's fatal pause at Ore allowed the FMG time to rethink, regroup, and reorganize their armed forces, and reinitiate international assistance. The ease and speed of the Biafran capture of the Mid-Western Region shocked Nigeria out of its complacency. Intense military recruiting by the FMG began immediately, and these new recruits were assigned to the newly formed Second Division under Lt. Col. Murtala Mohammed. The FMG's Third Marine Commando Division on Bonny Island were under Col. Benjamin (Black Scorpion)

Adekunle, and he was instructed to put troops ashore at Escravos and drive inland even as the Mid-Western Region was being invaded. This was a pincer movement to threaten the economic heart of Biafra.

Under duress, Gowon attempted to purchase additional military arms for his expanded forces from several countries. Britain, shocked by the Biafran military successes, had informed the FMG that the U.K. had decided to reexamine their past policy of refusing large arms sales to the FMG. But the Soviet Union, implementing their new African involvement policy, immediately agreed to sell additional arms to the FMG. Although the United States had declared an arms embargo, Gowon thought that the new military situation required a new policy. Mathews, who agreed with Gowon that this was an emergency situation, tried several times to unsuccessfully secure some change in the U.S. arms embargo policy. The degree of insecurity and uncertainty toward Nigeria's future was vividly expressed on August 10 by Gowon when he announced that the previous "police action" against the secession was now total war.

The U.S. hesitancy to support the FMG military requests during this crisis resulted in the FMG's decision to actively seek needed armaments from the Soviet Union. The Soviet government was all too willing to trade with Nigeria. "The decisive factor, which brought the Soviet Union down irrevocably on the Federal side, seems to have been a combination of the refusal of the Americans and British to supply the arms the Nigerians requested and its assessment of the likely outcome of the war at the end of July when Chief Enahoro arrived in Moscow. The West's nervousness about embroilment in the crisis left a partial vacuum."[15]

The Nigerian military contracts for Soviet hardware ranged from infantry arms and ammunition to MiG planes and tanks.[16] Such Soviet military assistance to Nigeria, absent before the civil war, grew quickly in 1967. Soviet and Communist-bloc arms supplies, particularly aircraft, were welcomed by the FMG as an alternative to British planes, which had been requested and denied. In addition to aircraft and arms, Soviet military technicians were sent to Nigeria. In a remarkable intelligence coup, the Biafran press reported on August 10 the names and passport numbers of 26 Soviet military experts who were then en route to Nigeria and added that 24 more Soviets would shortly follow.

These arrangements were of obvious concern to the British and American governments. Palmer inquired, through informal channels at the U.K. Embassy in Washington on Tuesday, August 15, if Britain could take possible action in Moscow to delay or negate the Soviet arms deal with Nigeria. He also asked if the British could initiate or stimulate some African mediation in the Nigeria conflict in the interim. By the time the U.K. Ambassador reported back on Saturday "negatively on first and time not ripe on second," both the British and Soviet governments had publicly announced their intentions to sell arms to the FMG.

Although the FMG were sending delegations to Moscow and the Biafrans were taking to clients in Beijing, the United States contented itself with statements of "regretful" condemnation for Soviet involvement.[17] The low-level U.S.

response to Soviet involvement was based on two important
factors. First, the State Department's belief that the
Soviet military contributions would not be sufficient to
disrupt or penetrate the staunch Western ideology of Nigeria. Second, Washington assumed that Britain, which had
made the decision to greatly increase its military support,
could sufficiently supply the FMG so as to counter any
Soviet involvement. According to Table 1.3 the Americans
were correct in their analysis. Nonetheless, the United
States continued to monitor the Soviet activity in Africa.
Cronjé speculates that Nigeria bartered cocoa for Russian
arms, which might explain why the official <u>Nigerian Trade
Summary</u> never listed the U.S.S.R. as an arms supplier.[18]
Smith, in his comments a year later to an American humanitarian group interested in Nigeria's conflict, expressed the
belief that the United States was concerned with the Soviet
involvement but that the British had a greater fear of a
possible Russian foothold.

Diplomacy had had its brief moment, now the FMG was
interested in military activity. With the British and
Soviet arms distributed to the new recruits under Mohammed,
their first test was to recapture the town of Ore. This was
accomplished by August 29, and by the end of September the
Biafran forces had retreated back to the original boundary
of the Eastern Region at the Niger River. "The really
tragic side, though, was the fate of the Mid-West Ibos. The
elites who planned the pro-Biafran coup and ruled the roost
during the brief occupation all got away safely to the East
before the Nigerians returned, leaving the innocent mass of
the people to face the red-eyed wrath of the civilians and
Federal troops. The Mid-Western Ibos who had been, through
no desire of their own, dragged into the eye of the storm
were to be buffeted mercilessly for the rest of the war."[19]
The humanitarian problems were incrementally mounting--the
refugees of 1966, the 1967 July FMG military offensive, the
August Biafran military offensive, the September FMG recapture of the Mid-West--to create inestimable numbers of
battle casualties, prisoners of war and refugees. But only
a few government bureaucrats were concerned with the rapidly
increasing cost of the conflict in human lives and material.

The FMG were particularly angry with America because of
the U.S. decision to deal with Biafra as though it were on
an equal diplomatic footing with Nigeria. Mathews reported
that a real "deterioration of relations has occurred between
the U.S. and Nigeria...and the even-handedness ranks high in
the Nigerian distaste for the U.S."[20] Other items that
irritated the FMG, according to Olson, were the U.S. refusal
to sell 106-mm ammunition in early 1967, the U.S. refusal to
withdraw A.I.D. projects and Peace Corps volunteers from
Biafra, the lack of official denunciation of Hank Wharton on
the occasion of his October 1966 plane crash with military
arms, the lack of U.S. attempts to control the American
press and individual groups that supported Biafra, and the
belief that there would soon be an American extension of <u>de
facto</u> recognition of Biafra. In lieu of these accusations,
Palmer tried to assuage some of these FMG fears by publicly
instructing Barnard to hand deliver a special diplomatic-
pouch letter to Ojukwu affirming U.S. confidence in Ambassa-

dor Mathews.[21]   The letter also urged Ojukwu to assist the
Organization of African Unity (OAU) initiative to develop
some peaceful settlement. Ojukwu, fully aware that African
recognition was the most effective tool to justify outside
involvement and help, called on the OAU to intervene and
strongly lobbied the summit meeting in Kinshasa in September
1967. The State Department had used British anxiety for the
success of the FMG to gain U.K. support for an attempt to
bring the OAU into a mediating position between Gowon and
Ojukwu. But the OAU itself was soon to become a pawn in
this struggle.

As August ended the FMG became worried that the OAU sum-
mit meeting scheduled to meet in the Congo (now Zaire) might
formally discuss the conflict. The Nigerian Ambassador in
Addis Ababa was instructed to made it clear to Emperor Halie
Selassie that the FMG would oppose consideration of their
crisis under Article 3 of the OAU charter. On September 2,
Gowon made a speech stressing that the Nigerian conflict was
an internal affair. This statement, publicly supported by
Mathews,[22] was a reaction to Ankrah's invitation to the
Cameroon, Chad, Niger, Upper Volta, Dahomey, and Togo heads
of state to meet in Accra, Ghana, on September 4 and 5 for a
discussion of Nigeria prior to the OAU meeting. This particular effort, however, was frustrated by the reluctance of
Nigeria's neighboring leaders Amadou Ahidjo of Cameroon and
Soglo of Dahomey (now Benin) and by the lack of time for
coordination and planning.

When the OAU conference convened on September 11 it soon
became clear to the Nigerian delegation that discussion was
inevitable. Along with William Tubman of Liberia and Ankrah,
the East African states desired OAU action. Kenneth Kaunda
of Zambia was particularly adamant, threatening to walk out
if Nigeria did not agree to closed-door sessions on the war.
Haile Selassie prevailed on Obafemi Awolowo, who headed the
FMG delegation, to consult Gowon, who finally agreed to the
discussions. This arrangement was possible because Awolowo
was guaranteed the job of wording any resolution that might
come out of the conference. Ojukwu and the eastern leaders
were also willing to see how far the OAU negotiations would
go, now that the FMG were in the midst of militarily winning
back the Mid-western area.

After consultation with Gowon, who proposed some additional wording, an OAU draft resolution was finally passed
condemning secession, recognizing the internal nature of the
conflict and establishing the Consultative Mission, which
included Haile Selassie, Ahidjo, Tubman, Ankrah, Sese Seko
Mobutu of Congo, and Diori of Niger. The Mission members
assured Gowon of the OAU's desire to safeguard the territorial integrity and unity of Nigeria; even the substance of
the resolution was in effect a paraphrase of the FMG position. But the fact that the draft resolution was passed was
a partial victory for Ojukwu because it gave international
recognition to the civil war.

Before the passage of the OAU resolution creating the
Consultative Mission to Nigeria, Palmer had instructed the
U.S. Embassies in each of the countries represented at the
OAU meeting to express American gratification for the pro-
posed mission and the expectations that they must get on

with the African preservation of peace in their delicate
diplomatic activity. The American officials also were to
stress the appropriateness of continued U.S. noninvolvement;
the State Department having publicly denied arms sales to
the FMG on September 13. Mathews hurriedly telegraphed
Washington that Gowon reluctantly agreed with the "draft"
resolution, but that the FMG needs amendments in which "the
rebels must renounce secession and accept federal solution
before mediation."[23]

When the eyes of Africa were turned to this high-water
mark of OAU summit diplomacy, Palmer and Smith turned to
their embassy in Nigeria to straighten out the disruptive
and arrogant reporting, which was beginning to undermine the
One Nigeria policy. In fact, Palmer flew to Lagos to talk
to Mathews and embassy staff about their clientism problem.
He was accompanied by Charles Runyon, a State Department
legal adviser, who was assigned to somehow straighten out
this sensitive situation. The tension between the U.S.
Embassy and its Enugu Consulate finally ended on October 2
when Barnard closed the post and evacuated with his staff as
the FMG troops were fighting to capture the city.[24]

During the two months of abortive efforts to arrange a
satisfactory date for the OAU Mission to meet in Lagos, the
State Department constantly emphasized the importance of an
early meeting. The arrangement to meet in Lagos was complicated by the busy schedule and travel plans of several of
the mission members and by the FMG desire to delay a meeting
as long as possible in order to secure a greater military
advantage. In October, for example, when Ankrah was in
Canada on a state visit, the FMG argued that any replacement
of Ankrah with one of his Ministers would be an infraction
of the final OAU resolution, which authorized only the Heads
of State to convene. Nonetheless, Palmer stressed urgency
to Dahomey's Foreign Minister Zinsou and Niger's President
Diori during their state visits to America in October.
Diori told Palmer that he regretted the U.S. arms supply
policy toward the FMG, but agreed that an FMG military victory would be dangerous for those living in the eastern sectors of Nigeria. For this reason, Diori agreed to assemble
the OAU Mission Ambassadors in Paris to instigate definitive
joint action before the end of October.[25] The next day
Mathews, freed of any further contrary Enugu reports, cabled
Washington that it would be better to activate the entire
OAU Mission Ambassadors in Lagos, than in Paris.

The desire to keep the process under the control of the
FMG was obvious once the tide of battle had turned in favor
of the federal forces. As October wore on, though, the FMG
began to fear that its resistance to the OAU Mission was
causing sympathy for the Biafrans, which could result in
recognition by several African countries.[26] In early November Okoi Arikpo publicly deplored the postponements and now
urged the mission members to agree to a meeting without all
six if necessary. "Though the [OAU] group was originally
scheduled to arrive in Lagos around September 27, the mission was postponed until October 5 and then again until
November 12."[27] The first delay coincided with the unex-
pected success of the FMG in winning back the Mid-West and
the second delay occurred during the period when the federal

troops were attempting to capture the Biafran capital of Enugu and, it was hoped, end the secessionist war. When the OAU Mission finally did meet in Lagos, Biafra was an enclave surrounded by Nigeria.

The OAU Mission finally convened from November 22 to 24. Despite the urging from the U.S. Embassy in Monrovia, Tubman did not come. He claimed a long-standing speaking engagement.   The U.S. Embassy reported, however, that "Tubman is disgruntle because a letter from him to Gowon resulted in Nigerian press accusations that he is inserting a 'Trojan Horse' into the Nigerian conflict."[28] Mobutu also declined to come because of his Congolese anniversary celebrations.

The report of the mission findings were overwhelmingly favorable to the FMG, but it completely emasculated any trust in the OAU by either combatant. The FMG continued to look with disfavor on the OAU intervention and did not cooperate with any future OAU attempts to mediate their internal affairs. It should be noted that, because the mission did not consult with Ojukwu or any leader in Biafra, the Biafrans also distrusted future OAU suggestions.

State Department officials who had frequently met in a private capacity with Biafran representatives on a "listen only" basis since the fighting began continued to urge the Eastern Nigerians in the direction of talks and toward more flexibility in their negotiating position.[29] If the Biafrans would show some flexibility in their demands then the State Department hoped that the FMG would follow suit, if only in regard to the problem of medical supply deliveries.

The ICRC was initially permitted by the FMG to become involved in their internal conflict because it traditionally approached all conflicts, with the combatants' permission, for prisoner of war care and medical supplies.[30] Acting under the ICRC charter to offer such humanitarian assistance to both sides, the ICRC sent 30,000 Swiss francs worth of medical equipment to the Nigerian Red Cross representatives in Lagos and Enugu. Two medical teams were also to be sent to help with the battle casualties; one to the Nigerian side and the other to the Biafran side.

Medical and food supplies on hand for both combatants at the beginning of the war were spent by the end of the year. Any transportation of the medical team and supplies into the secessionist area was soon impossible because there was no land or sea access to the Biafran side made available by FMG to the ICRC. When Biafra lost its contact with the Cameroon border it had become a total enclave within Nigeria. Krakow was distressed by these worsening events, especially when the African Bureau did an about-face vis-à-vis Palmer's July note on the possibility of increased war victims. Krakow incredulously reported that "State says it repeatedly warned me that this is certainly going to lead to a blood bath, all the more reason why we [ARC] should support the ICRC in its efforts in Nigeria."[31] Ramone Eaton, ARC executive vice president, who had received Krakow's memo from John Wilson, jotted a personal handwritten note to Wilson on Krakow's memo urging "a contribution of $10,000 immediately for Disaster Relief/Nigerian Civil War; we have every assurance of their [ICRC] doing a good job."

Observers on the ground began to notice the growing visible signs of starvation and medical problems on both sides
of the battlefront. This was particularly true with respect
to church leaders who were committed to the well-being of
all Nigerians. What was possibly one of the more crucial
decisions made by these religious groups when the conflict
erupted was the decision by a large number of Catholic Holy
Ghost Fathers and Holy Rosary Sisters to follow their Ibo
communities deeper into the Biafran enclave. The religious
groups who were permitted to remain and work on the federal
side of the conflict knew that they were there only at the
sufferance of the FMG. This made these religious groups in
Nigeria cautious in both word and action. Therefore, the
Holy Ghost Fathers' unique position of being outside the
reach of the FMG control allowed them to be the uncontested
"news" of what was happening behind the federal lines. In
response to the reported observations by these religious
groups, relief organizations began to gear up for serious
operations on both sides of the Nigerian conflict at the end
of 1967. American agencies, however, had to abide by the
U.S. policy of pro-FMG neutrality. This was especially true
of the ARC and the Catholic Relief Services-United States
Catholic Conference (CRS-USCC).

Lorimer continued to stress the State Department's
demand in two separate meetings held with Krakow during
November that the ARC restrict its support to and through
the ICRC. Palmer felt these strong sentiments needed to be
expressed to the ARC inasmuch as Gowon had allowed the ICRC
to send a medical team into Biafra by way of the banned air
flights the weekend of November 18 and 19. (This action was
also meant to impress the OAU Mission with the humanitarian
concern the FMG had for all Nigerians.) The FMG cease-fire
had permitted the ICRC relief plane to carry medical supplies and a medical team pass the blockade. The United
States was "most appreciative for the ICRC involvement, particularly since they are maintaining an impartial role and
they are working on both sides." However, after a November
21 meeting Lorimer "stated quite categorically they [United
States] would feel very uncomfortable if the ARC were to
become involved in a one-sided support";[32] meaning, of
course, any nonmatched relief to Biafra would be outside the
policy restrictions. It was also quite clear that any humanitarian relief assistance would have to come under the
umbrella of the ICRC authority.

Palmer and the entire State Department were shocked when
they learned during the first week of December that the ARC
relief shipments intended for Nigeria had actually been
shipped to Biafra. Smith was told by Palmer to issue an
immediate directive to Krakow that the ARC must send an
identical ARC shipment to the FMG.[33] The ARC complied with
the U.S. government's directive, but they also conveyed to
Palmer their deep concern for those caught on the eastern
part of fighting. One factor of major importance to the ARC
at this time was Dr. Francis Ibiam's tour through Europe and
North America. As an elder Biafran statesman and Vice President of the World Council of Churches, his public charges of
"genocide" by the FMG heightened already existing fears of
ethnic warfare. A second factor was The New York Times

article that had reported 5,000 people killed in revenge
slayings and the <u>Washington Post</u> article that had reported
that up to 2,000 Ibos had been massacred by vengeful minority tribes in Calabar, without apparent interference by FMG
troops.[34]
These "bloodbath" concepts were not only expressed by
sensationalism seekers, the concept of possible "genocide"
had also been heard from academics and government officials
who spoke both publicly and in confidential personal meetings at home and abroad.[35] Three respectable academics in
New York, Stanley Diamond, Audrey Chapman, and Conor Cruise
O'Brien, visited Biafra in September 1967, and on their
return they issued a warning that the civil war could very
easily lead to genocide. They also urged a cease-fire and
U.S. recognition of Biafra. The first Congressman to mention the Nigerian problem was Joseph Y. Resnick (D-NY).
Resnick spoke before the House of Representatives on March
20, 1967, concerning the growing tension in Nigeria and the
possible breakup of the federation.[36] He had just returned
from a one-week tour of Africa, during which he had sought
to explain the U.S. role in the Vietnam conflict. One month
later Resnick himself was seeking to understand the U.S.
role of neutrality in Nigeria. "Is this compliance by the
U.S. Government with the internal air blockade by Lagos
against eastern Nigeria the first step in an involvement by
the U.S. on the side of the Lagos Government against its
eastern region? Is this the first step in our becoming
involved with one side of a dispute, as we did in the
Congo?"[37] Six months later, after the FMG forces had
repelled the only Biafran military offensive and were rapidly condensing the secessionist territory, Resnick noted a
change in the conduct of the war.

> So long as this remained a war between two mil-
> itary groupings, the United States' proper role
> was to stay out. What we see happening now is
> of a different reaction. Instead of soldiers
> killing soldiers, innocent civilians, women and
> children as well as men are being murdered--
> there is no other word for it. Reliable sources
> reaching me indicate that these killings
> already are on a large scale, and carry the
> clear warning that unless there is a cease-fire
> in the next 10 days, they will reach the pro-
> portions of genocide.[38]

Resnick summarized his interest in the conflict by
introducing a bill the following month. It asked that "the
President of the United States be requested to take such
action as may be necessary to transmit to the belligerent
parties, to the Organization of African Unity, to the United
Nations and to the International Red Cross the earnest plea
of the United States that all appropriate bodies join in
seeking a halt to the hostilities and take measures, including the dispatch of impartial observes, to protest the lives
of the civilian population of the area."[39] Although this
third factor of U.S. official congressional concern was
denied as having any substantive truth by the State Depart-

ment's "African experts," Palmer would not allow any official comment on the fourth international factor that spurred
the ARC to send the relief to Biafra.   The ARC had also
received from Catholic missionaries in Biafra a copy of a
memorandum ("For Eyes Only") sent by Bishop James Moynagh of
Calabar and Bishop Godfrey Okoye of Port Harcourt to the
Pope.   "(1)   There has been in fact a conspiracy of silence
by the World Press and by the Great Powers to cloak over the
terrifying attack on basic human rights and dignity since
1966 and there has been systematic and organized slaughter
of any Ibo civilians found in federal areas."[40]
     Based on these factors the ARC had decided to send the
relief to Biafra and accept the inevitable rebuff from the
State Department. Inside the secessionist eastern enclave
evidence of starvation grew increasingly worse as the year
drew to a close. The loss of vital transportation access for
food imports, the loss of internal food-producing lands, and
the overloading of the extended family system with constantly increasing refugees were compounded by the total FMG
blockade of Biafra.   The ICRC estimated that approximately
100,000 Nigerians on both sides of the fighting needed immediate help. But the humanitarian relief impasse was bound up
by the issue of political sovereignty. The FMG insisted on
inspection rights of all imported items and foreign personnel to the former Eastern Region, and Biafra refused to
accept anything inspected by Nigeria because it violated its
independence. Such was the horse trading of humanity for
political and economic power.

Notes

1. St. Jorre, The Brothers' War, 100. The author also refers to the "Nsukka secessionist
group."
2. INTERCROIZROUGE, Geneva, Switzerland, to AMCROSS, Washington, D.C., telegram dated Nov. 6,
1967.
3. U.S. State Department Deptel 13730 to Accra, July 27, 1967, stated that a stalemate in Nigerian fighting would result soon because of the serious Biafran military losses of important towns
and cities. This would likely increase receptivity on both sides for mediation efforts and relief
assistance. The African Bureau based their belief in greater Biafran receptivity on Mathews's
Telegram 827, July 25, 1967, which discussed how moderate Eastern civilian leaders were urging a
cease-fire despite Ojukwu's bawling out, and on Mathews's Telegram 908, July 26, 1967, which discussed Awolowo's views on how to restore unity and end the war.
4. National American Red Cross, General Records, July 19, 1967.
5. Ibid., July 25, 1967, Samuel Krakow's note to John C. Wilson, Executive Vice President.
6. Ibid., June 13, 1967.
7. Lagos, Telegram 827, p. 3.
8. Deptel 13730 to Lagos, July 27, 1967, p. 1.
9. Accra, Telegram 315/03035, Aug. 1, 1967; Lagos, Telegram 314/11495, Aug. 2, 1967; Ibadan,
Telegram 59, Aug. 3, 1967; and Kaduna, Telegram 130, Aug. 3, 1967.
10. Lagos, Telegram 1091, Aug. 1, 1967, p. 3.
11. Kaduna, Telegram 139, Aug. 7, 1967.
12. Accra, Telegram 315/02755, July 14, 1967, and Accra, Telegram 315/03035, Aug. 8, 1967.
13. Lagos, Telegram 1319, Aug. 9, 1967.
14. London, Telegram 1110, Aug. 16, 1967, "Escalation has prompted British press to call on HMG
to take initiative in bringing about negotiations"; London, Telegram 1216, Aug. 18, 1967, "Wonder
if it possible to cut off arms supply?"; London, Telegram 1329, Aug. 23, 1967, "British anxious to
get fighting stopped."
15. St. Jorre, The Brothers' War, 183
16. Cronjé, The World and Nigeria, 268-269.
17. "Neither the United States nor the Soviet Union has in the past been an important supplier
of arms to Nigeria. Consistent with that fact, the United States decided for its part on the outbreak of the current hostilities in Nigeria that it would not sell or otherwise supply arms and
ammunition to either side. To have done so would have risked deepening the conflict and introducing an element of great-power competition in the internal affairs of a friendly state.
The United states has adhered fully to that policy. Its refusal to supply arms has been stated
publicly and is well known to the Soviet Union. In these circumstances, it is a matter of regret

to the United States that the Soviet Union has not shown the same forbearance but, on the contrary, has decided to engage in the supply of arms in this internal conflict."   Colwell, "Biafra," 15.
18. See Cronjé, The World and Nigeria, 392-392, tables and charts in Appendix 2.

Year	Nigerian Imports for U.S.S.R.	Cocoa Exports
1965	£ 281,709	£ 2,215,787
1966	5,210	--
1967	1,101,248	3,987,146
1968	₦ 897,063	₦ 5,411,867
1969	1,628,188	7,772,977

19. St. Jorre, The Brothers' War, 173.
20. Lagos, Airgram A-469, Mar. 7, 1968, "Nigeria: Annual U.S. Policy Assessment 1967," p. 4. A candid postscript that was classified as "Secret," declassified for analysis.
21. Deptel 41507 to Enugu, Sept. 21, 1967.
22. Lagos, Telegram 2137, Sept. 1, 1967.
23. Lagos, Telegram 2535, Sept. 14, 1967.
24. Barnard's problems with Mathews and Olson were not over when he returned to Washington. He received highly critical efficiency reports from both the Ambassador and the embassy Deputy Chief of Mission. Olson, in particular, charged Barnard with emotional involvement in the Biafran cause. These efficiency reports are vital to a healthy FSO career, and anything less than laudatory destroys a career. Yet, on his return to Washington Barnard was awarded the State Department's Superior Honor Award. Palmer and Smith originated the recommendation and cited Barnard for vigor and clarity of analysis, recommendations and independence of judgment.
25. U.S. Mission to the United Nations Organization, Telegram 1281, Oct. 9, 1967.
26. Kinshasa, Airgram-TDCSDB 315/03741-67, Sept. 18, 1967, "Kaunda threatened to quit and recognize Biafra unless Nigeria agrees to mission" and Nairobi, Airgram-TDCS 314/14537-67, Sept. 28, 1967, "Kenyatta, Nyerere, Ankrah prepared to recognize Biafra if FMG doesn't agree to meeting."
27. Colwell, "Biafra," 16.
28. Monrovia, Telegram 2010, Nov. 19, 1967.
29. State Department, Memo, "U.S. Activity on Behalf of Peaceful Settlement," Apr. 20, 1968.
30. Thierry Hentsch, Face au Blocus: La Croix-rouge Internationale dans le Nigeria en guerre (1967-2970) (Geneva: Institut Universitaire de Hautes Études Internationales, 1973).
31. National American Red Cross, General Records, Oct. 2, 1967.
32. Ibid., Nov. 21, 1967.
33. Ibid., Dec. 5, 1967.
34. "Race Hatred in Nigeria," The New York Times, Oct. 22, 1967, p. 2E. "Massacre Reported," Washington Post, Nov. 3, 1967, p. 7B.
35. National American Red Cross, General Records, Krakow to Eaton, Oct. 2, 1967, contains a reference to the State Department's belief in a "bloodbath" in Nigeria/Biafra; but this phrase was not part of the usual wording style for the African Bureau unless they meant to hasten aid by force of fear.
36. Mar. 20, 1967, Congressional Record, 90th Cong., 1st sess., 113:7317. "The position of the U.S. Government has been to adhere steadfastly to the maintenance of Nigeria as an integral nation without trying to tell the Nigerians how strong or weak a federation they should have. I found the role of the United States misunderstood by many leading Nigerians."
37. Ibid., Apr. 13, 1967, 113:9517.
38. Ibid., Oct. 17, 1967, 113:29109.
39. Ibid., Nov. 13, 1967, 113:32289.
40. "Memorandum Submitted to the Pope on Behalf of the Archbishop and Hierarchy of Onitsha Ecclesiastical Province by Bishop James Moynagh of Calabar and Godfrey Okoye of Port Harcourt." This "For Eyes Only" xerox copy of the "Memorandum" (dated approximately fall 1967) is part of the Nigeria/Biafra Clearing House papers, Swarthmore College Peace Collection, Swarthmore, Pennsylvania.   Bishop Godfrey Okoye, C.S.Sp., interview with author, Villanova, Pennsylvania, August 7, 1976.

3

Initiatives for Reconciliation

The new year began with more disturbing reports of massive
military losses and civilian deaths in Nigeria. When The
New York Times's Monday, January 8, 1968, article, estimated
that about 2,000 civilian Ibos had been killed in the south-
eastern fighting around Calabar,[1] the FMG Second Division
was also about to lose more than 2,000 of its troops in the
northwestern sector of Biafra because of multiple and disas-
trous attempts to cross the Niger River for a frontal attack
on the Ibo market town of Onitsha. However, the world attention was not riveted on this conflict and its loss of life.
Rather, American soldiers fighting to recapture the U.S.
Embassy in Saigon and the battle for Hue--these were the
number one news-making events. But the struggle in eastern
Nigeria, although remote, was important for Nigeria and
those throughout the world interested in humanity and
involved in relief activity.

The dimensions of the relief task for Nigeria and Biafra
grew quickly. The ICRC submitted a second request to the
FMG for a sorely needed medical supplies relief flight into
Biafra. Actual permission for the ICRC planeload of medicine
and personnel was secured from the FMG on Wednesday, January
10, but the ICRC were then refused permission by the Biafran
authorities because of inspection problems. Five days
later, when permission was canceled by the FMG, it was followed by a Biafran agreement on January 17--a seesaw pattern
that was to prevail throughout the conflict. Despite these
deliberate political vacillations and the many rumors of Ibo
genocide by the FMG troops, Joseph Palmer continued to
insist that the State Department be in total control of all
U.S. relief activity so as to preserve their pro-FMG neutrality policy. Robert McCloskey, the spokesman for the
State Department, issued a statement in support of the FMG
the same day as the ICRC received news of their flight
denial.

> We've been concerned with a number of insinua-
> tions recently alleging United States support
> of the "Biafran" regime. I wish to make
> very clear that the United States continues to

> recognize the Federal Military Government as
> the only legal government in Nigeria. We do
> not recognize "Biafra" nor, as far as we know,
> does any other government in the world. We
> have, from the outset of the Nigerian Crisis,
> regarded it as an internal conflict which, in
> the last analysis, only the Nigerians them-
> selves can resolve.[2]

But the United States and the U.K. did respond to the cancellation of the latest ICRC flight request with six weeks
of secret negotiations. News of increased killings and
civilian deaths in Nigeria began to concern officials in the
State Department, international humanitarian organizations,
and relief personnel stationed in Biafra and Nigeria.

The Nigerian crisis also became a concern for the American Negro Leadership Conference on Africa (ANLCA). This
civil war was their "first attempt to deal with an African
problem unrelated to freedom or development."[3] However, it
was not until the summer of 1967 that the ANLCA Executive
Director Whitney Young and three other delegates had made
several trips to Nigeria to arrange an Afro-American mediation mission. Their discussions with the FMG, OAU leaders,
and Mathews did not produce any concrete suggestions or support.[4] But when the ANLCA judged that the U.S. involvement
was evolving into humanitarian indifference in early 1968,
they sent their representative to Lagos on February 13 to
pave the way for an immediate ANLC visit. His request that
the future ANLC trip include a visit to Biafra was denied
because of "personal security problems."[5] The urgency of the
trip was then stressed by the announcement that Martin
Luther King, Jr, would himself lead the mission. At the end
of March, King appointed Ralph Abernathy to replace him on
the ANLC team, which was scheduled to arrive in Nigeria on
April 15. The mission was forestalled by King's assassina-
tion, but their plans demonstrated a real concern for all
Nigerians.

The Vatican was also concerned enough with the Nigerian
crisis as described by the two Biafran Bishops that it sent
two papal envoys, Monsignor Rochau of Caritas Internationalis (the Vatican's relief agency) and Monsignor Conway of
the Irish College, to visit Nigeria and Biafra. These envoys
had told Yakubu Gowon in December 1967 that they had come to
arrange for the distribution of food and clothing, that
their task was not political, religious, diplomatic, but
purely humanitarian.[6] Gowon did not grant any cease fire to
allow these envoys to fly into Biafra for the same reason
that the ICRC were denied permission--the FMG could not
guarantee their safety. When the monsignors chartered a
Pan-American plane to fly them at their own risk into Port
Harcourt, the FMG issued a specific prohibition of all use
of airplanes into Port Harcourt. The envoys began to believe
that the second part of their trip to Biafra was insurmount-
able when Pan-American backed down from their contract under
pressure from the FMG and the U.S. Embassy.

The Catholic bishops in Biafra did not agree with the
Vatican envoys that the situation was hopeless. Father
Anthony Byrne, a Holy Ghost Father who was the Director of

Catholic Social Services in Biafra, was asked by the Biafran bishops to find a way to bring the monsignors pass the FMG blockade.   Following in the recent successful footsteps of Reverend E. H. Johnson of the Presbyterian Church in Canada who had chartered space on one of Hank Wharton's arms flights into Biafra, Byrne worked a special deal with Wharton.   Byrne arranged for an "exclusive use" charter for one of Wharton's planes, which flew from Lisbon to São Tomé and then to Port Harcourt. He also arranged that the Catholic envoys be accompanied into Biafra by six World Council of Churches representatives and several tons of medicine provided by Caritas Internationalis.[7]   Thus the "illegal" relief flight pattern into Biafra was established for the duration of the conflict.

During this period, a less action-oriented and more diplomacy-oriented   approach was proposed by the State Department. Commonwealth Secretary General Arnold Smith was again conjoled by the Americans to work as an intermediary between the combatants. Although the Commonwealth efforts of exploratory talks had been temporarily put aside after the OAU summit meeting in Kinshasa and the OAU Mission, which failed to materialize any peace initiative, Smith and his Deputy remained convinced that both sides still sufficiently trusted the Commonwealth Secretary's role that their efforts might prove more fruitful in some third attempt.

Using the news of the war casualties and the canceled ICRC flight as an emergency crisis to reopen talks between Gowon and Odumegwu Ojukwu, Smith took a new approach to the possibility of secret meetings. Gowon, with Okoi Arikpo's urging, again agreed to assign FMG Permanent Secretaries Allison Ayida, Philip Asiodu, and Joda to the proposed Commonwealth talks; and Ojukwu designated the Biafran representatives Mojekwa, Udofia, and Dike. This time the Commonwealth Secretary General served as an intermediary, ferrying proposals back and forth between the two sides in an attempt to narrow the area of disagreement as a prelude to meaningful discussions. Supported by the United States, Smith also sounded out the Canadians and the British about the possibility of some contribution to a Commonwealth peacekeeping force. When Gowon and Ojukwu did not express opposition to the principle of a peacekeeping force providing that only non-African troops were used, Commonwealth Secretary General Smith began to look for appropriate volunteers.

Believing that the FMG position would soon harden if reasonable progress were not evident, Elbert Mathews encouraged the Commonwealth Secretary General to put together a "loose package" of five points that would accept a single Nigerian entity, give safeguards to the Ibos, and bring about a cease-fire policed by a Commonwealth peace force. On February 10, Smith flew to Lagos to hold a personal meeting with Gowon. The meeting was a disaster and the aftermath bitter when a representative at the meeting decided to leak some of the sensitive secret terms to a Manchester _Guardian_ journalist.   The consequent scoop article reported that there was a Commonwealth plan to have 3,000 peacekeeping troops assembled from the West Indies, India, Pakistan, and Malaya. The ensuing public debate on these Commonwealth troops allowed Gowon and Ojukwu to reject the Commonwealth's proposals. The State Department's INR concluded soon after these events, that because the commissioners had not worked together successfully the Commonwealth Secretariat had lost its potential as a future viable mediator.

Gowon and Ojukwu used this diplomatic discussion period to feign compliance to the cease-fire agenda because they both knew that Britain was not about to change its policy of arms shipments to the FMG and the United States would defi- nitely continue its support for pro-FMG neutrality. The State Department reaffirmed this support on February 5 by stating that the United States "has in no way encouraged or otherwise supported the rebellion in Nigeria." Once again it was reiterated that the United States "regards the break- away movement as an internal conflict."[8]

The U.S. Embassy staff in Lagos were also becoming dis- enchanted with events, even as Gowon and the FMG worked slowly for a military resolution of the conflict.   In the embassy's annual assessment of its policy toward Nigeria, Gowon was now portrayed as "not having transformed into a charismatic, electrifying leader...but he does provide quiet, steady leadership; and the FMG militarily is if'y."[9] Throughout the 17 pages of the embassy woes due to the con- flict, Mathews listed only one major American casualty of the Nigerian Civil War--the U.S. Peace Corps.[10] Peace Corps volunteers were not being allowed to reenter Nigeria because of their support of Biafra since the beginning of the war. Given this token of grief, the embassy went on record that the United States "would settle for a loose political struc- ture for Nigeria in the hope that economic ties would lead to closer political ties." Mathews believed that economic convergence would bring about political unity, and with that belief he reported that American "attempts at reconciliation were frustrated by three major factors: Ibo estrangement, Ojukwu's intransigence, and FMG ineptitude."[11] On the only positive page of the document, the embassy begged for increased assistance from the International Bank for Recon- struction and Development (IBRD) for Nigeria to meet its short-range balance of payments.   Based on the embassy's arguments, the United States eventually agreed to fund $62 million of the Nigerian $225 million six-year reconstruction plan. In one of the rare condescensions to reality, Mathews allowed the staff to insert the possibility that "if the [Ibo] heartland is invaded for occupation, there will be tragic loss of life."[12]

President Lyndon B. Johnson, when he accepted the new Nigerian Ambassador's credentials in March, emphasized the need for a peaceful end to the savagery.

> Mr. Ambassador [Joseph Iyalla], the United
> States has always wished to see a prosperous
> and united Nigeria growing in strength and
> vitality. For this reason, it is today sin-
> cerely sympathetic to the desire of the Federal
> Military Government to preserve Nigerian unity.
> At the same time, we have grieved with you over
> the lives being lost in the tragic war ow rag-
> ing in your country.   We have also ardently
> hoped for the earliest possible peaceful reso-

lution of a conflict which has brought so much
pain and suffering to the Nigerian people and
for the beginning of a period of national rehabilitation.[13]

This pain and suffering for the Nigerian people was about to
turn the corner and confront the long-term condition of massive starvation.
     On the battlefield,   it was only when Murtala Mohammed
decided his FMG troops should cross the Niger River further
north at Lokoja and   come southeast through Awka that the
federal troops were able, on March 21, to capture the Ibo
city of Onitsha.   Now firmly established in the capital of
the Biafran territory, the FMG announced the immediate
implementation of the new 12 states of Nigeria. The Biafran
army, however, did not surrender because they had lost
another city, which was a European symbol of the secessionist's capital. They just moved further into the Ibo heartland.   But, in this spirit of increasing security the FMG
began to be more accepting of the upcoming international
appeal by the ICRC for Nigerian Red Cross (NRC) relief activity throughout the country.   It should be remembered that
at this period of the ICRC's development, the traditional
relief activity of the ICRC was still conceived primarily as
a medical and prisoners of war activity and not as a crisis
food supplier during a famine.
     On April 6 Mohammed's First Division troops captured
Abakaliki,   the provincial headquarters and main food-
producing area within Biafra. This had a more devastating
effect on Biafra than the loss of Onitsha because all other
sources of protein had already been cut off by the war.
Imported beef from northern Nigeria had been discontinued
for a year and the southern fishing industry was under FMG
control since late 1967.   The loss of Abakaliki and its
large yam supplies was the severest blow to the food supply
of all those living within the shrinking Biafran borders.
Dr. Ikejiani reported that the Biafran Food Directorate
"failed to evacuate large quantities of food such as yams,
rice, from the food producing areas when these areas were
threatened by Nigerians. That they failed to do so and store
food in safe areas inside Biafra was a tragic error. Had
this been done, there would have been enough food to keep,
at least, the army going on for sometime without much starvation.[14]   The loss of this food depot town sharply
increased the Biafran starvation and gave greater substance
to the existing rumors of genocide.
     The ICRC relief appeal of April 10 responded to the new
famine situation by going beyond its traditional role to
include all aspects of war relief, including food. This
action was initially supported by the FMG and the NRC
announcement from Lagos that the country's situation was
considered critical wherein "more than two million children
and 1.6 million nursing mothers were in danger of malnutrition and starvation." The NRC also predicted that every
week more that 25,000 additional war victims would need
immediate relief care. Gowon agreed that the ICRC should be
given the official task of coordinating all of Nigeria's
relief, including the secessionist territory, because of the

obvious lack of experience by the NRC in medical and food relief. But if the NRC was inexperienced in relief activities, their officials became even more disoriented when the disorganized ICRC led them into a realm beyond the abilities of the ICRC leadership.

Robert Smith informed the ARC the following day (April 11) that the U.S.A.I.D. office would begin work immediately on the possible utilization of Public Law 480 (P.L. 480 or "Food for Peace") for Nigeria.[15] The fact that Palmer knew that the African country of Tanzania was about to officially recognize Biafra may have also influenced the State Department's humanitarian decision to provide food. However, Mathews hesitated to assist in any implementation of a P.L. 480 plan because in his opinion it would be an embarrassment to declare Nigeria a "disaster area" and publicly question NRC competency and FMG sovereignty. But Mathews knew in early April that Nigerian relief efforts in the recaptured territory were suffering dismally from undisciplined troops and officers. For the usual clientism reason this pertinent information was never relayed by the embassy to Washington.

Accurate and vital information on the Nigerian crisis had become so confused for the senior State Department officials that they ordered Palmer to prepare a classified report specifically on its peacemaking activity for Nigeria. Palmer, in turn, ordered Roy Melbourne, the Country Director for West Africa, to draft this document. As bureaucracy will have it, the actual job fell to Dane F. Smith, a new assistant on the Nigerian Desk. This document, which was his first FSO assignment, presented only the positive diplomatic negotiations of the United States with regard to the Nigerian conflict.

The seven-part document contained no new information or insight into American activity because it was a simple compilation of messages between embassies, consulates and Washington.[16] But it did become one more item that Secretary of State Dean Rusk used in his discussion with the heads of the African Bureau and the West African Section, the Nigerian Desk officer, and Mathews who was called back to Washington to explain the confusion and unprofessional approach to events in Nigeria.

The media's reporting of the high cost in human lives for the eventual FMG victory at Port Harcourt, the existing morass of NRC relief activity, and Nigeria's request for international relief and medical supplies were some of the major reasons why Rusk took steps to question the U.S. Embassy's ability to accurately report events as well as the African Bureau's awareness of events in that country. Even during the preliminary stages of the second OAU conference, scheduled to be held May 23 to 31 in Kampala, Uganda, the OAU staff were complaining to Washington about the pressure put on it by the U.S. Embassy.

The first result of these official investigations was to send Palmer and his staff off to Africa and Europe for a seven-week fact-finding trip. A second decision was to schedule a special declaration of American assistance to the Nigerian relief effort on Sunday, May 26, 1968--the first official U.S. rift in the hands-off neutral policy approach toward Nigeria. Clinton Olson, acting on direct orders from the State Department and in the deliberate absence of Ambassador Mathews who was in Washington, officially declared a disaster in the whole of Nigeria and authorized the use of U.S.A.I.D. contingency funds for relief activity.

Palmer took immediate steps to control any possible overreaction by American relief agencies. Mathews (still in Washington to explain his embassy's point of view) and Alan Hardy, one of the newly assigned Nigerian Desk officers, were sent by Palmer to have a personal talk with the ARC international section. The purpose of this May 31 meeting was to ensure the ARC's continued support for the ICRC relief and other programs in the various affected areas. Although Mathews owned up to Ramone Eaton and Samuel Krakow at the meeting that it did not appear that the Nigerian Red Cross was actually functioning inside of Biafra, Mathews inserted his typical downplay-the-conflict approach by adding that the 600,000 people reported by the ICRC as being refugees in Biafra actually were on federal territory.

There was a far deeper reason why the United States insisted on the ICRC as the primary official relief agency in the Nigerian conflict; outside of it being the only foreign relief operation recognized by the FMG. The major compelling reason for this unwavering American support was based on the belief that the United States was chiefly responsible for the ICRC being initially involved in the expanded relief system. While in Switzerland during the spring of 1968, Deputy Assistant Secretary for African Affairs Robert Moore believed that he had convinced the ICRC authority that they should accept a much broader role of coordinating all the Nigerian and Biafran relief. Moore had returned to the State Department with the strong recommendation that the United States government guarantee support for this magnified role of the ICRC in Nigerian relief. The State Department, therefore, had avoided direct involvement in the conflict by propping up the ICRC as a "legal" involved third party, with the promise that the ICRC would be in control of all American relief.

This procedure of having all relief activities under the authority of the ICRC's coordinating umbrella also allowed American officials to use vague or misleading statements. For example, during the State Department July 3 briefing when McCloskey was asked by a reporter if the United States was getting involved in the relief efforts in Biafra, he gave the official reply that "we have made certain contributions in that connection...and it was designed or intended for victims on both sides in the civil strife in Nigeria." His response also referred to the U.S. total of $1,327,000 in disaster relief funds and foodstuffs. What the State Department failed to reveal was the fact that this total amount was only going to the FMG. A more honest answer should have been--the U.S. has no involvement whatsoever in Biafran relief!

The U.S. contributions were government funds donated to the ICRC and the ARC, neither of which were able to supply any relief to Biafra because of U.S. policy. In a close reading of the State Department's July 11 briefing McCloskey's statements demonstrate this point. "Other foodstuffs, including the $1.1 million we have furnished under the Food

For Peace Program, are being positioned in places in Nigeria (Enugu, Calabar and Benin) from which truck convoys <u>could</u> move the food into Biafra <u>when</u> a land route <u>can be</u> arranged between the opposing forces"[17] (emphasis added). The truth of the matter is that the United States was earmarking relief for people and places that were inaccessible at the time of the announcement. The food and supplies were in Federal Nigeria to be used if and when the FMG decided to feed and heal their enemy. Therefore, direct relief for Biafra was not officially initiated by the United States until August 1968--fifteen months after the civil war began.

Despite original guarantees, U.S. support for the ICRC began to wane in May. Krakow, during one his then-frequent meetings with members of the State Department, noted this subtle shift in policy and recorded his impressions.

> The Ambassador [Mathews] seems to be somewhat critical of the ICRC since they seem to be too closely allied with or seem to be emphasizing the needs of Biafra rather than the needs of other parts of the country as well. The Ambassador also indicated that since Mr. Hoffman left [ICRC] there has not been as good liaison with the Nigerian Government in Lagos as might be desired. His replacement apparently does not speak English too well. Further, the Ambassador was most disappointed that the ICRC had insisted that the Nigerian Government lift the blockade in order to allow ICRC supplies to come into Biafra. This, he felt, was an error since the lifting of the blockade represented a military-political position of the Nigerian Government, whereas the ICRC would have been better advised to limit its requests to the Nigerian Government to make such temporary arrangements which would allow the passage of their relief supplies.[18]

Because the ICRC was not doing the job expected of it, U.S. support was initially more public verbiage than hard cash. The first direct cash donation of $100,000 to the ICRC by the U.S. government was in June 1968, two months after the ICRC was actively involved in Nigerian relief programs. This delay of cash donations had a disastrous result on the ICRC work in the relief work, for its credit was questioned. "The slowness of government to move into Nigeria/Biafran relief is clearly reflected in the ICRC's monthly income and expenditure figures for its operation there...the cumulative deficit through November amounting to nearly 5 million francs."[19]

There was also the coordination problem for the ICRC. As a representative of a relief agency noted after a September 12 meeting;

> The ICRC has not always been gracefully accepted by voluntary agencies who have been on the scene. They intend to remain and like operations to be identified with them. Volun-

> tary agencies CARE, CRS, CCN, Save the Chil-
> dren, OXFAM, hold regular weekly meetings with
> ICRC and Nigerian Red Cross....Voluntary
> agencies do not appear to quarrel with the fact
> of ICRC role as overall coordinator, but do
> believe they have qualified people experienced
> in both relief operations and on local scene
> who can be used more effectively within the
> ICRC structure. In general they believe ICRC
> administrative staff must be strengthened with
> not only more personnel to do the job, but with
> more personnel experienced in relief work.[20]

Although it was understood by all American voluntary
agencies that they came under ICRC coordinating authority,
the American agencies also knew that they were responsible
for the acquisition, distribution and control of all U.S.
government relief assistance after consultation with the
ICRC Director. Therefore, as the ICRC developed more and
more organizational and logistical problems in dealing with
these strong-willed American relief agencies, both internal
and external pressures built up against the role and work of
the ICRC.[21] Nonetheless, Mathews urged the ARC in May 1968
to send funds and personnel to assist the NRC and the ICRC,
which he stated was reasonably well organized. This later
proved to be another totally inaccurate judgment; both the
NRC and the ICRC were in the same shape--confused and disorganized.

Mathews also reiterated the promise to Eaton and Krakow
that the U.S. government would conduct all relief activity
through their ARC organization to the ICRC. This would
include the authorized shipment of $1.1 million worth of
food to arrive in Nigeria during July, a plane for use in
relief work, and trucks to deliver food to the affected
areas. In return, the ARC was asked to become more actively
involved in pressuring various members of "the ICRC to work
more closely with the Nigerian Government since, in his
[Mathews] opinion, in the final analysis, in view of the
deteriorating situation in Biafra, there would be no other
way of meeting the needs of the Ibos who, at this point,
seem to be completely surrounded."[22]

The $1.1 million was intended to go directly to the CRS--
USCC programs in Nigeria. CRS-USCC humanitarian programs in
Nigeria had been in operation since 1959. They had maintained a field headquarters representative in Lagos and had
worked in the Eastern Region through locally employed CRS
staff. When the civil war erupted it was reported that
despite some inconveniences the local CRS Eastern representatives were able to distribute 50 tons of foodstuffs and 67
tons of clothing to refugees before the end of 1967. But,
because of the final total FMG blockade, the CRS distribution centers in Biafra eventually ran out of supplies.

The CRS-USCC representative in Lagos, following instructions from his headquarters in New York, did not seek access
to the blockaded Eastern Region. CRS-USCC officials did not
want to jeopardize their programs in the federal territory
by seeking to enter the secessionist territory, thereby publicly offending the FMG. Therefore, as the CRS-USCC

depended on their field reports to request relief supplies,
any calculation that would omit the Eastern Region's needs
would result in a severe reduction of supplies. So it happened that the CRS-USCC programs in the Eastern section of
the conflict soon became depleted.

The U.S. contribution of $1.1 million to the CRS-USCC
through the ARC for relief work in Nigeria was a great boost
to CRS-USCC prestige and programs. This public acclamation
of confidence was used by the CRS-USCC officials as a
rationalized justification for keeping their past donations
secret; for the CRS-USCC had made private donations of
$22,000 in January and February 1968 to particularly needy
and influential individuals working in Biafran relief.   The
CRS-USCC had made the decision not to inform the U.S. of
such covert funding of Biafran relief because it would have
caused political and legal problems for all CRS-USCC programs that received U.S. funding.

One feature of the CRS-USCC work is that they are an
independent relief agency registered with the U.S. government for the distribution of U.S. supplies and foodstuffs in
disaster areas under Title II of P.L. 480. When U.S.A.I.D.
inaugurated a contract with CRS-USCC to work in Nigeria it
restricted the CRS-USCC distribution of U.S. relief within
the policy guidelines of the U.S. government. In this case
it meant working only on the federal side of the battlefront. CRS-USCC could not legally authorize any P.L. 480
food to be distributed inside Biafra due to the FMG blockade, and because U.S. policy lacked both official and tacit
recognition of Biafra. Even private funds to Biafra would
have threatened the CRS-USCC role in Nigeria's relief programs.

To outmaneuver this impasse, the CRS-USCC wanted the
Nigerian civil war declared a "disaster area" as quickly as
possible. Obtaining the P.L. 480 food free of charge for an
officially declared disaster would enable CRS-USCC to hold
their own funds for the purchase of other necessary supplies
and to pay for transportation costs. CRS-USCC relief workers also knew from their past experience that there was a
strong possibility that U.S.A.I.D. would eventually pay all
or part of transportation costs for P.L. 480 supplies used
in such disaster situations. But the CRS-USCC would continue
to be legally bound to seek a special exemption from U.S.
A.I.D. if it sought to publicly expand its relief activity
to Biafra.   Even if U.S.A.I.D. gave its consent, the CRS-
USCC would also have to be sensitive to the demands of the
FMG, and the degree that any such potential Biafran relief
would affect CRS-USCC's larger Lagos operation.

No political, only legal, strings can to be attached to
U.S. government assistance distributed through the P.L. 480
program. CRS-USCC understood these official policies, but
in this situation political intervention and relief activity
were inseparable due to the total blockade of Biafra by the
FMG.   Any CRS-USCC food or medical relief supplies to reach
the enclave would have to violate some FMG-held territory or
air space.   Therefore, the CRS-USCC could not supply any
relief needs by air, land, or water because it would violate
FMG sovereignty, which in turn would immediately be incon-
sistent with the U.S. government's demand that all relief

agencies follow all FMG directives.

There were few who needed food more than the starving and malnourished people in the secessionist territory of Biafra, and there were probably no more compactly produced high-protein foods suitable for the feeding of large numbers of people than P.L. 480 supplies. Unfortunately for the thousands in the grip of famine, the CRS-USCC officials decided in favor of long-term political expediency by agreeing to the contractual demands that the distribution of P.L. 480 foods take place only in federal-held territory. These considerations did cost lives and were directly related to the political hesitations by the CRS-USCC whereby the decision to save human lives came second to the political survival of the Catholic bureaucratic programs.

Bishop Edward Swanstrom, Executive Director of CRS-USCC, felt personal misgivings with the agency's decision. He approached Vice President Hubert Humphrey in early May 1968 to discuss how the American voluntary agencies could best help the relief problems of both Nigeria and Biafra. The Vice President's office informed CRS-USCC on Tuesday, May 7, that Under Secretary of State Nicholas Katzenbach and Palmer would meet with the CRS-USCC staff concerning the entire Nigerian relief system. In preparation for that meeting, CRS-USCC asked Palmer for a clear indication of the possibility of extending the declaration of a disaster area to Biafra. Palmer replied that a dispatch would have to be sent to Lagos seeking the embassy's reaction to such a request. Palmer did not see fit to tell CRS-USCC that a positive reply was unlikely, especially since Mathews was presently in Washington. What Palmer did convey to CRS-USCC was verbal support and concurrence that the eastern territory should be declared a disaster are if all CRS-USCC reports were accurate. In return, Palmer asked CRS-USCC to see what assistance could be expected from the ICRC for the CRS-USCC operation. It was well known at that time, however, that the ICRC was wary of all church relief aid because they were reported to be involved with mixing-up relief with Wharton's military shipments into Biafra.

Other reasons for Palmer's delay tactic included the sudden official recognition of Biafra by the African countries of Gabon (May 8), the Ivory Coast (May 15), and Zambia (May 20). A second ICRC international appeal (May 14) for humanitarian relief funds also weakened Palmer's position. If these diplomatic and humanitarian events strengthened the political will of Biafra, the FMG's strength was in military victories, especially the federal Third Division capture of Port Harcourt and the entire oil fields by Sunday, May 19. Although this FMG military success ended any possibility of an economically viable Biafra, it did not break the Biafran spirit. Just prior to the fall of Port Harcourt, which was Biafra's only large airport after the loss of Enugu, the Biafrans had built several airstrips during the rainy season in anticipation of future needs. One of these airstrips, Uli, which was a converted stretch of road west of the town of Orlu, eventually became the most internationally famous as the symbol of the Biafran's positive fighting spirit.

This spirit of determination was strengthened by the negative aspects of the Nigerian air warfare. "One of the

things which hardened the Easterners' determination to fight
to the last man, if necessary, was the Federal side's use of
air raids. Nothing had contributed more to the prolongation
of the war than the indiscriminate activities of the Federal
Air Force for the greater part of the civil war.   It was not
until the last few months of the war that they relented
somewhat in the bombing of civilian populations and concentrated on the war fronts and military targets."[23]   The
indiscriminate FMG air raids affected not only the normal
population but also the many refugees who had fled into the
Biafran enclave.   At the beginning of June the FMG estimated
that there were 140,000 refugees in the federally controlled
Calabar area alone.
     Lord Shepherd, the British Minister of State for Common-
wealth Affairs, met Gowon in Lagos on June 7 to discuss this
humanitarian crisis.   But the State Department showed little
evidence of a sense of urgency, which forced the frustrated
ARC and CRS-USCC to abide   their   time.   Swanstrom remained
curious as to why the CRS-USCC continued to receive negative
responses from U.S.A.I.D. on the use of P.L. 480 supplies
even after the May declaration that Nigeria was a disaster
area. It was during a brief scheduled meeting in New York
City on June 12 that a senior U.S.A.I.D. officer Steven
Tripp openly stated that the CRS-USCC request for relief
supplies for Biafra would have to be refused because there
was no legal way the United States could transport goods to
the enclave territory. CRS-USCC continued, nonetheless, to
pressure the United States for a more broad application of
relief to the Nigerian situation.
     CRS-USCC officials, when they met formally with U.S.
A.I.D. officials on June 24, were handed a hastily prepared
three-page "Disaster Memo Number One."[24]   It was compiled by
John Street, Acting Disaster Relief Coordinator in the
U.S.A.I.D.   Office of Private Resources/Voluntary Agencies
Division, from the A.I.D. Seventh Report on Foreign Disaster
Emergency Relief. One item of special interest was the fact
that the actual U.S. government contribution to the Nigerian
relief was only 14.5 percent of the total amount, i.e.,
$502,800 of the total $3,457,531 promised.   Obviously the
promised millions were still a negotiable item.
     On returning to Lagos, Mathews telegraphed Washington
that Lord Shepherd and Sir David Hunt, the British High Commissioner, had informed him of their plans to fly to Biafra
on a soon-to-be-arranged relief fact-finding mission.   This
potential British mission encouraged the African Bureau to
ask the American relief groups to take further action on
Nigerian relief.   Tripp called Krakow, informing ARC that
"$3,000 was being set aside to cover transportation and
maintenance for an American Red Cross disaster specialist to
be seconded to the ICRC."[25]   Tripp also mentioned that he
was working on another $10,000 contribution, which would be
made to the ICRC through the ARC by June 28.   The United
States was, therefore, in a very convenient position to
offer additional humanitarian assistance to Nigeria when the
British mission returned to Lagos and issued a joint commu-
nique with the FMG. Their report urged that an immediate
negotiated settlement was necessary in order to avoid the
loss of thousands of civilian lives.   Heinrich Joggi, the

Chief ICRC delegate in Nigeria, estimated that 3,000 people a day were dying in Biafra and that at least 200 tons of food a day were required to offset the potential massive starvation. He concluded that a relief airlift was the only working alternative because of ground hostilities.

During this British mission, the CRS-USCC were holding in-house meetings to take stock of their own approach to Nigerian relief. One CRS-USCC action in particular held potential problems for the organization vis-à-vis future P.L. 480 supplies. Holy Ghost Father Byrne, who had been promised CRS-USCC support for Biafran relief, had already authorized 24 Caritas flights of relief supplies to be flown from the island of São Tomé into Biafra by June 20.[26] CRS-USCC decided to delay their promised payments for these "illegal" flights until the U.S. policy could be altered to accept relief flights into Biafra.

A telephone call from the Vatican to the CRS-USCC Geneva office expressed dismay that nothing had been done by the American CRS-USCC with regard to the suffering in Biafra. The CRS-USCC representative immediately telegraphed the New York City headquarters to relay the message he had received. The Catholic Bishops from the Eastern Region had written to Rome indicating that they wanted to hear nothing more of CRS-USCC. They believed that a fundamental principle of humanity was involved here, and in the face of it the agency was asked to make a stand. Their challenge was: "could not CRS/USCC take a risk and help on both sides?" Swanstrom sent $20,000 from CRS-USCC personal funds to Caritas the next day (July 3), and another $6,600 thousand gift was made on July 10, with further contributions thereafter.

It had become an embarrassment to CRS-USCC to operate in the non-Catholic area of the FMG and not in the Catholic area of Biafra. Compounding the CRS-USCC problem was the knowledge that the "illegal" relief assistance and food being airlifted into Biafra were conducted by the Holy Ghost Fathers, most of whom had been CRS relief officials within the eastern territory before the civil war. The FMG especially did not appreciate reports that Catholic relief groups might be mixing their relief supplies in the same military shipment aircraft for Biafra. Nonetheless, the Biafrans did not appreciate the tremendous influx of CRS assistance to the FMG, and some anti-Catholic feelings were being reported in both Biafra and Nigeria.

CRS-USCC knew that there would be more severe and dangerous criticism of their agency if they did nothing during a humanitarian crisis than if they looked the other way during an "illegal" but humane activity. Swanstrom decided, therefore, to follow the Vatican envoys' approach to assist both sides in the conflict while trying to convince the U.S. government that humanitarian relief and political recognition were two separate entities. Together with six other interested relief groups, CRS-USCC sent a telegram to Rusk on July 8, 1968. The telegram emphasized that the crisis in Nigeria had reached the point that thousands were dying every day. The only realistic means of assistance on a practical scale would be opening of the shortest possible land route into Biafra. Sufficient supplies for immediate short-term relief were available in São Tomé and Fernando

Po. CRS-USCC urgently requested the U.S. government to use its strongest diplomatic pressures on both sides in Nigerian conflict, and all concerned governments, to effect an immediate solution. Senator Thomas Dodd (D-CT) sent a letter to Rusk that same day that raised the question of using the United Nations Organization as a mediator in the Nigerian Civil War. Other congressional signatories supported Dodd's proposal to have American medical and food assistance under the umbrella of the OAU and/or the U.N.[27]

Palmer responded to this increased pressure from the congressional and humanitarian relief agencies for some additional positive American initiatives in Nigeria and in Biafra by asking Rusk to see if it would be possible to receive some White House support with a presidential statement. Johnson's eventual message, however, seems to suggest that humanitarian considerations ought to be put above all other factors. "While we have no intention of interfering in Nigerian affairs, we do not believe innocent persons should be made the victims of political maneuvering. Deaths caused by warfare are tragic enough. But mass starvation that can be prevented must be prevented."[28]   The same day Johnson's message appeared, both the Senate and House of Representatives also expressed the need for the United States to become more involved in greater relief efforts. This sudden outburst of government concern, legislative and executive, was, in all likelihood, in anticipation of the next day's cover story and photographs of the Biafran starvation in the July 12 issue of <u>Life</u> magazine.[29]

Responding to a private White House demand that an immediate announcement be made on some positive government relief action in the Nigerian civil war, McCloskey read the following statement prepared for the State Department's daily briefing of the press: "The United States Government today approved the donation of 5,000 tons of food to UNICEF, which will be made available to the International Committee of the Red Cross to further the relief effort for all the victims of the Nigerian conflict. The dollar value of the food amounts to $1.3 million. UNICEF is now making arrangements to ship the donated foods."[30] A long-standing UNICEF (United Nations Childrens Fund) request for Nigerian relief assistance, submitted to the State Department in 1967, had been officially turned down just a fortnight earlier. Therefore, the American UNICEF officials were amazed to learn through the press that their relief requests for the Nigerian conflict was granted only four days after it had been resubmitted to the State Department. The remarkable about-face announcement by the United States emboldened UNICEF officials to immediately request an additional 5,000 tons of relief foods; but the United States would quietly deny this request.

Given the magnitude of the Nigerian crisis and the humanitarian ideals of the U.N. charter, the minimal involvement of the U.N. in the Nigerian Civil War is intriguing. The United Nations High Commissioner for Refugees never took any action with respect to the substantial refugee problem throughout Nigeria, nor did any other agency (for example, the Food and Agricultural Organization, the World Health Organization, or the United Nations Educational, Scientific and Cultural Organization). It is true that Article 2(7) of the charter prohibits the U.N. or its agencies from intervening in internal affairs, but that is only if it is narrowly defined.

This was exactly what Secretary General U Thant did in the Nigerian case. Out of possible fear of another Congolike embroilment, Thant made it quite explicit to all members of the U.N. and U.N. agency staffs that he would not tolerate any involvement in the Nigerian relief programs operations.[31] His insistence that there was no possible U.N. role in Nigerian affairs produced an atmosphere that did not invite international bureaucrats to get involved, lest they loose their job. However, the UNICEF action was the result of leadership, humanitarian pressure, and channeling the U.S. relief food through the legally accepted ICRC.

Notes

1. Alfred Friendly, Jr., "Pressure Rising in Nigeria to End Civil War As Military Standoff Continues," The New York Times, Jan. 18, 1968, p. 14.
2. Colwell, "Biafra," 19-20.
3. John Davis, "Black Americans and United States Policy Toward Africa," International Affairs 23, no. 2 (1969), 242.
4. Deptel 66699, Nov. 8, 1967, notes "Department non committal, do not recommend Gowon see ANLC reps" and Lagos, Telegram 4663, Nov. 26, 1967, notes "Embassy, asked to consent on ANLC initiative on behalf of 22 million American Negroes, was polite but cool."
5. Lagos, Telegram 6761, Feb. 16, 1968.
6. Africa Research Bulletin (Dec. 1967): 933; and Mary Cavanagh, "Tragedy and Force in Nigeria," The Tablet (London), 222, no. 6670 (Mar. 23, 1968): 278.
7. John Horgan, "The Church and the War, III," Irish Times, Mar. 21, 1968, p. 10. Caritas Internationalis had provided the $25,000 to charter the special plane. It is also reported that the envoys also brought a $20,000 donation to the Biafran Emergency Aid Fund.
8. "Nigeria," Facts On File: 1968 (New York: Facts On File Inc., 1969), 189.
9. Lagos, Airgram A-419, "Nigeria: Annual U.S. Policy Assessment," Febr. 11, 1968, p. 6.
10. There were some 750 Peace Corps workers in Nigeria at the beginning of the civil war. By the middle of 1967, around 1,500 Peace Corps volunteers had worked in Nigeria, the largest contingent of them in the Eastern Region. Mar. 20, 1967, Congressional Record, 90th Cong. 1st sess., 113:7316.
11. Airgram A-419, 2.
12. Ibid., 3.
13. U.S. State Department, Press release, Mar. 5, 1968.
14. "Food For Biafra," West Africa, June 29, 1968, p. 739.
15. Jack Plano and Milton Greenberg, The American Political Dictionary, 5th ed. (New York: Holt, Rinehart & Winston, 1979), 356-357. "Food for Peace--A special foreign aid program that provides for the disposal of American surplus food to needy countries. Congress established the Food for Peace program by Public Law 480 in 1954 to reduce American farm surpluses, to increase foreign consumption of American products, and to strengthen United States foreign policy abroad....Under the act, the President is empowered to provide emergency food aid following natural disasters and during famines."
16. State Department, "Activity in Search for Peace in Nigeria," April 20, 1968. The enclosures included
    1. General Activity, January - September 1967
    2. U.S. Activity Since Fighting, July 1967
    3. OAU Activity Since Fighting, July 1967
    4. Other African Activity Since Fighting, July 1967
    5. CS [Commonwealth Secretariat] Activity Since Fighting, July 1967
    6. Private Activity Since Fighting, July 1967
    7. Special Enclosure with More Limited Distribution
17. Lyndon B. Johnson, Statement of the United States Government on the Problem of Nigeria. no. 1 (1968), 23.
18. National American Red Cross, General Records, May 31, 1968, p. 1.
19. Peat, Marwich, Mitchell and Co., International Committee of the Red Cross: Report on Relief Operations in Nigeria (Geneva: ICRC, July 1, 1970), Schedule IV.
20. National American Red Cross, General Records, Sept. 12, 1968.
21. Sources tend to summarize the ICRC logistic problems as eight in number concerning their involvement and procurement of relief supplies and the seasoned personnel to surmount such logistical problems. All of this is complicated by the real question of how effectively the ICRC could respond in view of the FMG military priority in the conflict. It was also observed that Lindt (ICRC) and Bulle were aware that they had a tiger by the tail and could hardly confront the enor-

mity anticipated in the Biafran need in that they were unable to overcome the obstacles already existing in the liberated areas.

22. National American Red Cross, General Records, May 31, 1968, p. 2.

23. Nietyong Akpan, The Struggle for Secession, 1966-1970 (London: Frank Cass, 1971), 107.

24. The "Disaster Memo Number One" is in the Nigeria/ Biafra Clearing House Papers, Swarthmore College Peace Collection, Swarthmore, Penn.

U.S.A.I.D. Disaster Memo Number One: Nigeria/Biafra
June 24, 1968

U.S. Government
P.L. 480, Title II, Food for Freedom
Reported diversion of food commodities from CRS has
reached over 2,000 tons, valued at . . . . . . $ 396,500
In addition, to be administered by CRS, in co-operation
with ICRC and the NRC, is approximately 1,100,000
Cash contribution to ICRC 100,000
A funding level to provide assistance 100,000

                                              $ 1,696,500
Catholic Relief Services
From its own resources . . . . $ 1,096,129
Church World Service
[a]Also, A.I.D. is paying transport charges of .   6,300
American National Red Cross
Two cash donations totaling   25,000

Total USG and Voluntary Contributions
Reported to Date . . . . $ 3,457,531

[a This item was not included in the total amount of
$3,457,531 (although paid); whereas, the $1.1 million was
included in the total amount (although not paid).]

25. National American Red Cross, General Records, June 19, 1968.

26. Holy Ghost Father Dermot Doran, Coordinator of the Sao Tome-Biafra Relief Airlift, interview with author, Vilanova, Penn., June 28, 1974.

27. July 12, 1968, Congressional Record, 90th Cong., 2nd sess., 114:20973. The "Famine in Biafra" entry consists of letters and articles, of which Dodd's letter stated, "Specifically, I urged the State Department to ask for an emergency session of the United Nations Security Council to consider the terrible famine in Biafra and the threat it poses to the security of the area. It is my earnest hope that the Security Council will vote unanimously to instruct the Secretary General to use his good offices, in consultation with the OAU, in an effort to break the impasse between the Nigerian and Biafran authorities on the question of food shipments to Biafra."

28. Johnson, Statements of the United States Government on the Problem of Nigeria, "White House Statement, July 11, 1968," no. 1, 22.

29. David Robinson, the author of the July 12, 1968 cover article in Life magazine, also wrote "Blockaded Biafra Facing Starvation," The New York Times, June 30, 1968, p. 1.

30. Johnson, Statements of the United States Government on the Problem of Nigeria, no. 1, 21.

31. According to a UNICEF staffer, U Thant once met with UNICEF personnel to give them explicit instructions not to rock the boat. The staffer also claimed that UNICEF, to bypass possible interference from the Secretary General's office, had several telephone lines that did not go through the UN switchboard. An interesting contrast to this African position by Thant was his explicit involvement in the Pakistan-Bangladesh crisis of 1971.

4

Humanitarian Pressure
for Change

The world was startled with the July 12, 1968, Life magazine cover story and vivid pictures of marasmus and kwashiorkor, which depicted the existing malnutrition and starvation in Biafra. Marasmus, which is caused by a general lack of food, produces the living skeleton; a person whose body just simply shrivels away. Kwashiorkor, the more permanent and deadly malnutrition of the two, is caused by protein deficiency. John de St. Jorre noted that "the great majority of civilian deaths on both sides of the fighting came from kwashiorkor," and "the Biafrans, never short of a propaganda phrase, called this terrible phenomenon 'Gowon's Boots'" because the skin peeled off and down the leg like a fleshy boot.[1]

Public attention was centered by media reports on the plight of the starving Biafran, but the ICRC also estimated that a minimum of 1 million people in liberated territory were also in desperate need of assistance. Unfortunately, as the relief planes began to ferry in and out of Biafra, no similar programs or medical attention were directed to the starving people under FMG control. News of this particular situation was treated with less media sensationalism and, when it was reported, these accounts were never front-page news. Those articles that did make publication were often along the lines that claimed the FMG was preventing international relief agencies from feeding hundreds of thousands of starving refugees in Biafra. The basic charge was that all relief supplies were delayed by the politically corrupt practice that required a person to "dash" (bribe) FMG officials at every stage of the relief distribution process.

The gravity of the situation on both sides of the conflict was supported by Edward Marks, a U.S.A.I.D. official who had traveled with the ICRC convoy throughout the FMG controlled territory from Lagos to Enugu. From among the volumes of official ARC records, which are almost always brief and precise internal distribution memorandums for those who already have a good grasp of the crisis, there is a rare narrative record of the growing enormity of the famine:

Ed Marks (former refugee coordinator in Vietnam and now with American Embassy in London), accompanied ICRC convoy of land rovers and trucks moving seven team members and medical supplies from Enugu to Yue and also through 25 mile sector of Cameroons. Apparently they went all the way to Ekot Ekpene and other areas in the southeast State. He visited with Labouisse and Gendron. The largest cluster of refugees near Nsukka is a Nigerian Red Cross camp whose population of 438 is down from a high of 750. They have had no food in the past month from the army, but receive meager and sporadic rations from the ICRC representative who also visits 45 nearby villages. ICRC medical people consider refugee hunger in liberated areas east central State not as acute as in southeast State, where there is more local food available. There are very many Ibos in the northwest sector who are in the bust area; therefore, it is difficult to assess the situation, but the hope is that new ICRC teams and supplies will arrive to ease the situation.

Most urgent problem is plight of 250,000 refugees in the mainland southeast State west of the Cross River. As result of Biafran counterattack on June 22 some 86,000 refugees who had been in Ekot Ekpene since late March and others from nearby border areas have fled southward. Refugees living in squalid surroundings. All suffering from deprivation of food and many in need of medical attention or hospitalization. There is a well developed network of expatriates and Nigerian Catholic priests and nuns who provide limited hospital services and relief assistance to refugee camps when supplies are available.

Need for food still paramount. ICRC, Nigerian Red Cross and Catholics trying sustain like with limited distributions of rice, garri, beans or milk in some combination. If received in quantity and DD-4 can airlift, the tempo must be increased substantially to meet the estimated minimum requirement of 250-300 tons weekly for these refugees. Central feeding is limited to medical institutions and a few special categories. Lack of mass cooking equipment and limited personnel for supervision are two factors, but refugees own preference is for family rations they can prepare. Labouisse urges weekly target of 500 tons; this figure probably not too high in view increase in visible refugees and likelihood many more will emerge especially when adequate food distributions begin. Military action could also drive new refugees to the south. Some hospitals now

without doctors or medical supplies needed to
cope with mounting kwashiorkor and other hunger
based diseases. Two hospitals report 60% of
patients have kwashiorkor. Ed Marks visited
hospitals and burial grounds and feels there is
no reason to question the estimate of 200 to
300 deaths daily in this area.[2]

When Marks returned to Lagos and submitted his preliminary
report to Washington,[3] the U.S. Embassy staff was concerned
that this report would give Washington clear proof that the
starvation and death rate in the surveyed region was
steadily climbing. These official observations of deprivation, starvation and death figures for Nigeria were well
above those reported by the British and U.S. Embassies to
their respective governments. Marks's observations, however,
confirmed the reports of private relief agencies. Believing
they were vindicated by this official report, the relief
agencies once again pinned their hopes on the prospect that
Ed Marks's report would be the lever that would allow a
breakthrough in the political negotiations for a land relief
corridor. The humanitarian groups believed that a neutral
land route was the only means to provide systematic, massive
relief necessitated by the needs of the suffering population
on both sides of the fighting. But negotiations continued
to drag on, until it became quite clear that there would be
no quick agreement.

Even if the land corridor had been approved, the logistical situation in Nigeria threatened to sharply limit
relief flows. Mathews was reporting to Washington that the
Lagos harbor was a mess; it did not even have the proper
capacity for the cargo volume it was already receiving. Any
relief material coming into the Nigerian capital by sea had
to compete, often unfavorably, with the import-export arms-
for-cocoa trade. There were limited dock facilities and
transportation trucks. If the relief supplies were unloaded
for road or rail, there were atrocious supply lines from
Lagos to the Eastern Region. In addition to the logistical
horrors, there was a significant loss of relief material to
theft and spoilage. No one had anticipated or requested the
apparent buffer supplies necessary to compensate for those
diverted to the black market, lost or spoiled while in tran-
sit.

Although the land corridor discussions were stalled, the
relief groups continued to press ahead with the only thing
they had available--the illicit and dangerous airlift into
Biafra. For the most part, the relief airplanes flew unham-
pered in and out of the widened country roads of Uli or
Annabelle. But continuing to share these airstrips with the
relief flights were the gun-running shipments by Wharton.
Despite the fact that relief planes flew fairly predictable
routes and schedules, charges abounded that weapons and
relief were always intermingled.

In an effort to sidestep the sensitive issue of mixing
relief and arms on the same aircraft, the ICRC and other
relief groups turned to the United States for better and
larger planes, especially the easy loading C-130 aircraft,
which would increase the volume relief. Instead, the United

States provided a million dollars in reserve funds for ICRC
activity. It was clear that the United States was not going
to disrupt relations with Nigeria by providing relief groups
with military or civilian equipment.

The House Subcommittee on Africa was to hear the State
Department's familiar theme of a military neutrality policy
in support of a united FMG Nigeria during Joseph Palmer's
report to Congress on Tuesday, July 23.   Palmer had just
returned from a seven-week tour of Africa and Europe (he was
in Nigeria between July 4 and 8, 1968).   "The main purpose
of my trip," he reported, "was the Nigerian situation."
Palmer continued to define American policy by stating that
the only solution favored by the State Department was one
that maintained "the unity of Nigeria, which we have supported from the beginning."[4] He then went on to attack
Father Kilbrid's presentation of the CRS-USCC and other
religious groups' perceptions of Nigerian and Biafran relief
needs.   In effect, Palmer and the State Department were not
only struggling to control congressional understanding of
the crisis, but more importantly the public announcements of
the relief lobbyists that were attempting to change U.S.
policy.   Strong public statements were made during the two
weeks following the _Life_ article, including Senator Thomas
Dodd's (D-CT) conspicuous submission in the _Congressional_
Record concerning the Zambian official recognition of the
Republic of Biafra.[5]

Some members of Congress believed that the State Department's inaction toward the Nigerian and Biafran starvation
was a deliberate attempt to avoid disrupting the established
relations with organizations in Africa. Congressman John
Rarick (D-LA) asked: "Can it [U.S. silence] be because of
the State Department's fear of upsetting the extremist left-
wing OAU--Organization of African Unity--that facts have not
been properly reported to our people?"[6]   Other Congressmen
rejected what they believed to be the argument of logistics
as the main consideration. Senator Harrison Williams (D-NJ)
went on record with these remarks:

> I have been informed of all the political and
> logistical difficulties in mounting an airlift
> of sufficient size to bring to those who are
> starving and dying enough food and medical sup-
> plies to relieve the situation. Frankly, the
> logistical difficulties do not impress me as
> being insoluble. Difficult, yes--insoluble, no.
> If necessary, because of ground fire from the
> Nigerian forces or because of lack of loading
> facilities, an airdrop operation might be
> required. The political difficulties I believe
> we should ignore--in the name of humanitarian-
> ism.[7]

Such statements from Congress encouraged American civilian
groups to increase their support for relief activity in the
form of funds and material. Senator Edward Brooke (R-MA)
summarized the belief of the American relief groups when he
said that a "clear distinction between humanitarian necessi-
ties and political considerations must be made."[8]

The buffeting Palmer had received from the House Foreign Affairs members for the lack of the government's ability to generate more movement in relief efforts, even while the peace talks were presently underway in Niamey (July 15-26, 1968), motivated the State Department to hold a special briefing for the press to engender more positive public support for the One Nigeria policy approach. During this media briefing (July 25) on Nigeria, Palmer admitted that "an air corridor is important psychologically. I hope very much that the arrangements can be worked out. The essential problem here is one of finding some sort of a formula that will enable relief supplies to be flown in, without that same airstrip being used for the transportation of military supplies."[9] If Palmer's hope for the unfamiliar famine relief is to be compared to his hope for the familiar grasp of the Nigerian political situation, then there are serious questions as to his understanding of both issues. Palmer told the press, "I certainly did everything that I could to encourage the Federal Government to be just as flexible as possible to try to reach a negotiated settlement of the problem and, I think, that they will hold off while this is being explored. I think this underlines the importance of the meetings that are now going on in Niamey. I would hope very much that they will be successful."[10] These statements were uttered while he had in his hands official reports that the Niamey talks were deadlocked and would end the next day on the issue of sovereignty.

Fact sheets and maps were distributed to the press during the briefing. Stephen Tripp's first fact sheet on food and medical relief, "Disaster Memo Number Two," was also distributed to the reporters. The information in the 14 pages, an improvement on the first memo of three pages, maneuvered the total U.S. relief contribution to an exaggerated amount of $5,300,000; twice its actual contribution.[11] This fabrication was made possible by assigning funds to be used in the secessionist area, but that never could be used because humanitarian aid was not allowed to circumvent the political considerations for the One Nigeria policy. Therefore, Dean Rusk could state in his press conference, "the dispute over how to get supplies through the lines of fighting has thus far permitted only small amounts of assistance to reach the areas of actual conflict."[12]

The day after Palmer had derided the relief work of the CRS-USCC in front of Congress, a particularly significant incident occurred that would affect the future American relief activity. On July 24, 1968, Rabbi Mark Tannenbaum, National Director of Interreligious Affairs for the American Jewish Community, wrote to Mr. Van Hausengoten of Church World Service (CWS). Tennenbaum wrote that he was grateful for the privilege of having discussed the Biafran problem with such dedicated and competent people as Father Anthony Byrne, Father Raymond Kennedy, Monsignor Andrew Lande, Jim Norris and Van Hausengoten. In the name of the American Jewish Community, Tennanbaum responded affirmatively to the proposal for creating a joint Catholic, Protestant and Jewish effort to meet the needs of helpless people in Nigeria and Biafra. As a result of the Tennenbaum and Van Hausengoten meeting on Friday morning, that is July 19th, a number of initiatives were undertaken that quickly became productive. American Jewish Community President, Morris B. Abrams, received permission to contribute a grant of $10,000 to the cost of an air flight shipment of food, medicines and drugs to São Tomé.

CRS-USCC had already decided that it would have to do something public and positive in response to the Biafran starvation crisis or loose their leadership position among the relief agencies seeking assistance from the U.S. government. The result was a rushed shipment of 14 tons of high-protein foodstuffs valued at $35,000 for Biafra. The plane left New York's JFK airport after much publicity, and after a change of aircraft in Amsterdam, it arrived in São Tomé on July 30. The CRS-USCC plane did not carry any P.L. 480 material because the United States did not allow American voluntary agencies to take such material into Biafra, especially those religious groups with possible links to illegal shipments into Biafra. Whether the obstacles were difficult or insoluble, the State Department never deviated from its insistence that the logistical problems and consequent personal dangers were reasons enough for hesitation on the part of the United States to become more involved.

Senator Walter Mondale (D-MN) did not accept this excuse of a bottleneck of famine relief and asked that humanitarian assistance be separated from political considerations. "The death of thousands, most of them protein starved children, will continue each day until the United States abandons its cautious approach based on the niceties of political intervention." Mondale accepted humanitarian intervention, but went on to offer these possible alternatives.

> I believe that the United States can assist by endorsing and seeking the immediate implementation of an internationally policed demilitarized zone. The United States can offer food, with suitable guarantees to the Nigerian Government that no arms will be included in the shipments to Biafra and that food shipments will be internationally supervised. The United States can make available food and transportation facilities to neutral, international agencies and charitable relief organizations.[13]

There was a burst of humanitarian concern from Congress on August 2, 1968, the day it adjourned for the presidential campaign conventions. While only Congressman Barrett O'Hara (D-OH) spoke on the floor of the House, there were four other Congressmen who slipped some extended remarks into the Congressional Record.[14] Senators Wayne Morse (R-OR), George McGovern (D-SD), Dodd (D-CT), and Williams (D-NJ) spoke about the Biafran crisis on the Senate floor. The most interesting entry was a letter by McGovern to President Lyndon B. Johnson with seven signatures: "We wholeheartedly support our Government's present policy of strict political neutrality in the Civil War. At the same time, we believe firmly that the resulting starvation should not occur if it is within our power to prevent it. Therefore, we urge you to offer assistance through the United Nations or voluntary religious and humanitarian organizations to enable them to deal with the food shortage that has resulted from the conflict."[15] One of the three possible courses of action offered in McGovern's letter suggested the United States provide relief agencies with aircraft to have supplies reach the starving peoples.

Three perspectives emerged from these congressional discussions. First, members of Congress did not argue against the vague U.S. military neutrality toward the Nigeria-Biafra conflict but they did expect the United States to urge international agencies to become involved in attempts to establish relief operations. Senator Williams voiced the group's perspective in that "they [U.S.] will say 'wait for the parties involved to work out arrangements to permit relief operations to be mounted.' My answer to them is that we cannot wait."[16] These legislators wanted the U.N. or the OAU to be the third party mediator for the relief system between the combatants with guarantees of U.S. assistance.

The second perspective, which argued that the systemic weakness of the U.N. and the OAU would never sufficiently protect the human rights of the starving civilians, demanded that the United States support the private organizations presently involved in the Nigerian relief programs. The third perspective moved beyond America's indirect support through other agents to having the United States government act directly in bring assistance to those suffering in the conflict.[17] This third group argued that humanitarian assistance could be separated from political consideration and that the humanitarian principle was more important then the political requirements of diplomacy.

Sunday, July 29, the day two British refugee workers were killed in Biafra, there was a rally on the Boston Common, Massachusetts, to muster relief for the starving in Nigeria and Biafra. Senator William Proxmire (D-WN) mentioned this rally in Congress. The rally would "demonstrate the concern of Americans for the deplorable conditions in Nigeria-Biafra. The rally is under the auspices of the U.S. committee for UNICEF, CRS and CWS."[18] Three individuals at the rally became especially interested in forming a group to assist the relief agencies in their fund-raising events. At the same time in New York City, the CRS-USCC had finally convinced CWS and the American Jewish Committee (AJC) to form a joint effort for relief assistance to both sides of the conflict. But these events, important as they would be in the months ahead, did not immediately affect the State Department as much as the July 31 public statement by the French government that tacitly recognized Biafra as an independent and sovereign state.

Rusk issued an official statement the day before this French proclamation as a way of showing the strength of the U.S. commitment to the One Nigeria policy. But when the leaders of 15 prominent American religious relief organizations sent a telegram to President Johnson urging that the United States undertake a massive helicopter airlift of relief to counter the Biafran famine, the White House National Security Council asked Rusk to arrange a private meeting with these relief individuals. The delegation (which consisted of Morris Abrams, President of the AJC;

Robert Bilheimer, Director of the International Affairs Pro-
gram for NCC; Monsignor Bordelon, Director of the Division
of World Justice and Peace of the USCC; George Hauser,
Executive Director of the American Committee on Africa;
Bertram Gold, Executive Vice President of the AJC; Rabbi
Rudin, President of the Synagogue Council of America; James
McCracken, Executive Director of CWS; and Bishop Edward
Swanstrom, Executive Director of CRS-USCC) met Rusk on
August 6 to express its concern for the moral issues
involved in the Nigerian crisis. CRS-USCC stated at the
beginning of the meeting that it was their purpose to seek
an increase on the part of the United States in such relief
assistance. The relief delegation believed that the tragedy
of Biafra could not resolve itself; the simple fact was that
if the Biafrans did not starve to death they would be
slaughtered by the FMG troops. The U.S. Embassy in London
had also reported this strong possibility. The question to
ask was what will the United States do to stop it, if this
happens?

Secretary Rusk responded that the United States was
using its best efforts in such a way as to encourage action
among other nations with better relations with Nigeria, for
example, the present peace talks at the Addis Ababa Conference. Haile Salassie, leaders of the OAU, and the ICRC had
all put their prestige on the line to reduce the fighting in
Nigeria and to provide care for the victims of the conflict.
Rusk went on to ask that the interfaith group not precipi-
tate any addition pressure on the United States by emotional
public statements on the situation. Palmer, who had been in
attendance at Rusk's request, explained that there had been
agreement between Nigerians and Biafrans in July on a land
corridor, but at the very end of the meeting the Biafrans
suddenly made the agreement on the land corridor contingent
on an agreement for an air corridor. The State Department
did not know the reason why they did so. Nonetheless, it
was clear from the tone of the entire meeting that the
United States continued to be guided by its basic policy of
nonrecognition of Biafra and of nonintervention in a way
that could escalate the war.

Tripp handed out the hastily prepared "Disaster Memo
Number Three"--a seven-page reiteration of "Disaster Memo
Number Two"--to the interfaith members. Two interesting
additions to this memo were the front-page freehand drawing
of the now minuscule-sized Biafra and a full page detailing
how and when CRS-USCC had shipped food to Biafra. Palmer
then stressed that the United States was overlooking the
"illegal" activity of CRS-USCC. He said that the United
States would not allow itself to be placed in an awkward
position by publicly supporting any church group that was
known to give assistance to Biafra. Ignoring the blatant
threat, Swanstrom stressed that the only government that was
in a position to deal effectively with both sides in the
civil war was the United States. Britain was hopelessly wed
to the FMG, the Soviets were temporarily supplying Lagos
with modern weapons of destruction, France was engaged in
surreptitious support of Biafra, which included sending arms
and tacit diplomatic recognition, and the issue of famine
relief at the Addis Ababa talks was a consideration only in

the event that all or most of the other problems were resolved. Therefore, the United States was the last resort for those suffering on both sides of the conflict.

The interfaith group had also agreed, before seeing the Secretary, to propose that the United States government call a conference of experts in relief and logistics if they were to remain steadfast in their policy. The organization leaders believed that the United States did not have to become politically involved if a nonpolitical humanitarian relief conference could be assembled (and through it have the United States release P.L. 480 supplies to the interfaith group rather than directly to the ICRC and the NRC, which were in an morass of logistical problems). But Rusk did not rise to this idea. Palmer expressed the State Department's belief that a conference called by the United States would place the government in too awkward a position in relation to other world leaders who were seeking to negotiate peace. Even the idea of a voluntary agency conference with invited government representatives was beyond support. The interfaith group left the meeting with the correct belief that the State Department had not moved at all on the issue of American relief assistance to Biafra.

But the rapidly developing starvation in Nigeria and Biafra forced Rusk and the State Department to rethink the U.S. approach toward the relief issue during the next week. Momentum for this change started with the secret meeting between the U.S. Embassy staff in London and British authorities. They arrived at pessimistic conclusions, which were telegraphed to Washington and which in turn were relayed to the ARC: "the French self-determination statement destroyed the possibility of Ojukwu's flexibility, the FMG is preparing a three-division operation into Ibo heartland ready to begin just as soon as adequate stockpiles are built up and the Addis Ababa meetings either break down or stalemate-- probably this cannot begin before August 10--and it is expected the offenses will be bloody and protracted."[19] In the London discussions, Marks's personal observations of the conflict and refugee areas were accepted as valid. The U.S. ambassador in London wired these conclusions to Washington along with Mark's evaluation, which were then eventually summarized in "Disaster Memo Number Four" and "Disaster Memo Number Five."[20]

The magnitude of the Nigerian famine could not be denied any longer. In anticipation of the change in the U.S. relief policy, Robert Smith was told to call Samuel Krakow and arrange a special meeting for August 12 at which these two questions would be asked of ARC Executive Vice President Ramone Eaton. "1. A probable request for the ARC to supply two C-130's. (For your information, State is trying to locate such planes in this country. They are having a difficult time. My guess is that they are not available at the moment in Europe.) 2. A rather sizeable request for ARC professional staff qualified to handle the relief operations aspect of the program."[21] On August 14, as the news reached America that ICRC Director Auguste Lindt had suspended the ICRC relief flights to Biafra, Bishop Swanstrom, Abrams, McCracken and Golfio of Cooperative for American Relief to Everywhere (C.A.R.E.) asked the White House for an interview with President Johnson stating that they were convinced that immediate airdrops followed by a U.S. offer, through Haile Salassie, of U.S. engineers, temporary landing strips and maps for one or more exclusively humanitarian airstrips, were the sole hope for life for the suffering millions of Biafrans. It was becoming increasingly obvious to Johnson and his White House staff that the American voluntary agencies were about to openly support the "illegal" airlift, and that they had gained public support for their activity. CWS had sent Charles Bailif to assist in the São Tomé relief; he arrived there on August 15. With him was the associate director of the CRS-USCC, who had been sent to be the CRS-USCC liaison representative to the Caritas airlift operation, and to coordinate CRS-USCC relief operations with those of other agencies about to join the relief effort.

Three days after Rusk denied government assistance to the interfaith group, he reversed his decision. The U.S.A.I.D. General Counsel office would now make P.L. 480 supplies available to the interfaith group's work in both Nigeria and Biafra.[22] The A.I.D. directive was to reimburse, either from A.I.D. or U.S. Department of Agriculture (U.S.D.A.) funds administered by A.I.D. overseas for the freight costs of registered supplies sent into Nigeria or Biafra through Fernando Po or São Tomé by CRS-USCC and CWS. It is not quite clear from the records exactly when P.L. 480 foods were first made available specifically for these interfaith groups working in Biafra, but sometime in August, CRS-USCC was given an allotment of 25 tons of P.L. 480 cheese. However, as was noted, the first moves by CRS-USCC to use these supplies for Biafra were restrained by the State Department.

Palmer and his African Bureau remained insistent that all humanitarian relief be coordinated through ICRC. Even Lt. Col. James Langley was clearly briefed on this issue before being sent to the U.S. Embassy in Lagos to replace the reassigned military attaché Arthur Halligan. This insistence was a last resort to bolster the FMG-supported ICRC relief activity; inasmuch as the State Department was now totally disenchanted with ICRC operations in Nigeria. As a consequence, the ARC was being pressured by the African Bureau to become more involved in relief activity to head off the growing involvement of the independent American relief groups. Krakow informed John Wilson of this pressure in his August 28 memo.

> Steve Tripp, at the meeting this morning, indicated his concern that there was so little ARC participation in teams of personnel in the Nigerian program. (as a contrast, he pointed out that the Swedes had offered to send 25 medical teams consisting of between four and six persons each, but the ICRC at the moment would prefer to hold this down to approximately five to six teams.)
>
> Mr. Tripp specifically suggests that the ARC immediately offer to the ICRC a complete medical team fully equipped in accordance with the

recommendations of Dr. Bulle. He also urges
that we immediately offer a sizeable staff of
disaster relief experts, particularly those who
are fully qualified to handle the logistics
problems in the receiving, warehousing, transportation and distribution of supplies, in setting up camps for displaced persons, and in
handling the many social and welfare problems
that arise with displaced persons.[23]

The ICRC bureaucratic bungling was now public knowledge,
as was its unorthodox political activity.   In anticipation
that further pressure might yet move the United States to
further changes, CRS-USCC also began to lobby hard for an
independent airplane to carry P.L. 480 supplies. CRS-USCC
suggested privately to the African Bureau that the U.S. make
available some DC-7 planes for relief shipments as the West
German government had done back in July.   The only reply
CRS-USCC received from the State Department was that the
suggestion would be taken into consideration.
The representatives of the interfaith volunteer relief
agencies met with Rusk for the second time on August 26, and
at this meeting they were given permission to call a press
conference at the CRS-USCC headquarters in Washington. At
the meeting with Rusk the delegation stressed that their
"bootleg" relief operation for Biafra would not overcome the
existing famine, and that the solution must be one that
included establishing neutralized land and air corridors
would be established. They did announce, however, that the
United States had made a second allocation of P.L. 480 food-
stuff for the stricken areas in both Nigeria and Biafra.
This time, food was made available to CRS-USCC and CWS, as
well as to UNICEF, but it was still given under the distribution of the ICRC.   In securing P.L. 480 food for Biafran
relief the interfaith group had passed the first major
hurdle.   Swanstrom also told the press conference that he
had suggested to Rusk that the United States make planes
available for relief shipments as the German government had
done, and the State Department had taken the suggestion
under consideration.
CRS-USCC, in cooperation with CWS and the American
Jewish Effort for Emergency to Biafra Relief, entered into
an agreement on August 30 with Count Carl Gustave Von Rosen,
a Swedish aviator, to further increase their relief airlift.
He agreed to charter a new route into Biafra,[24] which would
avoid the heavy Nigerian antiaircraft fire. This agreement
called for financial support from the interfaith group for
improvements in the larger airstrips on São Tomé and in Biafra in order to better facilitate takeoffs and landings, as
well as the handling of loading and unloading substantially
more aircraft in a briefer period of time. Also on August
30, another hurdle appeared to have been cleared when Wilson
Roadway informed Van Hausengoten that it was now permissible, under the voluntary foreign aid office, to secure
reimbursement office freight for P.L. 480 product shipment
shipped by CWS and/or CRS-USCC to Fernando Po and/or São
Tomé.   Likewise, it was possible to get ocean and/or air
freight paid for by A.I.D. for shipments going from Fernando

Po   or São Tomé for P.L. 480 products to Nigeria and Biafra.
It was, however, to be some time before these details were
fully worked out. Thus within two months, both CRS-USCC and
CWS, supported by AJC and numerous groups and individuals in
America,   had moved from their early position of caution to
an acceptance that if the only way they could discharge
their obligations to the suffering and starving Nigerians
and Biafrans was by disregarding the laws of bureaucrats--
then those rules must be disregarded. Bishop Swanstrom made
this stand very clear when he preached in St. Patrick's
Cathedral in New York City in September.

The more these Americans increased their pressure for a
change in relief policy, the more the African Bureau
demanded government support for the FMG in Lagos. These
demands inevitably made their appearance in the presidential
campaign.   The most vocal and strongest statement issued
came from the Nixon for President Committee on September 10:

> The terrible tragedy of the people of Biafra
> has now assumed catastrophic dimensions. Star-
> vation is daily claiming the lives of an esti-
> mated 6,000 Ibo tribesmen, most of them chil-
> dren. If adequate food is not delivered to
> these people in the immediate future, hundreds
> of thousands of human beings will die of hun-
> ger.
>
> Until now efforts to relieve the Biafran people
> have been thwarted by the desire of the Central
> Government of Nigeria to pursue total and
> unconditional victory and by the fear of the
> Ibo people that surrender means wholesale atro-
> cities and genocide. But genocide is what is
> taking place right now--and starvation is the
> grim reaper. This is not the time to stand on
> ceremony or to "go through channels" or to
> observe the diplomatic niceties....The destruc-
> tion of an entire people is an immoral objec-
> tive, even in the most moral of wars.   It can
> never be justified; it can never be condoned.
> ...The time is long past for the wringing of
> hands about what is going on. While America is
> not the world's policeman, let us at least act
> as the world's conscience in this matter of
> life and death for millions.[25]

Soon both Richard Nixon and Hubert Humphrey were calling on
President Johnson to act decisively and more vigorously to
increase American efforts to feed the starving and "to speak
out against this senseless tragedy."

Congressional pressures for change also intensified in
response to the increased public awareness, so much so that
the Senate Subcommittee on Africa met in executive session
on September 11 to consider the Nigerian Civil War. Palmer,
just back from another fact-finding trip to Nigeria to see
what affect the French arms shipments were having on the
conflict, gave testimony that was unwavering in its support
for the British policy of One Nigeria.[26] But Palmer did say

publicly for the first time, "I think that we should draw a
distinction--to the extent that one is possible--between the
political and humanitarian aspects of the problem."[27]
     The American Committee to Keep Biafra Alive had also
been advancing this dual policy approach even before their
legal creation during the summer of 1968.   It was after the
first American public appeal on July 29 in Boston, to muster
relief for the starving war victims in Nigeria and Biafra,
that three individuals became actively interested in forming
a private group to assist the relief agencies in fund-
raising events.   Paul Connett, a British student studying in
America, Susan Durr and Philip Nix, both former Peace Corps
volunteers just returned from Nigeria's Eastern Region, were
soon joined by other interested volunteers. This new group
conducted their first public event outside the United
Nations building on August 8 to demonstrate concern for the
suffering in Biafra and to petition U.S. Ambassador Ball to
work for increased American relief action in both Nigeria
and Biafra.   This rally and several others that followed
were held to demonstrate not "how" the government ought to
act politically, but "what they must do" to avert another
tragedy of famine.
     The group also sought professional and political advice
about what it had to do to be more effective in its chosen
field.   Six weeks after its creation, the American Committee
to Keep Biafra Alive Chairman Connett enlisted the services
of Young and Rubicam, Inc., a professional public relations
Madison Avenue consultant firm.   In a letter to Stephen
Frankfurt, president of Young and Rubicam, dated September
13, the group set forth its purpose: "The American Committee
was begun by returned Peace Corps Volunteers from Nigeria,
committed to the third goal of the Peace Corps which is to
bring back to the American people insights into our international obligations and to educate citizens to undertake pur-
poseful action. The Committee now consists of a full spec-
trum of volunteers including clergy, teachers, housewives,
students, and professional people....The major thrust of our
activity is to ask that the U.S. Government... initiate
humanitarian intervention in Biafra-Nigeria."[28] The fall of
1968 was a very busy time for the new group. Schools were
opening and clubs were looking for something around which to
rally old and new members. Membership association with the
American Committee to Keep Biafra Alive was not intended to
be a purely academic experience. It offered activities that
members found interesting and worthwhile, as well as offering the opportunity to be morally committed to a human
rights cause. Schools and civic organizations accepted the
well-formulated material and up-to-date information concerning the summer's big news story of Biafra.   Thus another
private group, which was quickly established throughout 40
states in America, developed specific public pressure on the
United States for increased humanitarian action. [29]
     It was during the week of September 23-26, 1968, that a
turning point occurred for the American Committee to Keep
Biafra Alive, which would eventually crystalize it into a
formidable player in future U.S. policy formation toward the
Nigerian crisis. On Monday morning Connett and Durr went to
Washington to talk to Dale De Haan and Shannon McDonald,

staff members of Senator Edward Kennedy's office. The two
Kennedy staffers insisted that the U.N. be a necessary
intermediate stage for increasing relief to Biafra. They
told Connett and Durr that Senator Kennedy (D-MA) would
insist on these conditions in his speech before the Senate
that day.[30] That same afternoon the two American Committee
to Keep Biafra Alive members spoke with State Department
Nigerian Desk Officer Smith. They jotted down these observations made by Smith: "1. It was in the long term interest
of Nigeria and the U.S. that the U.S. hold to a policy of
neutrality; 2. The general feeling in the State Department
is that the U.N. and the ICRC were worthless organizations
in this situation; and 3. The U.S. cannot work through the
voluntary agencies, especially the Catholic agencies,
because of their involvement in arms shipments to Biafra."[31]
The two American Committee to Keep Biafra Alive members
returned to the Hill to meet with Robert Sherman, Senator
McGovern's legislative assistant. His suggestions were also
recorded. "A. The voluntary relief groups should purchase
outright C-130 planes for relief; B. The relief groups
should get in touch with Matthew Mbu, the Foreign Minister
of Biafra who presently is in the U.S., formerly the first
Nigerian Ambassador to the U.S.; C. They approach sympathetic Senators and Congressmen for endorsement of their
goals; D. The group definitely change their name!"[32] This
last point was the third time that day Connett and Durr were
strongly urged to change the group's name, and they were to
hear the same advice on a name change during their entire
stay in Washington.

The next morning the American Committee to Keep Biafra
Alive members returned to the State Department to meet
Steven Tripp, the U.S.A.I.D. Disaster Relief Coordinator,
and Roy Miller, the U.S.A.I.D. Nigerian Desk Officer. The
sum result of this meeting was a laundry list of multiple
facts and figures concerning U.S. involvement in the relief
system. Tripp and Miller reiterated the official line,
which did not foresee any direct U.S. involvement in relief
because it would entail a major commitment on a priority
level equal to the Vietnam conflict. Such an undertaking in
Africa would require a much greater commitment by the U.S.
leadership, which Tripp believed was very unlikely at that
time. Connett and Durr were told, therefore, to lower their
sights so as to expand and improve their organization to
better inform the American public of what the government had
done and intended to do for Nigerian and Biafran relief.
Several other bureaucrats whom the committee members met
that afternoon and on the following day continued to restate
similar messages.

Three days of meetings with these bureaucrats did not
produce a single positive initiative. The American Committee to Keep Biafra Alive was looking for an informational
exchange with some government agency as well as some positive response to the group's plea for increased commitment
by the government. Frustrated and depressed, they were not
prepared for the energetic ideas and support that National
Security Council African Specialist Roger Morris expressed
on September 26. Their meeting lasted two and a half hours
and it ended with Morris's sun-bursting statement that was

recorded by Durr as a reminder for the difficult days ahead: "Biafra was a definite possibility ten years from now." They were also encouraged when they read Senator Proxmire's Senate Concurrent Resolution 80, which called for immediate action "to save the starving and diseased of Nigeria."[33]

The first issue of the American Committee to Keep Biafra Alive newsletter, Biafra Lifeline, October 9, 1968, summarized the two main ideas Morris had discussed with the group members that September day. "The United States government either (1) provide comprehensive material and logistic support to those organizations already involved in relief operations; or (2) initiate action in the United Nations and other international organizations to create a mandate for humanitarian intervention to end the starvation."[34] Both these points reflected the thinking of government policy makers that there must be logistic support with third-party involvement. Morris began using the American Committee to Keep Biafra Alive to generate a specific attitude among the public pressure groups. The American Committee to Keep Biafra Alive leaders went along with this arrangement because they had their "insider" informational linkup and a positive response from an important government official. When it was obvious that the U.N. would not take any action to become involved with the starvation in Nigeria, the American Committee to Keep Biafra Alive followed the advice of Morris, Harold Saunders, and Peter Flanagan (the latter two were National Security Council staffers who had been brought into the circle because they also believed in Biafra's viability) to aggressively force Palmer and the African Bureau into some action. Their lobbying effort was to build pressure on the State Department to balance its humanitarian support for Nigeria and Biafra while taking on more responsibility for the humanitarian problems in Biafra. At this time the American Committee to Keep Biafra Alive did not push for the political recognition of Biafra.

When Palmer and other U.S. officials arrived in Nigeria on October 1 there was no hint that any distinction between politics and relief was possible. Palmer made it clear on his arrival in Lagos that he carried no messages, suggestions, plans, or offers of mediation.[35] The U.S. team studied the relief situation and Nigeria's reconstruction and rehabilitation needs, recommending the appointment of a U.S.A.I.D. assistant for relief and rehabilitation to the U.S. Embassy, the allocation of $3 million for special relief projects, and the "Nigerianization" of relief. On leaving the capital, Palmer again assured the FMG of U.S. support for postwar reconstruction.

However, the continuing domestic pressure for additional positive action in the Nigerian relief programs eventually convinced Senator Eugene McCarthy (D-MN), Foreign Relations Subcommittee on Africa Chairman, to hold a one-day hearing on the Senate Concurrent Resolution 80--U.S. policy toward Nigeria. While he was an advocate of increased U.S. humanitarian assistance to the conflict, McCarthy remained on the sidelines during the entire hearings. It seems he held the hearings to allow the many grievances, which the State Department refused to acknowledge, to be aired and placed on record by a number of influential humanitarian groups.

The question was how needy were those caught in the ever
shrinking Biafran enclave and around the battlefronts. Not
surprisingly, there were conflicting reports on the number
of deaths and the extent of starvation and malnutrition submitted for public testimony. On one side, the United States
and the U.K. held to the low famine estimate: "Reporting to
Parliament on Lord Hunt's mission, Commonwealth Secretary
George Thomson stated that the Biafran starvation death rate
was 200-300 per day."[36] The African Bureau presented three
documents, all brief in-house surveys of relief operations
in Nigeria and Biafra, for the Subcommittee's consideration.
The "American Friends Services Committee Report," which gave
the impression that something positive was happening in the
worst areas of starvation, was the first report submitted by
the State Department. The second document was the African
Bureau's "Disaster Memo Number Eight," based on the most
recent information from the U.S. Mission in Nigeria regarding increased ICRC food tonnage and stockpiling. The third
document was the First Interim Report originally submitted
to the U.N. and signed by representatives of Canada, Sweden,
and the U.K. This document stated that "it did not believe
that Federal Nigerian troops intended to exterminate the
whole Igbo [Ibo] tribe in the current Nigerian Civil War."[37]
    Robert Moore, Acting Assistant Secretary of State for
African Affairs, testified at the Subcommittee hearing
against Senate Concurrent Resolution 80 "that a U.N. relief
force be organized to transport and distribute relief supplies."[38] Instead, the State Department believed that the
U.N. needed to be protected from handling any conflict of
such legal complexity. Rather than have the U.N. as an
actor to relieve a crisis, Moore preferred to advance the
pretext of protecting the U.N. image. "There is not sufficient support at the present time among the U.N. membership
for a useful consideration for this question here. In the
view of so many states, the humanitarian and political
issues are so intertwined that relatively few believe that
one could be considered without the other.[39]
    On the middle ground, Heinrich Joggi, Head Represent-
ative of the ICRC, reported that Biafran deaths by starvation had stabilized at 6,000 per day by September 26, 1968.
He also stated that 100 tons of food were being received
daily as a result of the relief flights. The identical
situation was reported by the ICRC President Samuel Gonard
in regard to the FMG-held territory.[40]
    On the other side, epidemic proportions of starvation
were presented by the humanitarian lobbyists. All other
witnesses who testified during the hearing presented alarm-
ist approaches to the starvation issue. Edward Kinney, the
Assistant to the Director of CRS-USCC and in charge of coordinating relief aid to both sides, told the Senators that
"because of governmental inaction, the religious-sponsored
voluntary agencies became 'bootleggers of mercy' in the name
of humanity." McCracken of CWS reported that at the existing
rate of airlifted foodstuffs into the areas of starvation,
the relief groups were 400 tons a day behind the minimum
requirement to sustain life. The opinion of Dr. Jean Mayer,
professor of nutrition at the Harvard University School of
Public Health is worth quoting: "As a nutritionist, I feel

that I should point out that the estimates of the State
Department down-grading the magnitude of the malnutrition
disaster in Biafra (only 200 deaths by starvation per day)
have no foundation in fact....My estimate due to the fact
that Biafra was not self-sufficient in protein foods in
peace time and that there are 5 or 6 million refugees, it
that we should be prepared to find the number of deaths is
well in excess of 10,000 per day."[41]   In this state of
confusion and imprecise information, the relief agencies
responded to the humanitarian crisis according to their
institutional perception of what they thought the needs were
in regard to medicine and food.

Senate Subcommittee members found themselves at odds
over the arguments presented by witnesses at the hearing.
Kennedy continued to urge that the government bring the
question of staging an international relief effort before
the United Nations.   Brooke, now a supporter of the One
Nigeria policy, doubted "whether it will be helpful to seek
U.N. action on this problem."[42]   But the members of Congress
refrained from making any additional official statements on
the Nigerian problem after the close of this very informative Senate hearing.   The explanation for this rare public
inaction might rest on some covert bargaining process that
has yet to surface, or it might be that the members of the
congressional and executive branches were more concerned
with reelection then famine as the election day drew closer.

During this domestic lull the U.S.A.I.D. put together
"Disaster Memo Number Nine," dated October 29, in response
to the mounting requests from private groups interested or
involved in famine relief.   Many of these requests were from
local groups that were part of the pressure used by Morris
and the American Committee to Keep Biafra Alive to force
some change in the U.S. relief policy.

Notes

1. St. Jorre, The Brothers' War, 236.
2. National American Red Cross, General Records, Aug. 9, 1968, p. 2f.
3. Lagos, Airgram A-1781, July 27, 1968.
4. Cronjé, The World and Nigeria, 229.
5. July 12, 1968, Congressional Record, 90th Cong., 2nd sess., 114:20977.
6. Ibid., July 17, 1968, 114:22185.
7. Ibid., Aug. 2, 1968, 114:25007. Senator Williams was supporting what Senator McGovern had
said earlier, that is, if the United States could find the logistical skill to drop weapons, then
the United States should be able to find a way to drop some of its abundant food when there was
starvation.
8. Ibid., 114:20817.
9. U.S. State Department, "Transcript Background Briefing on Nigeria by Assistant Secretary
Joseph Palmer 2nd," July 25, 1968, pp. 6-7.
10. Ibid., p. 10.
11. U.S.A.I.D., "Disaster Memo Number Two", July 24, 1968, p. 13. A copy of the memorandum is
as follows:

        U.S.A.I.D. Disaster Memo Number Two, Nigeria/Biafra

Summary
Emergency Assistance Provided by the U.S. Government
P.L. 480, Title II, Food
Value of 5,400 MT emergency food grant and
PL 480 food commodities for distribution by CRS
approximately $ 1,400,000
Following food approved for emergency feeding
through UNICEF: 1,500 MT nonfat dry milk;
3,504 MT of CSM and 500 MT of butter oil. Market
value $2,319,000. Estimated CCC value   2,700,000

AID Contingency Fund, Worldwide Disaster Relief Account
As previously reported in Disaster Memo One, a
$100,000 cash donation was made to ICRC to support
its relief operations and another $100,000 fund was
established for direct AID purchase of relief supplies,
medicines and transportation for a total of   200,000

[a]Due to great need for transportation, vehicles
and distribution facilities for relief supplies, a
reserve fund of $1,000,000 has been established
whereby ICRC will be in a position to draw on the
fund for essential high priority needs.
(Allocated as of July 24, $250,000.)   1,000,000

   Total USG contribution . . . . $ 5,300,000
   Total U.S. Private Organizations contributions
   to July 1968, estimated at   2,000,000

[a]U.S.A.I.D. had allocated only $250,000 of
the $1,000,000 and UNICEF still was waiting for
the promised $1.3 million.]

12. Johnson, Statements of the United States Government, no. 1, 17.
13. July 30, 1968, Congressional Record, 90th Cong., 2nd sess., 114:24158.
14. Ibid., Aug. 2, 1968, 114:25077-25078. Congressmen Robert McClory (D-IL), 114:25186; John Ashbrook (R-OH), 114:25303-25304; William Ryan (D-NY), 114:25458-25459; and Bertram Podell (D-NY), 114:25478-25480.
15. Ibid., Aug. 2, 1968, 114: 25006-25007. The other signatories were Senators Frank Church (D-ID), Fred Harris (D-OK), Walter Mondale (D-MN), Joseph Clarke (D-PA), Wayne Morse (R-OR), Harrison Williams (D-NJ), and Claiborn Pell (D-RI).
16. Ibid., 114:25007.
17. Senator McCarthy sent a letter to the American Committee to Keep Biafra Alive dated August 19, 1968, in which he wrote, "I have urged that our government go before the United Nations and seek the immediate establishment of an international relief force. If the United Nations is reluctant to act, the United States should take the initiative."
18. July 29, 1968, Congressional Record, 90th Cong., 2nd sess., 114:24003.
19. National American Red Cross, General Records, Aug. 9, 1968.
20. U.S.A.I.D., "Disaster Memo Number Four" and "Disaster Memo Number Five," Aug. 6, 1968.
21. National American Red Cross, General Records, Aug. 12, 1968.
22. A copy of the memorandum in the "U.S. Government" file of the Nigeria/Biafra Clearing House Papers, Swarthmore College Peace collection, is as follows:

United States Memorandum

   TO: PRR/PRDS/VAD, Mr. Howard Kresgo   DATE: August 15, 1968
   FROM: [deleted]
   SUBJECT: Memorandum of Telephone Conversation with AID's
            General Counsel's Office on August 9, 1968.

   In a discussion of the present emergency situation in Nigeria/
   Biafra, Mr. Bytan affirmed that AID may reimburse, either from AID
   funds or USAID funds administered by AID, overseas freight costs
   of registered voluntary agencies for emergency supplies sent into
   Nigeria/Biafra by whatever route is most expeditious. This will
   make possible shipment of supplies originating in the U.S. through
   Fernando Po (Spanish) or Sao Tome (Portuguese), Nigeria off-shore
   islands. Large quantities of supplies may be consigned to the
   islands from where they will be broken into smaller consignments
   to be transshipped by planes or surface into Nigeria/Biafra.

   Reimbursement will be made through the customary procedure on the
   basis of paid bills of lading covering each leg of the route into
   Nigeria/Biafra.

   Care should be taken to ensure that the commodities destined for
   Nigeria/Biafra are not distributed to the local populace of these
   islands.

   The registered agencies whose programs are validated for Nigeria
   are: CRS, CWS, and the SDAWS.

23. National American Red Cross, General Records, Aug. 28, 1968. W.F. Bulle, (MD) ICRC Coordinator for the Nigerian Red Cross, issued a detailed 17 page memo: "Memo to: ICRC Medical and Staff Personnel Preparing for Mobile Emergency Service in Nigeria," July 27, 1968,

24. Von Rosen reestablished the relief air bridge into Uli on August 12 by a personal heroic act. Without the proper codes and radio frequencies (Wharton would not release them), without Biafran foreknowledge of his mission, and flying just above the treetops to avoid FMG flack, Von Rosen and his crew (having been persuaded by Anthony Byrne's desperate pleadings and without any legal contract) successfully landed his DC-7 at Uli airfield. As a result of this action Ojukwu gave the landing codes for Uli to the church relief groups, thus breaking Wharton's monopoly.

25. Nixon for President Committee, News release, New York City, Sept. 10, 1968.

26. Colwell, "Biafra," 29.

27. Sept. 16, 1968, Congressional Record, 90th Cong. 2nd sess., 114:26866. Senator John Sparkmen (D-AL) submitted Palmer's entire testimony in the record.

28. Letter signed by Connett to Stephen Frankfurt, president of Young and Rubincam, Inc., dated Sept. 13, 1968, in the American Committee to Keep Biafra Alive file in the Nigeria/Biafra Clearing House Papers, Swarthmore College Peace Collection, Swarthmore, Penn.

29. Material on school participation is held in the Nigeria/Biafra Clearing House Papers, Swarthmore College Peace Collection, Swarthmore, Penn.

30. Sept. 23, 1968, Congressional Record, 90th Cong., 2nd sess., 114:27848-27850. The next day Senators Dodd and Proxmire would both support Kennedy's position (ibid., 114:27918-27919). Senator Pearson (R-KS) was against U.N. involvement and for OAU control (ibid., 114:28212-28213).

31. These notes are in the Nigeria/Biafra Clearing House Papers, Swarthmore College Peace Collection.

32. Ibid.

33. Sept. 24, 1968, Congressional Record, 90th Cong., 2nd sess., 114:27918.

34. Biafra Lifeline, Oct. 9, 1968, p. 1.

35. Benjamin Welles, "U.S. Mission, in Lagos, Affirms Fact-Finding Role," The New York Times, Oct. 6, 1968, p. 25.

36. The New York Times, July 31, 1968, p. 4.

37. U.N., First Interim Report (New York: United Nations), Oct. 2, 1968.

38. Oct. 4, 1968, Congressional Record, 90th Cong., 2nd sess., 114:29587. Senator Robert Byrd (R-VA), "U.N. Urged to Act on Biafra", p. 29587.

39. U.S. Congress, Senate Committee on Foreign Relations, Hearings, 90th Cong., 2nd sess., Oct. 4, 1968, p. 7.

40. The New York Times, Oct. 29, 1968, p. 3.

41. Colwell, "Biafra," 26. Jean Mayer went with Senator Charles Goodell to Biafra in 1969.

42. U.S. Congress, Senate Committee on Foreign Relations, Hearings, 90th Cong., 2nd sess., Oct. 4, 1968, p. 12.

1. Refugees moving deeper into Biafra. *Credit:* Gerard Klijn, Church World Service file of the Clearing House for Nigeria/Biafra Information, August 1968.

2. Relief food station within Biafra. *Credit:* Catholic Relief Services file of the Clearing House for Nigeria/Biafra Information.

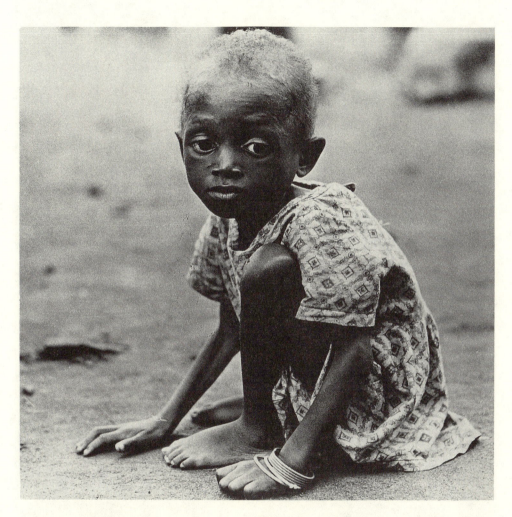

3. Biafran child sitting on ground. *Credit:* Catholic Relief Services file of the Clearing House for Nigeria/Biafra Information.

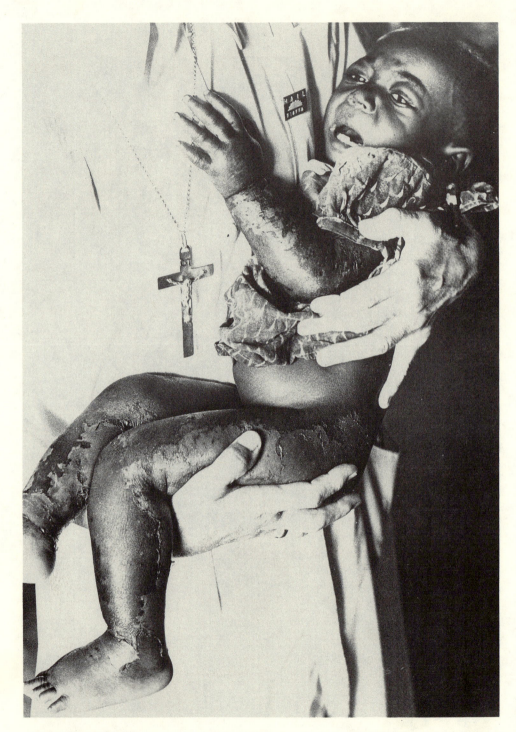

4. Catholic nun holding infant burnt by air attacks. *Credit:* Catholic Relief Services file of the Clearing House for Nigeria/Biafra Information.

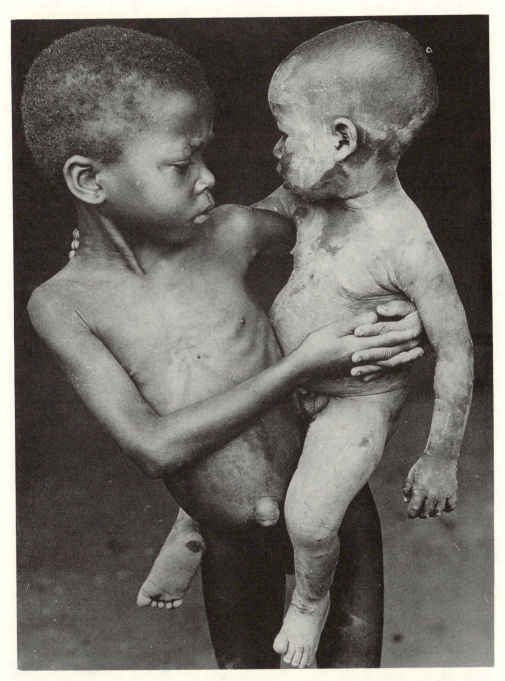

5. Boy holding starving infant. *Credit:* Gerard Klijn, Church World Service file of the Clearing House for Nigeria/Biafra Information, August 1968.

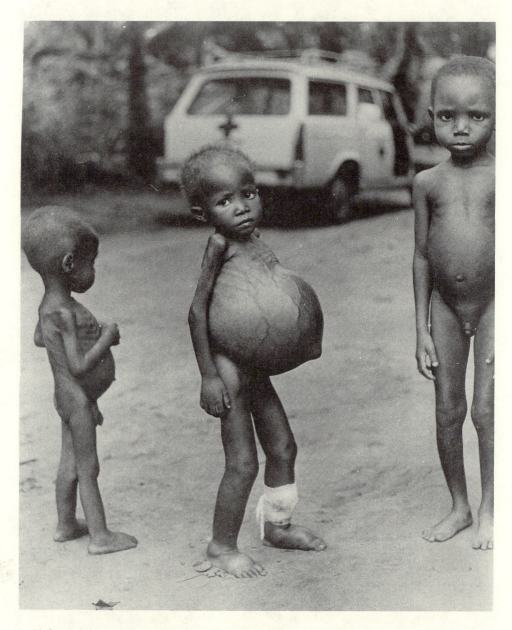

6. Biafran child with enlarged stomach. *Credit:* Church World Service file of the Clearing House for Nigeria/Biafra Information, August 1968.

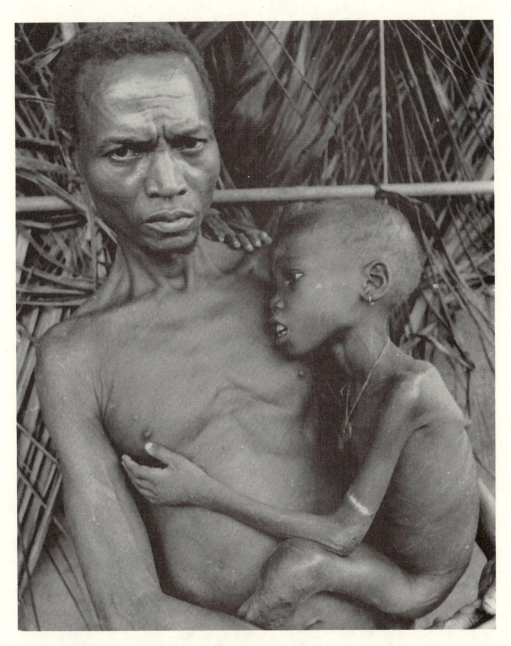

7. Father and starving child. *Credit:* UNICEF file of the Clearing House for Nigeria/Biafra Information.

8. Joint Church Aid-USA relief plane. *Credit:* Catholic Relief Services file of the Clearing House for Nigeria/Biafra Information.

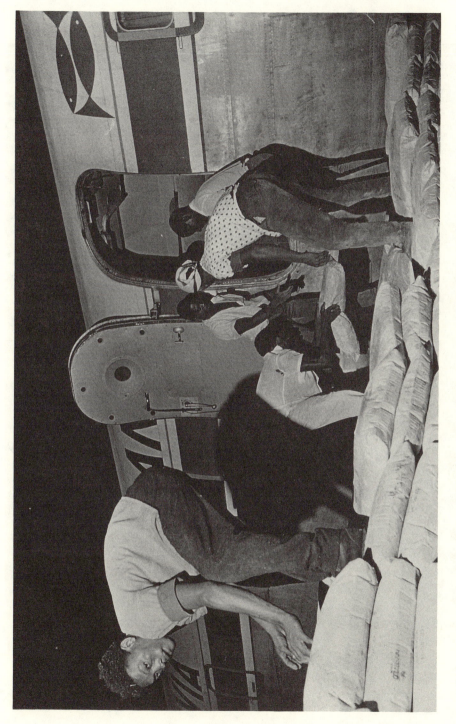

9. Relief workers loading JCA-USA plane for Biafra. *Credit:* Catholic Relief Services file of the Clearing House for Nigeria/Biafra Information.

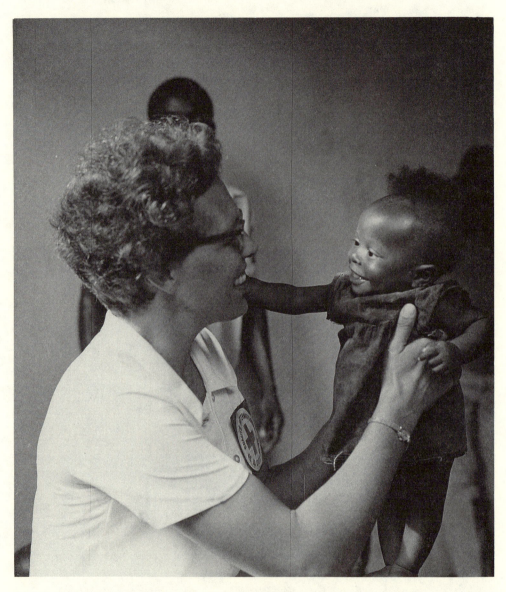

10. Nurse holding recovered child. *Credit:* UNICEF file of the Clearing House for Nigeria/ Biafra Information.

5

Political Pressure for Change

Richard Nixon created euphoria and renewed energy within all
the ranks of the American relief groups when he won the
election on November 5, 1968. They believed that this was
to be the touchstone for increased relief to Nigeria and
Biafra because Nixon was on record that he would do something about the famine relief: "The time is long past for
the wringing of hands about what is going on. While America
is not the world's policeman, let us at least act as the
world's conscience in this matter of life and death for millions."[1] The real margin between life and death for the
majority of people in and around the war zones was the
ongoing airlift of relief foods carried on by the church
groups. These church groups had sent representatives to a
meeting in Frankfurt, Germany, on September 20, 1968, to
discuss their open and active participation in the "illegal"
São Tomé airlift to Biafra. By November, however, the
relief situation had changed. Both CRS-USCC and CWS were
now playing major roles in obtaining essential food and medical supplies and equipment for the Uli airfield. Bishop
Edward Swanstrom continued to request additional government
assistance, most especially the use of Hercules aircraft
because of its increased load-carrying capacity.

> Our appeal for Hercules aircraft is addressed
> to our government since there is a possibility
> of acquiring this type of plane in view of the
> limited number of such aircraft commercially
> and the fact that their peak season for commer-
> cial operation is experienced each fall are
> both limited and more ordinarily costly.
> Consequently, the Church agencies are request-
> ing the two Hercules be made available for use
> in Sao Tome with a third in back up position on
> a charter basis, together with adequate spare
> parts and maintenance personnel. Operational
> crews and other operational costs will be borne
> by the Sao Tome Interchurch group.[2]

In anticipation of the State Department's usual request, Edward Kinney had already sent a letter on November 4 to the ICRC asking to explore ICRC's willing cooperation in this venture without the interchurch group losing status. He even went so far as to state that a paper agreement would suffice if it gained FMG approval.

It was important economically and symbolically for the American relief groups to have President Lyndon B. Johnson announce on Friday, November 8, a donation of $2.5 million to the ICRC to provide relief to both sides of the conflict. While this act publicly defended and supported the ICRC, the White House staff privately viewed the ICRC as only a legal cloak of U.S. involvement. But in their effort to neutralize the President's message, both Robert Smith and William Goug, a U.S.A.I.D. Administrator, replied immediately to Swanstrom's letter, which had suggested using Hercules aircraft in the Biafran relief supply system. Smith wrote,

> Although we are not able to provide Hercules aircraft for the Sao Tome to Biafra airlift, we are prepared to help you [CRS-USCC] in your efforts to charter the additional aircraft by providing $500,000 in A.I.D. financial assistance. We believe that a fully coordinated relief operation under the ICRC umbrella is necessary to guard against possible FMG military interception of church flights and to avoid jeopardizing continuation of present arrangements which permit the airlift of supplies to Biafra. We propose that our assistance be provided through the ICRC--it would be our wish to transfer the $500,000 to the ICRC with specific earmarking of this assistance for support of the church group airlift.[3]

Goug's memo was more blunt. "I regret that we cannot help by providing you with United States Government Hercules aircraft. The complexities and dangers surrounding the use of United States military aircraft in this kind of situation makes it inadvisable as I am sure you appreciate."[4]

Both bureaucrats went on to concede that CRS-USCC and CWS had been asking for some time, but at this stage it was politically required that any concession was dependent on the American agencies using U.S. aircraft or P.L. 480 supplies have open ICRC support. The interfaith group decided that there were too many conditions attached to the $0.5 million offer. Besides, they would never subject their relief flights to ICRC approval.

When, therefore, another church relief group meeting was called by Caritas Internationalis (Vatican relief agency) on November 8 and 9 in Rome, the attendance was far larger then had been at Frankfurt. Although CWS was absent due to a prior arranged meeting in New York, all those who were determined to keep the Sao Tome relief going sent representatives, despite the caution of governments, the ambivalent behavior of the World Council of Churches (WCC),[5] and the unwillingness of the ICRC to publicly acknowledge that it valued what Nordchurchaid and other churches were doing in the Biafran relief operations.

In August 1968, when Nordchurchaid was established, the various groups involved with the increasing complicated relief operation decided to adopt certain principles for cooperative action. First, all donated supplies were jointly shared and distributed in Biafra.[6] This avoided any inter-agency competition for relief supplies. Second, a rough division of labor was agreed on: the Scandinavian and German Churches shared the responsibility for flight operations, Das Diskonishe Werk (DDW) had responsibility for the composition of all aid shipments and CRS-USCC was responsible for information and publicity and agreed to serve as liaison with the ICRC.[7] Third, any relief group purchasing aircraft would assume its own financial responsibility for securing and maintaining the aircraft. At one point, in seeking their own chartering of a Hercules aircraft, Nordchurchaid had arrived at a limited centralized objective of joint owner-ship. However, because the aircraft did not materialize, incorporation never went beyond the CRS-USCC selection of a public relations name of Joint Church Aid International (JCA).

Once again in Rome, it was decided that Nordchurchaid would be responsible for the operation of and technical man-agement of any future aircraft, Caritas Internationalis would control the air list of supplies and personnel, and CRS would look after the press and information service. After a lengthy and important discussion of all aspects of the Sao Tome relief operation, the Rome meeting turned to the discussion of a name for the joint press service. These press releases were not intended to be in competition with those of the ICRC, their purpose was to make known the churches' activities in São Tomé. (There were already some 300 persons and organizations receiving the interchurch press releases.) The Rome representatives finally resur-rected the name of JCA and the insignia of two fish. Before concluding the meeting it was agreed that Kinney should arrange for Flight Test Research, Inc. (FTR) of Long Beach, California, to negotiate with Lockheed for some Hercules aircraft.

The agency representatives in Rome, without specifically intending it, had created a new ecumenical organization, which become known and accepted the world over. But it was soon discovered that the desired Hercules aircraft were unavailable because they had been sold to the Colombian gov-ernment (the result of a higher bid contract). FTR, there-fore, recommended to JCA that it purchase four C-119 Flying Boxcars as an alternative to the Hercules. Analysis by internal CRS-USCC staff showed, however, that the Uli air-strip could not handle these aircraft; so the suggestion for C-119s was shelved. CRS-USCC now began to consider another cargo plane--the C-97 military version of the Boeing Strato-cruiser.

CRS-USCC felt that the potential use of larger and faster planes would greatly increase the amount of relief sent to the suffering people of Biafra. Swanstrom was informed by colleagues who were associated with the National Guards of Oklahoma and Tennessee that C-97s were available from the U.S. Air Force, and, more important, they could be made available for the church relief airlift. These large planes were used surplus aircraft that were mothballed at a U.S. Air Force base outside Tucson, Arizona.

CRS-USCC decided not to approach the State Department or the White House personally with the C-97 request, especially after President Johnson issued a White House statement on November 8 that had stated that the political dispute under-lying this war is a Nigerian and an African problem--not an American one. Instead, Swanstrom presented the CRS-USCC case for C-97s to House Speaker John McCormack (D-MA) and Senator Edward Kennedy (D-MA). Personally convinced of the need for increased relief to the suffering people and armed with congressional support and public opinion for a more active U.S. involvement in the relief process, McCormack and Kennedy called on Johnson to urge him to use the office of the presidency to see if there were any possibility of such a transfer of planes for the Biafran and Nigerian relief.

After meeting the congressional leaders, Johnson called in Secretary of State Dean Rusk and Secretary of Defense Clark Clifford to discuss the Nigerian relief problem. The implication of this meeting was clearly understood by the Secretaries who knew how Johnson felt about the pressure from McCormack and Kennedy. The White House staff recalled that the President almost mandated that Rusk and Clifford work out the necessary arrangements whereby the C-97s could be given to the church relief groups. The Defense Depart-ment made it known to their staff that they were presented with a fait accompli.

When Colonel "Gene" Dewey was assigned by the Defense Department to the transfer of the relief planes, he found that the C-97s were well on their way to being given to the church relief groups. It was assumed by the Pentagon that there was no way to stop the process; because this had been a personal request from their Commander-in-Chief. This was not the attitude, however, adopted by the State Department. On November 13, when Swanstrom met with senior State Depart-ment officials concerning the A.I.D. offer of $500,000, he was told that the United States would insist that this offer would be conditional on the ICRC approval of the São Tomé operation. Publicly, however, the State Department was reporting that the relief airlifts into Biafra were extremely dangerous. Therefore, the government "realists" did not believe that an airlift of massive quantities of food into Biafra, for any reason, was feasible under present circumstances.

Informed by Roger Morris of an impending State Depart-ment in-house emergency task force meeting, the American Committee to Keep Biafra Alive called a press conference at the McAlpin Hotel in New York City on Thursday, November 14. At the end of the press conference Paul Connett posed two questions to the State Department, which were already sche-duled to be the two main points of the classified agenda of the task force, "1. Why [are there] no serious plans being made to move food to the disaster area in anything even remotely approaching the quantities necessary to avert the enormous starvation which will surely occur as this year ends? 2. Why will the U.S. Government give no plans to the relief agencies?"[8] A six-page explanation, "The Magnitude

of the Relief Problem," was also distributed by the American
Committee to Keep Biafra Alive to the press.

On November 21, Undersecretary of State Nicholas de B.
Katzenbach was appointed to head an emergency task force to
study the humanitarian aspects of the Nigerian conflict.
Other appointed members included Acting Chairman of the Task
Force Robert Moore; Deputy Assistant Secretary for African
Affairs and former Ambassador to Mali, Roy Melbourne; State
Department Task Force Director of Relief, Robert Smith of
the Nigerian Desk and his assistant Robert Wech; and Steven
Tripp as A.I.D. Disaster Relief Coordinator and his two
staff assistants Helen Wilson and John C. Wilson. In all
likelihood, the specific appointment of Katzenbach to head
the task force may have been primarily symbolic. It was
interpreted by the supporters of Biafran relief as a clear
signal that the Sao Tome operation would receive higher
priority within the government policymaking system. Nicholas
Katzenbach's appointment also pleased those Congressmen and
Senators pressuring for U.S. intervention because he was
known as Kennedy's closest friend in the State Department.
His appointment also buttressed the neutrality of the policy
review group, in as much as Palmer was conspicuously absent
from the group. The supporters of the FMG regime accepted
Katzenbach's position because there was an administrative
point there--it was not good to have the Chief of the African Bureau (Joseph Palmer) running such a controversial
operation as a review of Biafran relief.

But if Palmer was not running the policy review, neither
was Katzenbach. Most of the information and influential
contributions came from the U.S.A.I.D. team. Their analysis
of what the United States had done in Nigerian and Biafran
relief up to that point, described in "Disaster Memo Number
Ten", was accepted without question. The African Bureau
backed its earlier decision of minimum American involvement
and was hesitant to release surplus C-97s for the mercy airlift to Biafra. Although the task force requested more time
to study the consequences of giving American aircraft to the
CRS-USCC airlift outside the control of the ICRC, "Disaster
Memo Number Ten" hinted at a change of heart in firm U.S.
support for the ICRC. "There seems to be some impression
that the ICRC has had major responsibility for relief operations in Nigeria since the outbreak of hostilities. This
is not the case."[9]

It was obvious to Katzenbach's task force that the
United States had become more involved in relief assistance
for Nigerian and Biafran programs then they had initially
intended. From the beginning of the conflict until June
1968, the U.S. contribution had been minimal. But the public
outcry during the summer months, followed by congressional
hearings, had moved the United States to increase its relief
support. More than half (57 percent) of the U.S. relief was
committed after the public pressure for a policy change had
developed in the fall of 1968 (see Table 5.1). Even then,
the major part of U.S. relief to Biafra was in the form of
reimbursement for the voluntary agencies' shipping and
transportation, and that only since August.

Table 5.1. U.S. Contributions to Nigeria/Biafra Relief, June-November 1968

Time Period	Government	Percent	Voluntary Agencies	Percent	Total	Percent
Up to June 24	$ 1,721,500	10	$ 1,736,031	42	$ 3,457,531	16
June-July 24	3,539,426	21	149,189	4	3,688,615	18
July-August 19	2,039,074	12	262,238	6	2,301,312	11
August-November 25[a]	9,601,760	57	1,998,102	48	11,599,862	55
Total	16,901,760		4,145,560		21,047,320	

[a]This period can be divided only in approximate thirds as follows: U.S. government total, $3,200,587 (19 percent); U.S. voluntary total, $666,034 (16 percent); total, $3,866,621 (18 percent).

Source: Summarized from A.I.D., "Disaster Memo Number Ten."

Table 5.2. U.S. and Other Nations' Contributions to Nigeria/Biafra Relief, June-November 1968

Time Period	U.S. Total Per Period	Percent	Other Nations Per Period	Percent	Total Per Period[a]	Percent
June-July 24	$ 7,146,146	34	$ 2,488,775	22	$ 9,634,921	30
July-August 19	2,301,312	11	2,163,975	20	4,465,287	14
August-November 25[b]	11,599,862	55	6,401,372	58	18,001,234	56
Total	21,047,320		11,054,122		32,101,442	

[a]The U.S. contribution, by percent, to total amount per period is as follows: June-July, 74; July-August, 51; August-November, 64; and total, 66.

[b]This period can be divided only in approximate thirds as follows: U.S. total, $3,866,621 (18 percent); other nations, $ 2,133,791 (19 percent); total, $ 6,000,411 (19 percent).

Source: Summarized from U.S.A.I.D., "Disaster Memo Number Ten," 1, Table I.

Table 5.3.   Food For Peace Contributions to Nigeria/Biafra
              Relief

| | Tons of Supplies | | Shipping |
	Biafra	Lagos	Dollar Value
U.S. Government P.L. 480			
through CRS-USCC	none	6,761	1,752,081
through UNICEF	2,215	5,987	3,567,780
Dollars for CRS-USCC P.L. 480 Food Shipped			381,900
Total	**2,215**	**12,748**	**5,701,760**
Percentage of Total Tonnage (14,963 tons)	15	85	

Source: Summarized from U.S.A.I.D., "Disaster Memo Number Ten," 1, Table II.

Table 5.4.   Food For Peace Contributions Through Voluntary
              Agencies and UNICEF, June-November 1968

Destination	Tons	Value	Shipping Costs	Total
Lagos	85%	82%	56%	80%
Biafra	15%	18%	44%	20%

Source: Summarized from U.S.A.I.D., "Disaster Memo Number Ten," 1, Table I.

Another important comparison exists between the American contributions and all other contributions. The United States had an impressive 66 percent of the total value of relief sent to Nigeria and Biafra (see Table 5.2); but of this only 18 percent was channeled to Biafra (see Table 5.4).

The entire 18 percent of tonnage value of P.L. 480 sent to Biafra before November 25 was handled completely through the American Committee of UNICEF. The United States had contributed 8,202 tons of P.L. 480 supplies to UNICEF after May 26, with a shipping value of $3,567,780. Of this dollar amount, UNICEF had allocated 75 percent for Nigeria and 25 percent for Biafra.

The later 25 percent ($891,945) was important because it represents the total amount of P.L. 480 food and material to Biafra. Katzenbach's task force was very concerned how the "Food For Peace" was distributed by UNICEF because State Department guidelines were stringent--by providing the P.L. 480 material to UNICEF they were legally obliged to operated under the umbrella of ICRC. It was very disturbing for the task force to find that UNICEF had provided the ICRC with only 19 percent of the funds ($169,470) for Biafra and the remaining $722,475 to the independent church groups that were not working under the coordinating authority of the ICRC. Even though the ICRC was not everything the United

States desired, such UNICEF action placed them outside the task force's consideration when it developed an approach for better control of policy implementation.

The question of U.S. relations with the American church relief groups was the most difficult item on the agenda for the task force. The CRS-USCC and CWS were the two major affiliated organizations. One-third of the relief supplies, or $2,000,669 of the total relief contributions up until November, were from the personal accounts of CRS-USCC and CWS. Eighty percent of all American support for Biafra was attributable to the relief work of CRS-USCC and CWS; and 81 percent of that 80 percent was from the personal account of CRS-USCC. In addition to their own resources, the CRS-USCC was the only religious affiliated agency that was legally eligible for distribution of P.L. 480. One hundred percent of CRS-USCC's P.L. 480 resources had been delivered for use in Lagos as stipulated in the government contract. Another factor that would influence the task force was the knowledge that CRS-USCC worked in close cooperation with the ICRC for Nigerian relief and with Nordchurchaid for Biafran relief.

CRS-USCC had always tried to work closely with the State Department, not only to receive financial support but to assist the government in any of the problematic logistics of relief. For example, estimating and locating individuals and teams inside Biafra was fairly easy for the only American relief structure behind the lines. Although medical personnel who entered Biafra were in a constant state of mobility due to the active war front, the CRS-USCC always knew where they were because of their need for supplies. The State Department, therefore, began to rely on the CRS-USCC for accurate maps of medical projects, medical mission personnel, estimates of refugees, and death rates. Most religious who traveled from Biafra to America for one reason or another were always directed by CRS-USCC to specific U.S. bureaucrats for debriefings. In return for such a close working relationship the task force accepted CRS-USCC as the fastest source for relief to both sides of the conflict, with the consequent authorization for future release of larger volumes of relief supplies to CRS-USCC.

CRS-USCC had already been authorized 1,000 small food-drop parachutes in the eventuality that a crisis in Biafra would become imminent. By the end of September, Tripp had even authorized larger parachutes for CRS-USCC.[10] In early November A.I.D. had offered to provide funds to CRS-USCC to purchase their own aircraft (with the understanding that the aircraft would be put under the authority of ICRC). By the end of November, the task force was prepared to discuss new possibilities in the relief approach with CRS-USCC.

The final question before the task force was how to get these and other decisions out to the public for a measured response. As Palmer recalled,

> We felt in the African Bureau, and Nick [Katzenbach] agreed, that there was a real need for a comprehensive and definitive statement of the general situation in the area and what the U.S. had been doing and what our basic policies were. We felt there was insufficient under-

> standing on the part of a lot of people who
> just accepted blindly a lot of the assertions
> that were coming out of <u>Markpress</u>. This was
> the purpose of it [Katzenbach's speech].   I
> wouldn't say that anybody, I can't remember who
> specifically suggested he make the speech.   I
> remember Nick had been asked to speak at Brown
> and we decided this was a good topic, and a
> good opportunity to lay it out on the table.[11]

Before the task force adjourned, official "visitors"
were to be sent to the U.S. Embassy in Lagos to check on the
accuracy of the field information. John Rosenthal, an aide
to Katzenbach; Melbourne, the State Department's country
director for West Africa; Smith, of the Nigerian Desk; and
Oliver Troxel, from the INR Bureau, arrived in Nigeria late
that fall to question the reporting from the Embassy in
Lagos, as to whether it was even-handed. It was now evident
that the embassy was highly concerned with the real possibility of a successful African secession. Their prevailing
view was that should Biafra establish itself as a viable
sovereign state, the future would see bloody irredentist
movements breaking out all over Africa. This would make
shambles of U.S. diplomacy, which had long sought to foster
stability within established boundaries.
        However, Katzenbach's entire December 3 speech at Brown
University was confined to remarks about the Nigerian Civil
War and the problems the United States had in trying to
remain neutral. For the record, the United States managed
to avoid any direct humanitarian assistance to Biafra for
the entire course of the conflict.
        CRS-USCC anxiously analyzed this nine-page declaration
and decided that the most important aspect of the speech was
the following ambiguous statement: "The American interest in
the Nigerian Civil War is primarily and fundamentally humanitarian. We want to relieve suffering and end the killing.
We have already taken a number of steps to seek to do this
and are prepared to do more."[12] The question CRS-USCC was
concerned with was how much more was the United States prepared to do in Nigeria and Biafra. Especially intriguing
for CRS-USCC was Katzenbach's reference to their Gordian
knot: "The real difficulty, of course, is that the humanitarian aspects of the problem are hopelessly tied to its
political aspects. We would like to separate them; we should
like to convince those responsible that innocent persons
should not be made victim to power plays and political
maneuvering."[13]
        The challenge to CRS-USCC was to find an acceptable way
to separate the political and humanitarian aspects of their
relief. The U.S. open invitation and challenge to the church
relief agencies came at the end of Katzenbach's remarks: "We
shall help to intensify in every way feasible the existing
relief flights, but even this will not suffice to reach all
those in need so long as the fighting continues....I believe
that any solution must come within a framework that both
preserves Nigerian sovereignty and unity and guarantees the
future safety and development of the Ibo people."[14]

December was a month of important decisions for both
CRS-USCC and State Department bureaucrats. It began with
the December 5 press briefing by the State Department in
which they criticized the Biafran authorities for denying
daytime relief flights. CRS-USCC responded that the size
and number of relief flights were more important than the
hours during which they could fly.[15] Kinney reminded the
State Department that the church relief agencies were still
asking, unsuccessfully, for bigger and faster planes to fly
in the available P.L. 480 supplies.

When the German DC-7 relief plane crashed Thursday,
December 12, at Uli airfield, all options on U.S. aircraft
to be used for relief flights to Biafra were canceled. The
State Department and the Defense Department were now deeply
concerned over the possible misuse of the military C-97s
involved in relief work. They judged that it was now too
risky to allow the military version of the Boeing Strato-
cruiser to be used as a CRS-USCC relief aircraft.

Morris decided that the only way to get any movement in
the relief issue was to use his National Security Council
(NSC) influence to have the White House request an alternate
Biafran relief plan from the State and Defense Departments.
The result was a hastily drawn up plan for a massive land,
sea, and air emergency operation that would cost some $20
million. It was clear that the departments were in no rush
to provide viable assistance; probably to avoid the embarrassment the U.K. faced when the British military activity
in support of the FMG became public. But it was also clear
that Biafra's starvation and food problems were far from
over. Lacking massive deliveries through a land corridor or
a daylight airlift, the CRS-USCC insisted that the only way
to increase tonnage and reduce death rates was to augment
the air bridge. But the State Department backed their earlier course of minimum involvement and continued to be hesitant about releasing surplus C-97s for the Biafran airlift.

President-elect Nixon's staff, informed of the bureaucratic delays and pressured by all the relief groups, sent a
blunt letter to the State Department urging greater movement
on the C-97 deliveries. Senator Kennedy, who had long
pressed for a more active U.S. role, weighted in with the
eclipsing Democratic administration, writing Clifford to
urge the release of the idle C-97 transport aircraft to CRS-
USCC.

In spite of these pressures, the State and Defense
Departments insisted on examining two additional problems
before any transfer of military aircraft to active duty
would be finalized. The strongest objection U.S.A.I.D. had
to the CRS-USCC proposal for the purchase of the C-97s concerned America's neutrality toward the Nigerian conflict,
and America's neutrality and impartiality toward one or
another sectarian relief organization. The church groups,
therefore, had to prove their nonpolitical positions in
regard to their selection of goals. If any public relief
group or any of the religious groups were to be totally
responsible for the relief activity in one conflict area,
went the argument, then that agency's work might be placed
in jeopardy should it develop difficulties with the host
government. CRS-USCC believed that a better approach would

be to have several groups involved in both areas. But this presented a special problem to the church relief groups-- which religious group, if any, should be responsible for the relief operations in one or both areas?

When confronted by this stumbling block of which one of the American religious agencies should have authority over the future C-97s, CRS-USCC resurrected the concept of the very loose cooperative structure tentatively explored by Nordchurchaid and the Rome representatives--JCA. CRS-USCC presented this concept to both departments. The executive officers of the consortium would be from CRS-USCC, CWS, and AJC. CRS-USCC's assets were its A.I.D. P.L. 480 contracts, and CWS's assets were its experience and contacts with the many European relief groups and, just as important, it was non-Roman Catholic. The key factor that eventually allowed the government to follow through on the sale of these air- planes was attributed to the AJC's decision to join the work of CRS-USCC and CWS. Under such a joint venture there would be no basis for bias; nor could it be said that the move was anything but humanitarian. And so this all-American, human- itarian ad hoc venture of interchurch cooperation was to be formally known in America as Joint Church Aid-USA (JCA-USA).

Another problem raised by the State Department officials concerned the logistical positioning of the relief supplies and the airfield. But the interchurch group had already explored four possible working arrangements. The least advantageous location for JCA-USA to work from would be within the borders of the Cameroons. The FMG might ini- tially accept this arrangement, but the relief operations from Douala would be endangered because of the pressure the FMG could put on the Cameroon government to either reduce or suspend flights at any time. The FMG cancellation of ICRC flights in August and September 1968 justified this observa- tion.

A second option for the interchurch group would be to move its base of operations to the island of Fernando Po. But this would not only place the ICRC that was based there over the religious operation (which was the reason for the original CRS-USCC rejection of the U.S.A.I.D. offer of $500,000), it would also reduce the number of planes avail- able to the relief operations. Issues of airfield parking, repair, and landing facilities, the island of Fernando Po could not manage any additional large planes. The third option would be to fly out of the island of São Tomé, but stop at Fernando Po for inspection on the way to Uli. But this would have lengthened, of course, the flight time and thereby reduce the total volume delivered nightly. The fourth, and eventually the only acceptable of all possibili- ties, was to continue the relief airlift from São Tomé with some international inspection staff on the island to satisfy U.S. bureaucratic suspicions.

The State Department was not at all satisfied by this São Tomé base of operations for the future JCA-USA relief activity. But, unable to stem the political demand for some positive action on Biafran relief, Palmer insisted on one final bargaining position so as to maintain "neutrality." If CRS-USCC were allowed to purchase American aircraft for Biafran relief, then the ICRC should be allowed to purchase an equal number for their relief activity in Nigeria.

Sensing a political agreement, Morris encouraged the White House administration to go ahead with the sale of C-97s to the CRS-USCC with an equal number of planes for the ICRC. Overriding the final technical objections of the State Department, the Johnson administration announced on December 27 that it was selling eight C-97 Stratofreighters to enlarge the Nigerian and Biafran relief airlifts.

> As we have emphasized on past occasions, the situation requires the utilization of every possible channel of relief, including most importantly a surface corridor, which we continue to hope can be arranged. In the meanwhile, we continue to ask means of strengthening the airlift of relief supplies. We are therefore making available for the international relief airlift eight C-97 G "Stratofreighter" cargo aircraft which are no longer required by the U.S. Air Force. Four will be provided to the American Voluntary Agencies and four have been offered to the International Committee of the Red Cross.[16]

When this sale was announced, Palmer sent an immediate telegram to the FMG that this action did not reflect, either directly or indirectly on the U.S. political support of the rebellion, nor did it portent such support.

JCA-USA was incorporated on December 30, 1968, under the laws of New York State.

From December 1968 to February 1969, the Nigerian land war remained stalemated. But famine was about to launch another assault. Biafra's Chief Medical Officer, Dr. Rufus Nnaeto Onyemelukine, reported in <u>Medical World News</u> that "one million more persons--almost all of them children--will die of malnutrition within the next eight months."[17] Prolonged starvation, the physician said, opened the door to a host of other diseases. The land and sea blockade, the limited air access to Uli, and the denial by both Nigeria and Biafra for any arrangement on the delivery of medical and relief supplies contributed to the increase of the famine. The battle against disease and starvation, like the war with Nigeria, was a losing one for Biafra.

It would be an understatement to say that the FMG was angered by the U.S. decision to support the church airlift of relief to Biafra. Gowon summoned Mathews to listen to a strong Nigerian statement, in which the loan or sale of the C-97 aircraft would "directly and indirectly increase the arms carrying capacity of the rebels, encourage the rebel leaders to reject land routes which all international agencies agree to be the most effective means of relief, and encourage the rebels to think that the United States Government was now prepared to intervene in their favor, and thereby prolong the war."[18] Gowon then demanded that Mathews give a further clarification of the terms of the loan or sale of the American military aircraft. The U.S. Embassy in Lagos issued a statement the following day, New Year's Day: "The December 27 decision...was motivated solely by pressing humanitarian concern. In no way does this relief action reflect, either directly or indirectly, U.S. Government political support of the rebellion."[19]

It was Palmer who pointed out to the FMG that the sale of the C-97 planes to the relief groups was merely one step beyond what had been done before, that is, financing the Biafran relief planes. In an attempt to reassure the FMG that the eight C-97 planes would be used only for relief activity, Mathews promised Gowon that the United States would impose strict controls over the use of the relief air-crafts. In fact, Mathews reiterated the three conditional items mentioned in the December 27 announcement under with the voluntary agencies assumed responsibility of the C-97s. "Their use will be in accord with the strictly humanitarian purposes and operations of the total ICRC relief effort, they are to be used solely for the relief of non-combatants in transporting urgently needed food and other non-military supplies, and workable procedures will be instituted for inspection of cargoes."[20] Implementing these conditions were to cause considerable difficulty for the State Department.

George Sherry, the new State Department Nigerian Desk officer, called Krakow at ARC on Wednesday, January 15, 1969, to explain the extremely difficult and embarrassing situation in which the African Bureau found itself regarding the FMG and the recent sale of C-97s to the JCA-USA. Because the FMG had issued the strongest message that all planes that flew out of São Tomé had and would continue to carry arms and ammunition to Biafra (this was supported by cables from the U.S. Embassy in Lagos), the State Department was apprehensive that these new relief planes might also be used by the religious groups for that purpose. To eliminate this possibility, Palmer was attempting to assign acceptable and completely trustworthy inspectors at the airport on the island of São Tomé. Only in this way could the State Department ensure that the C-97 planes carried nothing other than relief supplies.

Sherry admitted to ARC officials, after some intensive questioning, that he had already explored this situation with ICRC officials. The ICRC had promptly informed Sherry that they were not willing to take on this assignment. The U.N. had also turned down the offer to inspect the relief planes. It was not too surprising, therefore, when General Collins of the ARC immediately and categorically disapproved of this proposed relief inspection assignment. He told Sherry that he would not hear of loaning ARC staff for the purpose of becoming a political investigatory agency. The official written reason that Collins sent to the State Department, however, described the agency's limited person-nel and the need to limit ARC activity to properly support the ICRC relief efforts.

Sherry's search did not end with the ICRC, U.N., or ARC refusals to provide inspection staff. The U.K. High Commis-sioner agreed with Mathews that impartial survey of relief supplies was necessary, but Britain surely could not help the United States inasmuch as the U.K. was openly providing arms to the FMG. Nonetheless, the U.K. promised to keep in touch and if the U.S. search failed, Britain had its own plan for relief inspection. Palmer recalled that at this

point in negotiating for an inspection team, "we first could
have informed the Federal Government about the Red Cross,
then we ran into trouble with the Portuguese. By that time
it was extremely difficult to go forward and say we didn't
trust the American relief agency."[21]

Although the State Department had to let their inspection demand disappear quietly that did not mean that they
came to trust the church group. The State Department did
not trust the church groups because CRS-USCC clandestinely
supported the initial Biafran relief, which may have shared
space on Wharton's planes, and because the relief groups
dared to challenge Palmer's One Nigeria policy. What seemed
an unforgivable action by the State Department staff, however, was the successful CRS-USCC pressure to obtain the
C-97s for their relief work. Some FSOs felt personally that
the CRS-USCC was publicly mocking the intelligence of the
African Bureau staff because, although there were other
groups in the JCA-USA, everyone knew that the principal
decision makers were the CRS-USCC staff. The working executive officers of JCA-USA were Bishop Swanstrom (CRS-USCC) as
President, Kinney (CRS-USCC) as Secretary-Treasurer, and
Eleanor Stein (CRS-USCC) as Assistant Treasurer.[22]

The State Department continued to delay the delivery of
the C-97s for these and other technocratic reasons. Palmer
insisted that the aircraft, purchased on January 8 at a cost
of $3,670 per plane, not be turned over to JCA-USA until
they had submitted the necessary official papers and insur-
ance documents to meet the State Department's Legal Bureau
requirements and the Defense Department's requirements. It
was January 10 before the first two C-97s were released to
the JCA-USA by the Defense Department, and the final two
planes were released seven days later. FTR, which was hired
by JCA to search for the additional relief aircraft, was now
hired by JCA-USA to operate, maintain, and fly the four
C-97s to São Tomé and then shuttle relief to Uli, Biafra.

Nixon was inaugurated into office during the C-97 trans-
atlantic flight. He had ordered, as president-elect, the
new NSC to prepare by January 21--the day after inauguration
--an extensive policy paper on the Nigerian conflict. It
analyzed the background to the conflict and the positions of
all sides including their myths, realities, and optional
approaches to an increase in relief supplies. Shortly after
receiving the document, Nixon ordered Secretary of State
William Rogers to conduct a top-to-bottom review of all U.S.
policy positions. This request temporarily immobilized the
entire State Department with paperwork, including the African Bureau.[23]

Rogers did not take immediate steps to fill the all-
important post of Head of the State Department Secretaries
because of this "busy work." But these important positions
are the eyes and ears of the Secretary of State in Washington politics. It was inevitable, then, that Rogers was not
fully aware of the activities of the new Special Adviser on
National Security, Henry Kissinger. It had been at the suggestion of Kissinger that Nixon had diverted Rogers to
"learning the ropes of the foreign policy trade," while
responding to the massive rewrite of American foreign policy. Such activity diverted Rogers from the inherent role

of foreign policy leader within the Washington power scene.
Rogers, busy with defensive action and learning how to cope
with big-league power politics, did not have the time or the
talent to create an offensive to stall Kissinger's moves to
assert a more influential role.

Rogers's inability to control the State Department
became evident early in his term. This was evidenced by the
long delay of normal ambassadorial and assistant secretarial
changes in the department. The bureaucracy in the department had also decided to delay its support until it saw who
would be the real decision maker, its actual boss.

Whereas Kissinger did not want to move too quickly into
a foreign policy utterance, the Senate's first policy advice
for Nixon came just twenty-four hours after his inauguration. The public statement of Senate Concurrent Resolution 3
was not on Vietnam, the source of the historic confrontation
between Congress and President Johnson, but in support of
the Nigerian and Biafran relief.

> That it is the sense of the Congress that:
> (1) the President should act to increase sig-
> nificantly the amount of surplus food stocks,
> relief moneys, non-combat aircraft, and such
> other vehicles of transportation as may be nec-
> essary for relief purposes; and this relief
> assistance should be made available to and at
> the request of the Organization of African
> Unity, UNICEF, the International Committee of
> the Red Cross, and such other suitable reli-
> gious and charitable relief agencies now or
> hereafter operating in the area with the con-
> sent of the responsible authorities; and
> (2) the Government of the United States should
> solicit the cooperation of other nations in
> this humanitarian effort.[24]

An identical House Concurrent Resolution 97 was offered by
Congressmen Donald Fraser (D-MN), Bradford Morse (R-MA), and
John Duncan (R-TN) in the House of Representatives with 90
cosponsors.   To add to the importance of the occasion, six
other statements were entered in the Congressional Record.

The day after the Senate and House Concurrent Resolutions were submitted to Congress, Nixon "ordered his Administration to prepare an urgent, comprehensive review of
United States relief efforts for civilian victims of the
nineteen month old Nigerian Civil War." Nixon also publicly
called for recommendations of what could be done to "enlarge
and expedite relief to the suffering."[25]   This second NSC
review of Nigeria and Biafra, ordered on January 24 and due
on January 28, was made within the context of urgency along
with the other policy priorities of Vietnam, SALT, and the
Middle East.

There were three new members attending these NSC meetings. The first of these was Kissinger as Chairman of the
NSC. As the Assistant to the President, Kissinger actually
controlled the American foreign policymaking process of this
number two priority issue of Nigeria--sometimes it was number one on the list of the top five problems in foreign

affairs. Although Rogers was physically present at the meetings as the Secretary of State, he was rationalized out of the Nigerian decision-making process because the issue was said to be too important for him to handle; it had to be kept under the President's and Kissinger's thumbs.

The second new NSC member was Dewey from the Defense Department. Dewey had been assigned by the Pentagon to work on the transfer of the C-97s to the church relief groups and to evaluate the needs required by this process. It was Dewey's analysis of the potential difficulties of the FTR organization handling the C-97s in the Biafran relief efforts, and his request for greater professionalism on the pat of the new JCA-USA organization that had added to the Defense Department's delay in authorizing the transfer of the aircraft.

The third new NSC member was initially Palmer, the FSO with the longest association with the Nigeria. He brought with him the 25 page U.S.A.I.D. "Disaster Memo Number Eleven", dated January 15. Having listened to Palmer and having read the information his team had prepared, Kissinger decided very early to replace Palmer with Under Secretary of State Elliot Richardson. Richardson was eventually, with Kissinger's approval, placed in full charge of policy decisions in regard to the Nigeria and Biafran relief.

The NSC study group recognized that the United States held leverage only with the FMG. Cognizant of the lingering fear of an earlier U.S. entanglement in Zaire, the NSC dismissed such fears as irrelevant and suggested the United States mount every effort to get relief into Biafra, mindful of both long- and short-run consequences and the limitations of the American role in ensuring a solution. Using the best information available on the scope of needs (which was admittedly fragmentary) the NSC group estimated the endangered population at between 1.5 and 3.5 million people for up to six months. They also placed relief needs at from 30,000 to 40,000 tons monthly. At the time of the review, some 18 aircraft in the Biafran air bridge (assuming the resumption of ICRC flights from Fernando Po) were capable of delivering a maximum of 4,000 tons. But due to the dangers of night operations, the technical flights never reached the 4,000-ton capability.

The review did not pose any happy alternatives. On one hand, military stalemate was actually producing horrible casualties among the noncombatant Ibo population. On the other hand, any FMG or Biafra military triumphs would likely increase the death toll and suffering. Therefore, what the NSC study emphasized was the need for greater U.S. humanitarian involvement. Pierre Gaillard, the ICRC Director, had already stated publicly that the ICRC needed an additional $2.2 million, by mid-December 1968, if they were to pay for the transportation and distribution costs for Biafran aid relief. The P.L. 480 food shipped to the FMG alone was over $5 million at the beginning of January 1969, compared to the token of $1 million to UNICEF for Biafra.[26] "In the areas under the control of the Federal Government, thousands of tons of food, medicine, and other relief supplies are stockpiled. Supplies are distributed from Lagos, Enugu, Calabar, Agbor and Port Harcourt by trucks and landrovers, cargo air-

craft helicopters, barges, and coastal ships."[27] The amount,
manner, and length of stockpiling had given the NSC group
cause for concern.

In the middle of January, the State Department received
embassy reports describing the FMG apprehension of three
expatriate ICRC workers from the Calabar-Uyo area. Eight
other workers, presumably Nigerians, were also arrested.
The State Department suspicions that relief workers were
stealing and selling relief supplies were now confirmed. All
the parties involved in the situation agreed, however, to
keep such incidents as quiet and as low keyed as possible.[28]
In the case of Calabar-Uyo, the ICRC representative issued a
press release stating that certain ICRC personnel were
merely being withdrawn from the area as a result of internal
reorganization.[29]   The ICRC also stated that it had no
knowledge of any misappropriation of ICRC funds or supplies.
Such illegal activity would have been hard to prove since
the Nigerian Rehabilitation Committee in the South East
State eventually dropped the charges against the ICRC
people.   The Nigerians caught stealing, however, did not
fair as well.   The only public record of the event is in the
Nigerian press, which reported that ICRC workers in Calabar
had stolen more than Ł 64,000 worth of stockfish and other
relief goods.[30] Spotty field reports, which the U.S. Embassy
in Lagos failed to properly "whitewash," did reach Washington and confirmed that this Calabar-Uyo incident was not an
isolated case.   Such loss of relief supplies and monies convinced the State Department that positive action must be
taken to convince the FMG and ICRC to accept professional
relief assistance.

The Biafran programs were experiencing similar problems
of relief control.   In one case there was a report from an
Order of Malta representative to the State Department concerning the loss of ICRC prestige and effectiveness among
the Biafran relief organizations.   The report attributes the
cause primarily to the ineptness of the ICRC personnel who
were poorly equipped to deal with the Africans. A corrobo-
rating ARC report presents the same picture of the ICRC
staff: "Personnel.   This situation is shocking from any
angle.   Personnel have been recruited and assigned who were
totally unfit for the jobs.   There are no job descriptions.
Staff have been arrogant and have shown contempt for the
Nigerians.   They have failed to use the national language
[English] even though able to speak it. Numerous staff have
had to be sent home because of lack of ability or violation
of regulations.   There is no plan for replacements on schedule."[31]   Other reports concerned the Biafran conviction that
ICRC representatives were engaged in military intelligence
reporting.   One ICRC representative was actually caught red-
handed gathering detailed data regarding arms airlifted into
Biafra.[32]

Replacement of these relief volunteers was very difficult.   Nigerians did not want to work for the NRC because of
low pay and unattractive promotions. This lack of skill and
experience compelled the ICRC and other relief agencies to
bring into Nigeria what they felt to be the necessary new
specialists to conduct proper relief programs. However, many
of these relief workers who had volunteered were prevented

from entering Nigeria. Even the officially accepted international and religious relief groups had to seek refuge in
the diplomatic pressure of the U.S. State Department to
resolve the Nigerian visa problem. The Deputy Chief of the
U.S. Mission in Lagos had a meeting with the Nigerian Federal Information and Labor Minister, Chief Anthony Enahoro,
in mid-January to set up a faster visa process.   Enahoro saw
the problem as a result of a cabinet decision whereby all
visas must be cleared by the Minister of Internal Affairs in
Lagos.   This change had been made at the urging of the FMG
Ministry of Internal Affairs and approved by the whole FMG
cabinet.   Inasmuch as this Ministerial position did not have
the necessary staff to administer such a situation properly,
long delays for visa applications could be predicted.   From
all accounts, the visa delays, permanent and unavoidable,
seem to have resulted from both bureaucratic inefficiency
and some intended obstructionism to foreign relief activity.
     Another factor that contributed to the general notion of
misuse of relief activity occurred at the end of 1968.   The
FMG's need for military mobility clashed with the ICRC's
relief needs.   The ICRC was working under the assumption
that relief planes were to be used solely for the transportation of relief supplies.   It was a surprise, therefore,
for the ICRC to be confronted by an order from Col. Benjamin
Adekunle on December 20, 1968, to cease all relief flights
to Calabar and Port Harcourt.   This order was issued because
one of the ICRC pilots had refused to transport some federal
military cargo and troops in an ICRC relief plane.   The ICRC
had assiduously avoided just such relief mixtures with military arms or troops because of the evident problems the
religious relief groups continuously faced concerning their
Biafra flights.   The ICRC was flying only relief and if one
combatant started the practice of using the ICRC planes for
military functions, the other would quickly follow.
     The order for the ICRC to cease all relief flights within
Nigeria was rescinded by the FMG six days later. It is still
to be explained why the FMG allowed the ICRC to resume their
relief flights within the federal territory on December 27,
the same day the United States announced the sale of eight
Stratofreighters to the ICRC and the religious relief groups
for Biafran relief.   The FMG most assuredly knew about this
impending American sale from Ambassador Mathews inasmuch as
the normal channels of bureaucratic information exchange
were being followed in regard to all such items concerning
relief programs and organizations working in Nigeria.
     Aside from trying to influence a delay in the U.S. sale
of the eight airplanes for Biafran relief, there may have
been another factor that allowed the FMG to permit resumption of ICRC flights in Nigeria. This factor was the FMG's
ability to make greater use of Nigerian Airways for military
movement within the federal territory.   Nigerian Airways was
directly linked with the American Industrial Development
Corporation.   It seems that the American corporation made a
concession to allow the federal military forces to use their
airline to preserve their lucrative Nigerian licence and
operation facilities.
     Another factor in the complex picture of relief programs
concerned the obstruction of relief shipments to Biafra from

the island of Equatorial Guinea. Equatorial Guinea, which included the island of Fernando Po, had become independent from Spain in October 1968. According to American reports, there was a complete lack of experience and knowledge by the new government of Equatorial Guinea in conducting foreign affairs. This inexperience had a direct effect on the ICRC's Biafran relief flights. The seaport and airport of Fernando Po used by ICRC continued to be run by the Spaniards under the new government of Equatorial Guinea--an untenable situation for any newly independent country. The government of Equatorial Guinea, to assure itself that the ICRC was really humanitarian, asked that the ICRC build a hospital in their country as a sign of the ICRC presence.

Auguste Lindt, director of the ICRC Nigeria-Biafra Relief, replied to the Equatorial Guinean government that such an arrangement would have to be negotiated outside the context of Biafran relief. The reason, as Lindt stated, was to avoid any future insinuation of blackmail. ICRC attempted to resolve the problem by working with three anti-Franco Spaniards on the island who were trying to set up a new bank for Equatorial Guinea. Lindt offered to deposit all the ICRC relief payments in the new Equatorial Guinean bank.[33] The inexperienced Equatorial Guinea government denounced this venture as traitorous and stopped all ICRC relief flights to the Biafran enclave. The dispute between the ICRC and the government of Equatorial Guinea, however, was presented in a different context to the public. "The Government of Equatorial Guinea refused to allow the ICRC to fly fuel to the airstrip near Uli, on the grounds that some of the fuel had been used by Biafran military vehicles."[34]

This dispute had an immediate effect. From a December total of 2,048 tons flown in by the ICRC, deliveries plunged to 304 tons in January, representing a loss of almost half the combined airlift.

When the Equatorial Guinea government stopped the ICRC airflights, which supplied relief to over 850,000 Biafrans, it also had a resounding effect on the humanitarian groups in America. Under public pressure, Secretary Rusk sent an exceptionally sharp note to the FMG asking intervention on behalf of restored flights. The government of Equatorial Guinea responded by informing the U.N. Secretary General U Thant on January 16, 1969, that it would allow the Santa Isabel Airport on Fernando Po "to be used as a private base for relief supplies to Biafra but it could not be used by the ICRC."[35] Two days after Nixon's inauguration, January 22, as his first official act as Secretary of State, Rogers took this issue to Equatorial Guinea's Foreign Minister. But, it was to no avail. The ICRC eventually came to use Dahomey as its base of relief operations for Biafra whereas the religious groups continued to fly out of Fernando Po and São Tomé.

Had the São Tomé and Fernando Po to Uli relief air bridge not existed, it is doubtful whether Biafra could have sustained its succession for any length of time. Why the Portuguese government and the Spanish/Equatorial Guinean governments allowed the Biafrans to use their islands was based on decisions made in Lisbon and Madrid/Malabo and can only be guessed at. But there can be no doubt that the Biafran government was dependent on these facilities for the survival of its people.

Notes

1. Nixon for President Committee, News release, Oct. 12, 1968, New York City, p. 1.
2. Quoted in the private collection material of "The Creation and Early Days of Joint Church Aid and the United States," by John A. Daly, C.S.Sp. and Anthony G. Saville, History of Joint Church Aid, Vol. 2.
3. Memos in "U.S. Government" files of the Nigeria/Biafra Clearing House Papers, Swarthmore College Peace Collection, Swarthmore, Penn.
4. Ibid.
5. The World Council of Churches (WCC) is a highly heterogeneous body, comprising 232 churches in 79 countries. Yearbook of International Organizations, 12th ed. (Brussels: Union of International Associations, 1968/9), 1069. The WCC was hoping to play the role of peacemaker, but the task of a diversified assembly to reach consensus on such a controversial issue was not easy.
6. Ingvar Berg, Nordchurchaid: A Report on Its Operations (Stockholm, June 10, 1970), 6-7.
7. Joint Church Aid, Report on the JCA Conference, November 8/9, (Rome, JCA), p. 5. Das Diskonische Werk (DDW) is a relief agency of the German Lutheran church.
8. The American Committee to Keep Biafra Alive, "News conference report," November 14, 1968.
9. U.S.A.I.D., "Disaster Memo Number Ten," Nov. 25, 1968, p. 7.
10. Norman Kirkham, "Biafran Food to be Air Dropped," Sunday Telegraph, Dec. 22, 1968, p. 7.
11. Palmer, interview with author, Chevy Chase, Maryland, July 23, 1975. Markpress was the Biafran information newspaper.
12. U.S. State Department, Press release No. 267, Dec. 3, 1968, "Address by the Honorable Nicholas de B. Katzenbach, Under Secretary of State at Brown University."
13. Ibid.
14. Ibid.
15. Remarks by Edward Kinney, CRS-USCC Executive Director, before the Catholic Apostolic Radio, Television, and Advertising, Dec. 6, 1968.
16. Johnson, Statements of the United States Government, "U.S. Will Make C-97's Available for International Relief in Nigeria," no. 2, 4.
17. Robert Corcam, "Medicine Versus Starvation," Medical World News (Feb. 28, 1969): 31.
18. "Lagos Warns U.S. on Aid to Biafra," The New York Times, Dec. 31, 1968, p. 7.
19. Johnson, Statements of the United States Government, 2, 2.
20. Ibid.
21. Palmer, interview with author.
22. The two executive Vice Presidents were James MacCracken of CWS and Bertram Gold of the AJC.
23. Rowland Evans and Robert Novak, "National Security Council Continues to Gain Influence under Kissinger," The Washington Post, June 18, 1969, p. A23.
24. Jan. 23, 1969, Congressional Record, 91st Cong., 1st sess., 115:,1468-1475.
25. Colwell, "Biafra," 12.
26. U.S.A.I.D., "Disaster Memo Number Eleven," Jan. 15, 1969, p. 1, Table I. The P.L. 480 to Biafra was the single contribution by the U.S. government to UNICEF for 1,755 tons of food.
27. U.S. State Department, The Nigerian Relief Problem (February 25, 1969), 4.
28. The State Department categorized these public Nigerian news stories as "classified" information. The American press also agreed to be silent on this issue. Only once did the American public and Congress express a reaction to a snafu story on supplies for refugees by Charles Mohr, "Nigeria Will Slash Food Distribution, The New York Times (Nov. 2, 1969), p. 9.
29. ICRC, Press release, Jan. 20, 1969.
30. Nigerian Post, Jan. 17, 1969, p. 1.
31. National American Red Cross, General Records, Feb. 12, 1969, p. 1.
32. Father Dermot Doran, Holy Ghost Father and Special Consultant to JCA-USA on Sao Tome, interview with author, Villanova, Penn., June 28, 1974.
33. ICRC, Field report to Headquarters, Geneva, Jan. 18, 1969.
34. Colwell, "Biafra," 11.
35. Ibid.

6

Politics of Relief

Relief that was intended for starving Biafrans continued to
be hamstrung by politics. The U.S. policy continued to be
pro-FMG, yet it was becoming more low key as the NSC review
group explored policy options that ranged from strict neutrality to all-out support of either the FMG or Biafra.
Lying between these two extremes was the choice of all-out
relief initiatives, a quiet pro-Nigerian political stance,
and peacemaking probes. The compromise option, with something for everyone, was the one eventually recommended by
Henry Kissinger.

There was apparent majority agreement during the NSC
meetings of January 24-28, 1969, on the need for more relief
and some sort of neutrality, but it did not pass without
telling bureaucratic skirmishes. Roger Morris and Harold
Saunders took the position that Biafran success might not
encourage other secessionist movements in Africa, noting the
peculiar circumstances of the Biafran breakaway. Joseph
Palmer, now cut out of these meetings, encouraged his staff
to demure for as long as possible with the humanitarian
argument of the domino theory pure and simple--"If you
didn't stop it here, even at this terrible price that you
had to pay, so many more would die." The Pentagon members
argued that the FMG would not come around on relief for less
than hefty U.S. political backing.

During the NSC discussions the African Bureau came around
to ally itself with the Defense Department to argue against
any moves that might encourage the Biafrans and to press for
a boost in public U.S. political support for Nigeria to
counterbalance stepped-up relief. The African Bureau, supported by Elliot Richardson, predicted dire consequences for
American-Nigerian relations and for the overall fabric of
American policy in Africa should the Biafran secession stand
as a result of humanitarian aid that strengthened Biafra and
lengthened the war. Given the options under consideration,
their effort was to head off any substantial reduction in
U.S. backing for the FMG through strict neutrality or, similarly, to avoid a commitment to Biafran survival beyond what
would be entailed by increased relief activity (for which
the African Bureau demanded compensation to the FMG). It

worked to a degree because America never formally recognized the Biafran political goals.

After their review of the medical and relief problems in Nigeria and Biafra, the majority of the NSC staff decided that the United States should be more actively "neutral." This decision was taken in response to American domestic political pressures rather than to any international crisis. Their decision would blunt the force of the strategic importance of this case to a considerable degree and give it the character of a momentary high priority political issue. The important fact is that the United States did not adopt any new policy nor change any old policy because of the NSC review study; it just stretched the existing policy to appease domestic political pressure. The expanded U.S. relief assistance was not destructive to the main systemic relation nor did it threaten the goal orientation of American-Nigerian relations at that time.

Together with a set of relief options, which ran the gamut from substitution of larger aircraft to daylight flights using 35 seventeen-ton payload airplanes to a land corridor, the NSC review was sent on to Kissinger. When the NSC had finished examining the relief programs and studies done by the Pentagon, the State Department, and U.S.A.I.D. concerning Nigeria and Biafra, several plans seemed promising. Kissinger immediately dispatched Gene Dewey to Nigeria and Biafra to examine these proposed plans in person on the ground. At the final full meeting of the NSC (Dewey was now overseas), Kissinger took control of the discussion on the options for Nigeria. He reportedly told the group that what they had was essentially a trade-off: for every relief move that strengthens Biafra, the United States should make positive sounds to the FMG; similarly, the nicer the United States is to the FMG, the more tangible should relief be for Biafra. President Richard Nixon concurred with this report.

But Nixon adopted none of the six options offered by the NSC report. Instead, a brief decision memorandum, drafted by Alexander Haig from notes of the meeting, called for continued political and military neutrality and a high profile on relief. The possibility of offering the FMG additional political support for relief concessions was held in abeyance. Senior White House officials understood that Nixon wanted a "two track" U.S. policy designed to take highly visible actions to reflect a deep humanitarian concern, including the appointment of a special relief coordinator from outside the government and to continue to look forward to an ultimate FMG military victory as best suited to American interests while carefully avoiding political involvement in the uncertain fortunes of either side.

The basic difficulty the United States had with American relief was the logistical control of Biafran relief. There was a need for a special person in the United States who would be the coordinator of all relief to both Nigeria and Biafra. Several capable choices were recommended. The NSC, therefore, ended its first series of discussions to await Dewey's field report and Nixon's choice of a special coordinator of relief.

Even as America's policy on relief was under NSC review, the FMG began to react to a perceived shift.   On Saturday, January 25, the day that the two U.S.-supplied C-97s arrived at São Tomé for relief duty, some 500 Nigerian students stoned the United States Information Agency Center and British High Commission in Ibadan in protest of foreign intervention.   That same day in a Lagos news conference, Nigeria's Commissioner of Information, Anthony Enharo, told newsmen that while past U.S. policy was directed at humanitarian problems, "now it seems more people are talking about keeping Biafra alive, which is a political question." The "slight shift," he added, caused a dilemma and "considerable concern" in Lagos.[1]

Their dilemma was based on the fact that as relief planes would come into Biafra at night to land at Uli airfield, Hank Wharton's arms planes would intermingle with them.   This was hardly in accordance with what the church relief organizations were trying to do to help the Biafra suffering.   In their zeal to get relief into Biafra, the interfaith groups gave inadequate recognition of the extent to which other groups, with far different motivations, might take advantage of the relief flights.   It was not just the intermingling of food and arms (which was a problem) that upset the FMG, it was also the fact that additional larger planes were being given to the groups supporting Biafran survival.

The very limited ICRC activity was accepted as a sufficient humanitarian effort by the FMG.   However, they did not ignore the efforts that supplied relief to the worst famine areas in the secessionist Eastern Region.   The ICRC had always received tacit political approval from the FMG for such airlifts of relief supplies to Biafra.   These flights were not considered illegal as they were not perceived by the FMG to be in legal violation of Nigerian airspace.   The conflict was with the church relief groups flying supplies into Biafra--this was seen by the FMG to be in direct violation of their requests and in violation on their airspace. Okoi Arikpo, who argued the FMG cause, went on record with the comment, "No humanitarian consideration can justify the violation of our airspace."[2]   Even though the church relief groups argued that their humanitarian airlift assistance was fulfilling a higher law of humanitarianism, the FMG viewed such action as political and as interference.   "In the view of some Nigerian officials, the Roman Catholic Church workers often seem motivated as much by politics as pity.... Gowon also said he would not tolerate political interference by any relief organization under the guise of humanitarianism."[3]   Therefore, any humanitarian act toward Biafra by the church relief groups working out of São Tomé and Fernando Po would have constituted an overt act of intervention according to the guidelines set out by the FMG.

The level of the military conflict was also reported to be on the rise.   Lllewellyn Chanter reported on January 25, "Russian arms and influence will back up the new assault which, I understand, the Nigerian Federal Government forces are about to make on Biafra. The next few days will probably indicate that this is under way."[4]   This military action in Nigeria caused ripples of concern in American relief.   At a

San Francisco investment seminar on January 27, Nigerian
Consul-General Peter Afalabi said his country would do
everything it could to "keep as many doors open and the welcome mat out to current and future investors as much as we
possibly can."[5]   Nigerian officials increased their quiet
approaches to American firms with financial stakes in Nigeria urging them to use their influence with the new Nixon
administration to gain a more pro-Nigeria policy.[6]   Meanwhile, senior U.S. officials and Nigerian Ambassador Joseph
Iyalla were reportedly urging key congressional leaders to
stick to the principle of One Nigeria.[7]

A member of Congress who actively sought to influence
America's role in the conflict was Charles Goodell, the mav-
erick Republican Senator from New York. He had assembled a
team of nongovernmental experts on nutrition, agriculture,
relief, and distribution and had flown with them into Biafra
in early February, following a brief stop in Lagos. The
Goodell team traveled throughout Biafra for several days,
gathering ad hoc indicators of health, nutrition, and relief
levels. Emerging from Biafra, the men bearded and haggard,
members of the group wrote their report while flying back to
New York. Goodell asked the team not to shave or clean up
before landing--he wanted maximum public relations impact.
When the humanitarian team landed, the reporters pressed
them with questions, but beyond the brief media moment (neither NBC, CBS, nor ABC ran the story nationally), the Goodell Mission won few converts. To those who already believed
in a humanitarian imperative, often in tandem with sympathy
for the Biafra experiment, Goodell's findings sustained
their views. But to those who viewed Goodell's public
statements as staged, it was just another Biafran public
relations coup.

The most serious congressional attempt to change this
established pro-FMG policy was the Senate Concurrent Resolution 3, introduced on January 21 by Senators Edward Brooke
(R-MA), James Pearson (R-KS) and 50 cosponsors.[8] Then,
Congressmen Bradford Morse (R-MA) and Donald Fraser (D-MN)
introduced their counterpart House bill two days later as
House Concurrent Resolution 96, and it was supported by more
than 100 Congressmen.[9] Both resolutions, which did add to
the pressure for increased U.S. relief to the starving and
suffering in Nigeria and Biafra, played heavily on the
humanitarian theme and urged an increased and more effective
U.S. relief role. But these resolutions were soon overtaken
by events.

Shortly after its introduction, as is the American cus-
tom, these congressional Concurrent Resolutions were sent to
the State Department for comment. Obviously the African
Bureau was not an enthusiastic supporter of the Brooke-
Pearson Resolution because they urged in their reply that
Congress should be cautious in this area of relief assistance. Although Palmer and Robert Smith had the necessary
data on hand--they had based their October 1968 presentation
to the Senate Foreign Relations Committee hearing on their
U.S.A.I.D. disaster relief memos and numerous official and
unofficial reports--the State Department report on Senate
Concurrent Resolution 3 was not returned until March 20;
nearly two months after submittal.

Since no visible or tangible relief assistance decisions seemed forthcoming from the State Department, Senator Thomas Dodd (D-CT) submitted his Senate Concurrent Resolution 8 on January 31, which called on the Nixon administration to "utilize all its diplomatic resources" to somehow implement an immediate cease-fire. "The United States Government, in the interest of putting an end to the killing and starvation, should lend its good offices and utilize all its diplomatic resources for the purpose of bringing about an immediate cease-fire."[10]   Congressman Donald Lukens's (R-OH) House Concurrent Resolution 127 of February 5 supported Dodd's group of 17 cosigners with an additional 25 congressional signatures. The announcement of Dodd's resolution coincided with the first ICRC flight from Contonou, Dahomey, being returned to its base without unloading its relief cargo in Biafra due to FMG military harassment.   The Dodd Resolution also had been referred routinely to the State Department on February 8 for comment, but the department never took any action on it.

One reason for this inaction was the U.S. Embassy's Annual U.S. Policy Assessment: Nigeria, 1968 forwarded to Washington on February 1.   In the report, Elbert Mathews emphasized the FMG suspicion that "since the U.S. is giving less than total support to the FMG it must be giving some support to Biafra in humanitarian terms."[11]   But, he went on, the United States cannot begin to consider any recognition of Biafra until two basic questions are answered:
(1) Who will determine the area of Biafra and where will the boundaries be fixed? and (2) Who is acceptable to negotiate peace between Nigeria and Biafra?

After finding someone they could trust the State Department decided it was now politically advantageous to publicly support an official congressional fact-finding mission to Biafra.   It consisted of Congressmen Charles Diggs (D-MI), Lester Wolff (D-NY), and Herbert Burke (R-FL).   Diggs was the Chairman of the House African Subcommittee and supported the One Nigeria policy and Burke had known Nixon since the Eisenhower administration.   This team was scheduled first to travel to Lagos on February 7, then to pay a 48-hour visit to Biafra, then to go back to Lagos via Dahomey, and finally to return on February 20 to America.

It was February 12 before the JCA-USA planes flew the Uli shuttle for the first time.   Forty-seven days between the sale and the use of the aircraft for relief does not imply any great urgency.   FMG indiscriminate bombing, which also began in February, on Biafran airstrips naturally caused increased American concern.   The news that Biafran women and children were killed and injured had Vietnam connotations.

It was after Congressmen Lukens, Goodell, and Allard Lowenstein (D-NY) returned from Biafra and during the official Diggs's fact-finding mission in Nigeria that the NSC met to update and evaluate the recent Nigerian findings. Dewey had cabled from Nigeria that of all the proposed relief plans, the Cross River Project was the best plan. The only other major plan that was active at the time, that is Lindt's ICRC Plan, was said (by Dewey) to contain too many problems.   Therefore, the implementation of the Cross River Project was to be the first objective of any future

relief decision. The United States decided to wait for the
right moment to go public with the new plan.
      Aware of the slow U.S. approach toward any involvement
in the Nigeria conflict, Lukens published a four-page record
of his visit to Nigeria and Biafra on Thursday, February 20.
His first impression of the conflict was that the United
States must use all diplomatic and economic resources to
bring about a cease-fire. This cease-fire was not the inhu-
mane British "quick-kill" policy that Lukens condemned.[12]
The much-publicized quick-kill concept began as an error of
personal interpretation by Lukens.   When Lukens went to
visit Mathews in Nigeria, Lukens mentioned that there were
some people in London who were saying that the way to solve
the Nigeria and Biafra problem was to make a quick-kill in
Biafra.[13] In this way, the argument went, the extended
suffering and killing would end quickly and the relief food
and medicine would reach the needy. Mathews recalled that
he nodded and mumbled in the affirmative, intending only
recognition of the concept, not support.[14]
      Lukens returned to Paris to recuperate from an illness
contracted while in West Africa.   During the recuperation
period he was interviewed by Lloyd Garrison of The New York
Times. It was from this interview that Garrison reported
that Mathews told Lukens that the Biafra problem could be
solved by a quick-kill policy. Because these statements of
a quick-kill were made public in Garrison's article, The New
York Times eventually published a retraction for the error,
but the concept continued even after the retraction and
after the end of the conflict.[15]
      If the quick-kill had been the official policy of the
British and/or supported by the United States, then the
activity of their relief systems and the United States arms
neutrality were contrary to such a policy. No evidence yet
exists to support the notion that the United States at any
time seriously entertained the policy of a quick-kill toward
Biafra. The Americans were more interested in getting the
relief food and medical supplies legally into the combat
area. The main issue always before the United States was to
do it properly and precisely, no matter how long it took.
      One way to get more food into Biafra, of course, was
through another airstrip similar to that at Uli.   Lukens
proposed that just such an airstrip be built by the United
States, which would be parallel to the proposed airstrip
sponsored by the Canadian church relief groups. Both the
airstrips would be operated by neutral authorities for
humanitarian purposes only. It was on Friday, the day after
Luken's eight-point pro-Biafran report, that Congressman
Lowenstein balanced the record with his own eight points.[16]
Lowenstein's first general observation, based on his two
trips to Biafra, was that the FMG was not engaged in a campaign of willful genocide.   Such an observation was also
publicly supported by Goodell and officially reported to
William Rogers, Richardson, and other State Department offi-
cials.   In return, Goodell decided to announce during his
National Press Club talk on February 19 that the State
Department officials had given him assurances that "the
United States Government will make available to relief
agencies on a feasible and emergency basis such cargo

planes, maintenance personnel, and parts as are found to be necessary to perform the humanitarian mission of getting food and medical supplies to the starving people in Biafra and in Nigeria."[17] Congressional staffers also reported at this time that the State Department was planning to send a representative to Umuahia, a Biafran administrative center, to act as coordinator for air shipments. Along these same lines, the FMG offered to open Obilagu airstrip to daytime relief flights. The FMG external affairs commissioner indicated that this offer was the result of steps taken by Lowenstein who made these arrangements in his travels between Lagos and Biafra. Lowenstein said the United States should "separate the military from the humanitarian question" and "commit itself more deeply to alleviating human suffering."[18]

The policies presented on February 22, 1969 by President Nixon were not, therefore, to a great extent new positions.

> Immediately after taking office, I directed an urgent and comprehensive review of the relief situation. The purpose was to examine every possibility to enlarge and expedite the flow of relief. This very complex problem will require continuing study. I am announcing, however, the following initial conclusions of the review:
>
> 1....additional support for the international relief effort.
>
> 2....a comprehensive, internationally conducted survey of food needs in that area (of Biafra controlled).
>
> 3....The main problem is the absence of relief arrangements acceptable to the two sides which would overcome the limitations posed by the present hazardous and inadequate nighttime airlift.
>
> 4....the humanitarian urge to feed the starving and have become enmeshed in those issues (political and military that divide the contestants) and stands in danger of interpretation by the parties as a norm of intervention.
>
> 5....It is this spirit (that is within the conscience and ability of man to give effect to his humanitarianism with involving himself in the politics of the dispute) that the U.S. policy will draw a sharp distinction between carrying out our moral obligations to respond effectively to humanitarian needs and involving ourselves in the political affairs of others. The United States will not shrink from this humanitarian challenge.

After these five points, Nixon announced the appointment of
Clarence Clyde Ferguson as Special Coordinator of Relief to
civilian victims of the Nigerian Civil War with a personal
rank of Ambassador.[19]   Kissinger had advised Nixon to personally announce Ferguson's appointment as Ambassador. This
action would take away from Rogers's role as Secretary of
State (and strengthen Kissinger's role) but it would at the
same time given Nixon the center stage of humanitarianism.
If Ferguson's appointment was a political move to appease
the domestic pressure of the American humanitarian lobbyists
who demanded some action-oriented position in the relief
sector it also supported the concept that relief could be
separated from the political and military aspects of the
Nigerian Civil War.

In announcing that the State Department would have a
relief coordinator (an act reportedly resisted by State
Department), Nixon charged Ferguson with assuring that the
U.S. contributions to the international relief effort would
be responsive to increased needs to the maximum extent possible and that they be effectively utilized.   At the same
time, Ferguson was enjoined not to seek or accept a charge
to negotiate issues "other than those directly related to
relief."   It was a deliberately narrow mandate. Nixon and
Kissinger, sharing a basic distrust of bureaucracy, wanted
to reserve a possible mediation role for the White House,
not the State Department.

Three days after Ferguson's appointment, the State
Department had prepared a brief five-page document for him,
"The Nigerian Relief Problem," which attempted to further
limit an already limited mandate. "He [Ferguson] will give
particular attention to ways and means by which the flow of
relief can be increased to the suffering on both sides of
the battle lines. He will work closely with the relief
agencies engaged in the international relief effort."

However, Goodell had prepared another rather lengthy
report on his study mission to Nigeria and Biafra, which he
also made public on February 25. His recommendation was to
have Nixon extend Ferguson's duties from the Coordinator of
Relief activities of man power and supplies in the Nigerian
conflict to a new level of internationalism. "For this and
similar situations which could arise in the future, the
President should be asked to designate a Relief Advisor to
work in a voluntary capacity as his consultant on problems
of international relief."[20]

Ferguson began assembling a staff shortly after his
appointment.   It was inevitable that friction began to
develop between Ferguson's office and other State Department
agencies, including the African desks and U.S.A.I.D.'s desk
of Central and West African Affairs. At about the same time
Ferguson was named relief coordinator, another in-house
shift of responsibility moved A.I.D.'s relief focus to the
Special Office for Nigerian Relief and Rehabilitation. Seeking continuity and greater expertise to execute his mandate,
Ferguson unsuccessfully sought administrative and technical
support from A.I.D. From December 1968 to February 1969 the
Central and West Africa Office tried to maintain primary
responsibility for Nigerian disaster relief as a normal
A.I.D. function.

From its inception the Ferguson office (coded U/CF) was
a peculiarly unique bureaucratic creature. Symbolizing the
"high profile" approach requested by the Nixon administration and attached to Richardson's office--and not to any
A.I.D. or African Bureau desks--it trespassed institutional
domains. While liaison with the State Department's political
offices was expected, regularized policy coordination was
infrequent.   "I never saw any regular consultation between
Ferguson, the Nigeria Desk, and other agencies," remembered
one Ferguson aide. The Special Coordinator for Relief also
ran afoul of the U.S. Embassy in Lagos, remembered a high-
ranking team member: "The Embassy's job was to maintain
relations with the Nigerians and their prime concern was
relief, so lots of things irritated them."   Ironically,
while Ferguson soon came to be regarded with suspicion by
the White House, State Department officials always suspected
that he was an agent of the White House intrusion into
international affairs.
     Possibly the most crucial congressional fact-finding
tour on problems of international relief was made by Diggs
between February 7 and 20.   Unlike the Goodell Mission,
Diggs's findings had substantial impact. The first recounting of Diggs's official trip to Nigeria and Biafra was a
brief interview with the U.S. Voice of America on February
27 in which he commented, "I am optimistic because, number
one, I think all of the principals concerned want to see an
early negotiated settlement of this whole matter....
Secondly, if the United States has a role to play, now is
the time for it to be played, while the administration is
new, without the kind of tarnishment which characterized the
other large parties."[21] It was evident that the Congressman
felt that the United States could play a role in the ending
of the conflict. However, in his official published report
on March 12, 1969, Diggs wrote, "It is...impossible that an
interested third nation such as the United States will be
able to act as the catalyst to bring about successful peace
talks which lead to a lasting settlement. The United States
is not likely to have any particular power of persuasion
over the Federal Government, which it continues to recognize."[22]
     The official "Diggs Report" presented an opinion similar
to that of the FMG and the State Department because it was
ghost written by the African Bureau. Its effect on the U.S.
Congress, the West Africa article stated, was "generally
agreed to have been considerable."[23] In no small part, the
timing of Diggs's Mission and the State Department's report
on the Brooke-Pearson Resolution contributed to that resolution's subsequent defeat by the March 20 House vote.
     Nonetheless, pro-Biafran Congressmen did not relent in
their quest for greater humanitarian concern. Such concern
led Goodell to have a meeting with Ferguson on Thursday,
March 6. This meeting led to an article in the Saturday
Review by Goodell, which put forward a clear humanitarian
interest in the Nigerian conflict.[24] Goodell agreed, however, that most Congressmen were content to give Ambassador
Ferguson time to improve the relief system in Nigeria and
Biafra.

Table 6.1.   U.S. Contributions to Nigeria/Biafra Relief,
            November 1968-June 1969

Time Period	Government	Percent[a]	Voluntary Groups	Percent[a]	Total	Percent[a]
Nov.-February 25	$ 8,089,940	17	$ 3,122,502	39	$11,212,442	21
Feb.-March 25	6,457,400	14	731,938	9	7,189,338	13
March-April 15	15,453,500	33	2,346,000	29	17,799,500	33
April-June 1	12,537,300	27	217		12,537,517	23
June-July 1	3,701,755	8	1,757,296	22	5,459,051	10
Subtotal	46,239,895	73	7,957,953	65	54,197,848	72
Table 5.1[b] Subtotal	16,901,760	27	4,145,560	28	21,047,320	28
Grand Total	$63,141,655		$12,103,513		$75,245,168	

[a]Percentage of total Grand Total.
[b]Table 5.1 summarized U.S. contributions to Nigeria/Biafra relief,
           June-November 1968.

Source: Summarized from U.S.A.I.D. disaster memos.

As Table 6.1 indicates, the March-April 1969 period did show
a 45 percent increase in U.S. public and private funds made
available to relief organizations.   Such relief involvement
met Goodell's request that the State Department combine an
"arrival of conscience with an assertion of action."[25]   The
Goodell article also asked for a separation of American
relief from any political implications of intervention;   a
humanitarian relief that was neutral in its activity.   As
was the case, Ferguson did pursue an independent course to
alleviate starvation in both Nigeria and Biafra.
    By mid-March Ferguson's efforts were totally focused on
Dewey's preferred relief plan--the water route up the Cross
River.   The river was judged to be the only way to substantially increase the relief tonnage going into the Biafran
enclave.   Based on the calculations and logistics work out
by Dewey, the Cross River Project was the major task of the
Special Coordinator's staff. Stephen Schott, U/CF Executive
Director, put together the staffers' hard work, which
included the detailed loading and unloading points along
Cross River, the storage areas, the two commercialized Landing Ship Medium (LSM) Dona Maria and Dona Mercedes and their
entire crews (see the Appendix to this chapter).   This final
report was the subject of Ferguson's first junket trip.   The
Cross River Project was taken by Ferguson to both Yakubu
Gowon and Odumegwu Ojukwu, and he reported that neither side
said no.
    The purpose of the Cross River Project was to offer a
surface relief route, adequate to satisfy Biafra's relief
requirements, and so it was configured and presented to the
parties that neither side could offer a credible logistic,
military, or political basis for a turndown.   It was always
viewed, responsible officials and ex-officials said, as
first augmenting and then replacing the existing dangerous
and illicit night airlift. Its success would offer appealing
outcomes for the State Department. Any dramatic breakthrough

on the Cross River Project would have deflected and reduced
domestic pressures on the government. A replacement of a
problematic airlift supported by U.S. money, goods, and
equipment would also ease a sore point in American-Nigerian
relations. The Cross River Project offered the best of both
worlds--relief supplies and good diplomatic relations.

     Yet for all its apparent promise, the Cross River Project
carried several distinct liabilities. One was the seasonal
variation in the water level of the river. During the dry
season the river level dropped to a point where, according
to one expert, payloads would be reduced from its calculated
900-ton capacity to perhaps 200 tons. While U.S. officials
were hopeful that the difference could be made up by truck
shipments from Calabar to Ikot-Okporo, such a proposal would
have also required the approval of both sides. The greatest
constraints to the implementation of the Cross River Project
were political. Both sides saw political or military implications, advantages or disadvantages, in all the various
relief initiatives offered. Therefore, U.S. officials did
not rule out negotiations for a land corridor, but they did
realize that such efforts must be accompanied by vigorous
attempts to professionalize and optimize the channels that
were open to the United States to get relief into Biafra--
principally the night airlifts.

     Among the usual items of Ferguson's discussion with
involved relief groups was the question of division of labor
in the relief effort of the airlift. Concerned with the
inadequacy of the existing program as well as the serious
consequences of continued American support for an airlift
regarded by the Nigerian government as illegal, Ferguson
suggested to Lindt in March 1969 that the ICRC concentrate
on a negotiated daylight flights agreement while Ferguson
sought a breakthrough on the Cross River Project. Lindt
agreed.

     The division of labor was not arbitrary. Assignments
were suited to values held by the institutions. The ICRC,
tradition bound and conservative by nature, viewed negotiated and legal daylight relief flights as a major goal. A
reluctant and tardy participant in an "illegal" mercy airlift, the ICRC was eager to erase its illicit past (it had
first sponsored flights during the summer of 1968, although
ICRC representatives in Biafra had reported an urgent and
immediate relief need as early as November 1967). The proposal for the division of labor held the prospect of ICRC
vindication by agreement and legality, and at the same time
the ICRC would not be embroiled in the Cross River Project.

     The JCA-USA was experiencing its own problems with the
airlift during the first months of 1969. An initial delay in
airlifting relief was due to the military position of the
C-97 crews. The pilots and crews hired by FTR were mostly
U.S. military personnel who had not been reclassified as
civilian pilots and crew. This had come about because of
the uniqueness of the aircraft and the experience required
to fly these planes.[26] However, the Pentagon did not want
its military personnel involved directly in this sensitive
situation of the Biafran relief. The hazardous wartime conditions of the Biafran air relief, therefore, forced the
C-97 crews to avoid any possible embarrassment to the U.S.

Defense Department. For these and other personnel reasons, the C-97 pilots and crews went on strike and refused to fly any of the relief missions to the Uli airstrip after the first night mission. What compounded the problems and pressures for the JCA-USA was the fact that the ICRC crews were making successful flights to Uli at this time.

FTR, hired in haste by CRS-USCC, was not able to handle either the crews' refusal to fly or the lack of C-97 spare parts. There was a definite lack of organizational staff within FTR, an inability to hire the necessary experienced pilots and crews to fly the C-97s as promised, and a lack of C-97 spare parts promised to JCA-USA by FTR. Such weakness could not be left unattended indefinitely if JCA-USA was to succeed in its mission. Edward Kinney was assigned by CRS-USCC to assume more and more responsibility as the FTR proved incapable of coming up with the necessary motivation and imagination to solve these relief supply problems.

The eventual departure of six of the initial 24 American crewmen was of minimal impact on the JCA-USA relief mission compared to the major problem of obtaining the all important and necessary spare parts and replacements for the C-97s. It was Kinney who eventually convinced Dewey to obtain the necessary aircraft spare parts from the U.S. Air Force. Kinney was also very aggressive in the Pentagon and State Department negotiations. He was eventually allowed to rent three DC-6s to transport the necessary tires, parts, and tools to São Tomé.

There was a critical shortage of aircraft for Biafran relief during these negotiations. The independent churches and humanitarian agencies working in Biafran relief made offers to charter or rent the inactive C-97s from JCA-USA. Caritas/DDW representatives in São Tomé expressed the desire to charter the C-97s that were sitting idle in the island, as did the relief group African Concerned (out of Libreville). The humanitarian and religious relief groups were run by individuals who were not always above petty politics, pride, and resentment of the potential monopoly the JCA-USA would exercise in São Tomé once it would become mobilized. The mere number of planes and their load-carrying capacity was indicative of future achievements.

In spite of the initial inability of the JCA-USA to kick off its relief operation as intended, the assigned CRS-USCC staff to JCA-USA was adamant in its refusal to panic. On January 20, Kinney was able to report to his JCA-USA colleagues that partial airlift subsidy by the State Department would be available to all carriers of U.S. supplies or goods donated by American groups and organizations. He was quick to point out that it would be to the financial advantage of all relief groups to permit the American agencies to supply the maximum amount of materials they could obtain.

The difficulties encountered by JCA-USA were transformed into challenges to be conquered. However, similar challenges to the ICRC seemed to drag it deeper into difficulties. Although it was understood by all U.S. voluntary agencies that they came under the coordinating authority of the ICRC, the American agencies also knew that they were responsible for the acquisition, distribution, and control of all U.S. relief assistance after consultation with the ICRC Director.

As the ICRC developed more and more problems with their
organizational and logistical dealing with these strong-
willed American relief agencies, both internal and external
pressures built up against the role and work of the ICRC.

One such ICRC pressure came from the State Department
through the ARC. In a February 12 memorandum, ARC Director
of Disaster Service Robert Pierpont summarized the ICRC
problems as observed by the State Department in three points
he had to discuss with his ICRC counterpart. "1. Organizational. There has been a very ill-defined structure with
overlapping controls and no single operational command
structure....2. Personnel. This situation is shocking from
many angles....3. Supplies. ICRC began the operation by
paying 12 shillings per ton to the Nigerian Government for
all incoming supplies when this should be free."[27]

The U.S. government finally had to force ICRC officials
to admit to a long-range possibility of the Nigerian Civil
War at the end of January 1969. In February, the State
Department presented the ICRC with a projected long-range
relief plan of six months. This plan, the product of the
African Bureau and the ARC,[28] was acknowledged as an ICRC
proposal with no credit given to the U.S. bureaucrats. It
took some doing, but the United States did convince the ICRC
that they (ICRC) were involved in a major operation.[29]

Early in March, the United States requested that the
ICRC increase its ability to transport logistic operations.
If the ICRC was to achieve even a minimum target in the six-
month proposed plan, the ICRC would have to enlarge its
experienced staff and alternate points of entry for relief
supplies. The State Department also wanted the ICRC to
access the Nigerian and Biafran food requirements as basic
to planning and budget. Reports had to reflect on-the-spot
assessments; the time for temporary, expediency measures
were proven by all involved to be over.

The carrot-and-stick method was used by the United States
to convince the ICRC to move in the direction of action. It
was no problem to point out to the ICRC the gaps of information that existed in their relief reports. "What is needed
for long range planning are the real and potential levels of
food production, the exact degree and extent of starvation
around the two battlefronts, etc." The "carrot" for the
ICRC was the guarantee that the United States would stand
financially behind the total relief and medical supplies
necessary to undertake such long-range emergency planning.
To ensure that the ICRC would continue to function and allow
the United States to be involved behind the scenes (as a
silent decision maker) the American government deposited $2
million to the account of the ICRC in March, an additional
$4 million in April, and another again in May.

The "stick" was the message from the State Department
that unless the ICRC program was improved substantially, the
United States would pull out all its Food for Peace supplies
and end all financial contributions to the ICRC. The ICRC
was forced by this threat to accept American administrative
and logistical skills to implement such a six-months plan of
relief. Also involved in the U.S. demands was the need for
the ICRC to set up an advisory coordinating relief committee. In this way ICRC and JCA-USA could be coordinated on

both sides of the conflict. The eventuality of one relief group being rejected by either the Nigerians or the Biafrans could be balanced by a cooperative coordinating relief committee. Therefore, any rejection of either relief group by either combatant would leave the other relief agency to take up the relief and be in a position to understand the relief policies.

Notes

1. Alfred Friendly, Jr., "Nigeria Charges U.S. Policy Shifts," The New York Times, Jan. 26, 1969, p. 17.
2. "Biafra Mercy Corridor for Supplies," The (London) Times, July 13, 1968, p. 1. See also Michael Knipe's article "Nigerians Starve As Well As Biafrans," ibid. p. 1.
3. Stanley Meisler, "Nigeria Views Relief Agencies as Political," Los Angeles Times, July 27, 1968, p. 18.
4. Llewellyn Chanter, "Russian Arms Will Back Up New Nigerian Assault," The Daily Telegraph, Jan. 25, 1969, p. 21.
5. William Pengra, "Nigeria Doing Everything Possible to Keep Doors Open for Investors," New York Journal of Commerce (Jan. 28, 1969, 3.
6. Benjamin Welles, "Oil Company Is Said to Sponsor Nigerian Official's Visit to U.S.," The New York Times, Jan. 29, 1969, p. 4.
7. Benjamin Welles, "Biafran Problem Gains a High Nixon Priority," The New York Times, Jan. 27, 1969, p. 10.
8. Jan. 22, 1969, Congressional Record, 91st Cong., 1st sess., 115:1468-1475.
9. Ibid., Jan. 23, 1969, 115:1632.
10. Ibid., Jan. 31, 1969, 115:2779.
11. Lagos, Airgram A-68, Feb. 1, 1969, pp. 5-6.
12. Feb. 20, 1969, Congressional Record, 91st Cong., 1st sess., 115:4113-4116.
13. Cronjé, The World and Nigeria, 246.
14. Mathews, interview with author, Washington, D.C., June 19, 1975.
15. The "quick-kill" theory can also be found mentioned in Lee Auspits, "Anatomy of a Bloody Mess," Ripon Forum 5, no. 2 (Feb. 1969): 4; Beal, "How the State Department Watched Biafra Starve," Ripon Forum 6, no. 3 (Mar. 1970): 17; and Elliot Richardson's reply, ibid, 28: "The Department of State has never followed a so-called 'quick-kill' approach, any charge to the contrary is not only false but outrageous."
16. Feb. 21, 1969, Congressional Record, 91st Cong., 1st sess., 115:4131.
17. "Statement by Senator Goodell before the National Press Club," Washington, D.C., Feb. 19, 1969.
18. Feb. 21, 1969, Congressional Record, 91st Cong., 1st sess., 115:4131.
19. Clarence Clyde Ferguson, a prominent Afro-American professor, Dean of Howard University's School of Law (1959-1964), and General Council on the U.S. Commission of Civil Rights (1961-1963), was working as a U.S. expert in the U.N. Subcommittee on Discrimination when he accepted the office of Special Coordination on Relief. He eventually went from this diplomatic position to become Ambassador to Uganda in May 1970.
20. Feb. 25, 1969, Congressional Record, 91st Cong., 1st sess., 115:1975-1987.
21. U.S. Voice of America, Information Office, Washington, D.C. Feb. 27, 1969.
22. Cronjé, The World and Nigeria, 233.
23. "The U.S. and Nigeria," West Africa, (June 14, 1969): 678-679.
24. Charles Goodell, "Biafra and the American Conscience," Saturday Review 52 (Apr. 12, 1969): 24-27.
25. Ibid.
26. Lloyd Garrison, "U.S. Pilot Revolt Perils Biafran Aid," The New York Times, Feb. 16, 1969, p. 10. "James Carter, a flight captain, cited two reasons for quitting. The first was political...money was another grievance."
27. National American Red Cross, General Records, Feb. 12, 1969, p. 1.
28. National American Red Cross, General Records, Feb. 28, 1969. Ambassador C. Robert Moore, the Deputy Assistant Secretary in the Bureau of African Affairs, brought his staffers, Walker, Tripp, Helen Wilson and Clark (from the Gabon Desk) to the February meeting with ARC officials John Wilson and Krakow to discuss the Nigerian relief problems and the ICRC. Despite the "very sharp criticism of the ICRC operation," Krakow did not believe "that the Department of State is prepared to really pressure the ICRC into making any major changes in the program" (p. 2). Part of the ICRC problem was the unwillingness of Nigerians to support the operation. "Helen Wilson confirmed that the ICRC is really making an effort to recruit Nigerians but is having a real problem. The Nigerians don't want to work for the Nigerian Red Cross because of low pay, and, obviously, those who are qualified can get much better jobs" (p. 1).
29. Ibid., p. 1. "Privately, Ambassador Moore said that the U.S. will, of course, pick up at least one-half of the total [ICRC] tab."

Appendix

Map 6.   Cross River, Nigeria

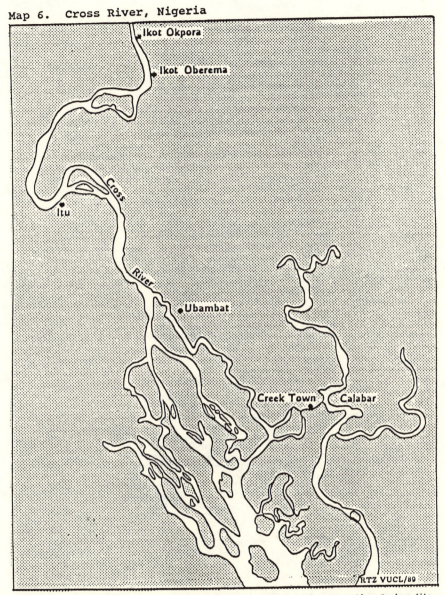

Source: Adapted by Villanova University Cartographic Laboratory from Cross River Project file, Nigeria/Biafra Clearing House Papers, Swarthmore College Peace Collection, Swarthmore, Pennsylvania.

Figure 1. Cross River Project Discharge Area

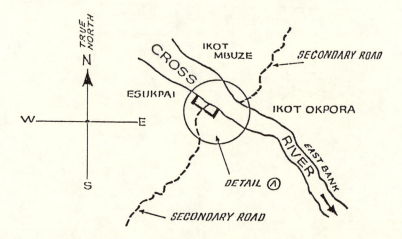

Source: Adapted by Villanova University Cartographic Laboratory from Cross River Project file, Nigeria/Biafra Clearing House Papers, Swarthmore College Peace Collection, Swarthmore, Pennsylvania.

Figure 2. Cross River Project Storage Area

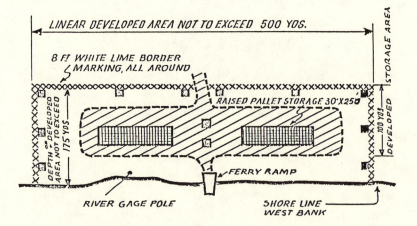

Source: Adapted by Villanova University Cartographic Laboratory from Cross River Project file, Nigeria/Biafra Clearing House papers, Swarthmore College Peace Collection, Swarthmore, Pennsylvania.

Figure 3.   Cross River Project Ships

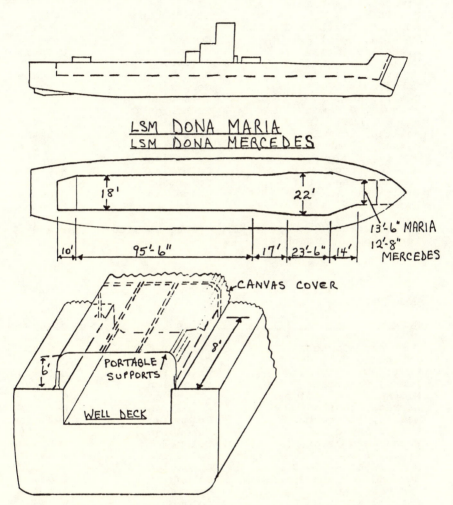

LSM DONA MARIA
LSM DONA MERCEDES

18'   22'

13'-6" MARIA
12'-8" MERCEDES

10'   95'-6"   17'   23'-6"   14'

CANVAS COVER

PORTABLE SUPPORTS

8'

6'

WELL DECK

Source: Adapted by Villanova University Cartoagraphy Laboratory from Cross River Project file, Nigeria/Biafra Clearing House Papers, Swarthmore College Peace Collection, Swarthmore, Pennsylvania.

119

Figure 4. Crew List

Dona Maria

Name	Nationality	Passport Number
Stephens, Henry	Colombian	D-91142
Stephens, Susana L. (wife of Captain)	Colombian	(Not Available)
Hamilton, Justine	Nicaraguan	246
Robinson, William	Colombian	D-63194
Pitalua, Angel M.	Colombian	D-54054
Archbold, Thomas W.	Colombian	D-55619
Watler, Radly A.	British	C-470850
Henry, Arosemena E.	Colombian	D-64069
Tory, Luis A.	Colombian	F-030814
Oneill, Noel J.	Colombian	D-94868
Francis, Orlando F.	Colombian	F-007746
Bilbao, Guillermo S.	Colombian	F-087080
Hawkins, Veranis A.	Colombian	F-024502
Miranda, Sanson M.	Colombian	F-076368
Davila, Enrique E.	Colombian	F-087216
McLean, Fernando E.	Colombian	E-023620
Jiminez, Isaac N.	Colombian	D-95347
Bryan, Dionicio T.	Colombian	E-009685
Hooker, Rofina L.	Colombian	F-091805

(All Colombian except Hamilton, who is Nicaraguan, and Walter, who is British.)

Dona Mercedes

Name	Nationality	Passport Number
Robinson, Gaston R.	Colombian	E-009365
Robinson, Orlando	Colombian	C-06437
Whitaker, Oberto	Colombian	D-64130
Ramos, Francisco	Colombian	F-084065
Medrano, Leovigildo	Colombian	C-69044
Barraza, Jose A.	Colombian	E-045361
Garcia, Federeco G.	Colombian	F-076289
Perez, Justo E.	Colombian	F-087395
Hernandez, Jeronomino P.	Colombian	F-053234
Campo, Lopez E.	Colombian	E-013554
Henriquez, Assia O.	Colombian	F-076372
Hernandez, Sergio S.	Colombian	E-004736
Prophete, Luc G.	Haitian	860
Suarez, Fernando E.	Colombian	E-045474
Rodriguez, Jose A.	Colombian	F-091223
Mercado, Hugo R.	Colombian	F-101893

(All Colombian except Prophete, who is Haitian.)

7

Relief and U.S. Diplomacy

Richard Nixon, who assumed the presidency with an immediate call for greater American activism in the humanitarian issue of the Nigerian conflict, grew impatient with the reluctant departments. Henry Kissinger, after meeting with Nixon in March 1969, told the NSC staff that the President was now seriously thinking of officially recognizing Biafra. This news played into the hands of Roger Morris and the American Committee to Keep Biafra Alive who were lobbying for greater relief involvement. The most recent U.S.A.I.D. report, The Nigerian Relief Problem, also gave Morris the leverage he needed to move the State Department into some action; especially by quoting the report's leading paragraph, "The best estimates available indicate that by May of this year [1969] as many as 4.5 or 5 million people on both sides of the battle lines may be in need of relief."[1] It was now up to the NSC to find a way to increase relief that would least harm the traditional U.S. relations with Nigeria.

The NSC first step was to require U.S.A.I.D. to deposit $2 million in the ICRC relief account for Nigeria. Kissinger also told the U.S. Information Mission to make an additional $4 million available in April and May to ICRC if Director Auguste Lindt would meet with Clyde Ferguson to implement the American five-point plan.

1. A comprehensive report of food and medical requirements from on-the-spot assessment; no more "reasoned estimates based on best guess."
2. More and better information on ICRC contribution sources.
3. Establish an ICRC Advisory Committee to work with JCA-USA and other relief agencies to develop relief delivery schedules.
4. Improve and appoint better top level management and leadership within ICRC senior officers.
5. Enlarge the ICRC transport and logistic specialists unit, thereby making it possible to have planning in advance for both sides.

Outside the White House councils, however, the State Department lobbied hard to deflect any such action that would interfere with their perception of the necessary and proper U.S.-Nigerian diplomacy.   On March 12 Steven Tripp went to Samuel Krakow to solicit ARC assistance in helping ICRC achieve even minimum targets in this five point plan.   Tripp stressed that ICRC would see to it that any U.S. funds given to church relief groups would be used "to purchase in the United States to the extent possible in order to minimize adverse efforts of our donations on U.S. Balance of Payments."[2]

An ICRC delegation met with Ferguson on Thursday, March 13, for four hours to discuss these points.   They finally agreed on priorities, and the first one was to push harder for daytime Biafran relief flights.   They also agreed that there must be closer cooperation between the ICRC, the League, JCA-USC, CRS-USCC, and ARC "to avoid Ojukwu playing off one against another."   The politics of food continued to plague all attempts to bring the necessary supplies to the starving civilians.

After his trip to Nigeria and Europe to meet those political and humanitarian leaders involved in the relief efforts, Ferguson discussed this separation of relief from politics several times during Congressman Charles Diggs's special African Subcommittee Hearing on April 24, 1969. Ferguson's first two general observations on the Nigerian situation before the Subcommittee concerned logistical improvements.   The extreme congestion in the relief supply lines and the improper management and storage of relief foods were considered more important in his testimony than the number of starving civilians.   It was expected, therefore, that these two recommendations would be a call for a new logistical officer to be placed in Lagos.   It would also require training and coordination of American relief efforts with the NRC. All this would then come under the coordinated authority of the State Department official assigned to the position of seeking political solutions to the conflict.

Another interesting line of questioning by Congressman Benjamin Rosenthal (D-NY) relates to this problem.

> Mr. Rosenthal. Can you, Dr. Ferguson, in your own judgment, divorce relief efforts from political efforts?   Can there be this clear distinction that I sense you have tried to make here this morning?
> Mr. Ferguson.   Well, sir, I think that it is impossible to make the distinction.   I realize that it is quite difficult in that I suppose traditionally in matters of foreign affairs, there has only been really one dimension considered and that is the political dimension. Everything else, economic development, humanitarian concern, even social development becomes subsidiary to the political objectives.
> Mr. Rosenthal.   But in this particular political situation, did you come away with the feeling that political and military situations had an overriding effect on relief efforts?

Mr. Ferguson. That is certainly true....
Mr. Rosenthal. From what I gather, you made the whole political circle....Is it the position of our Government and your position that your mandate was not to go beyond relief effort under any circumstances?
Mr. Ferguson. That is clear. The charge to avoid political issues under any circumstances does have a certain flexibility in it because I believe the terms of the charge were to stay away from those political questions not directly relevant to the relief effort.
Mr. Rosenthal. But all political efforts were relevant to the relief efforts.[3]

Publicly and privately Ferguson admitted that he went along with the State Department in the belief that a separation was not possible. But he was required by the White House political advisers to take a stand for the proposed distinction so as to allay the domestic pressures on Nixon for a much more action-oriented relief policy. The president's instructions to Ferguson, however, had left plenty of room for bureaucratic discretion, which generally turned out to favor the interests of established agencies over those of the interloper U/CF office. As was bound to happen, once the White House was again taken up by Vietnam the bureaucratic decisions of the State Department were to gain more strength, and they wanted to move away from this action-oriented policy initiated by the President.

During this period Joseph Palmer was not personally attending the NSC meetings on relief, but he continued to work on the political aspects of the Nigerian conflict and was never out of touch with the relief activity of Ferguson. Palmer insisted that he was always kept informed of the relief movements of Ferguson, and in return he always tried to keep Ferguson informed of the political and diplomatic activities of the State Department. Ferguson's statement during the Diggs Hearing that he was "not fully cognizant of all that had been going on the political side,"[4] was a public admittance of the uncooperative African Bureau.

Unfortunately for the many starving civilians in Biafra and Nigeria, Ferguson's staff was not linked to any of the normally traditional government agencies. Although established within the State Department by presidential order, the Ferguson Mission was distrusted by both; the NSC saw him as a puppet of the pro-FMG State Department while the State Department considered him a spy for the White House. To further complicate matters, Ferguson's intrusion into previously claimed turf gave rise to additional frictions and suspicion. The FMG viewed Ferguson as secretly sympathetic to Biafra, while the Biafrans considered him a captive of a pro-Nigerian State Department. Although his immediate legal response to Rosenthal's question "Who are you responsible to, Dr. Ferguson?" was, "I report directly to the Under Secretary and to the Secretary. Ultimately, of course, to the President," it would have been more accurate to have said he reported to everyone but he was responsible to those dying from the famine deliberately inflicted by the conflict.

Because of his mandate to assist the suffering an both
sides of the conflict, Ferguson called an emergency relief
conference at the State Department on May 7.   This meeting
had special meaning after an ICRC DC-7 plane crashed killing
four of its crew members. Ferguson told those at the meeting that he had informed Bishop Edward Swanstrom on Friday,
May 2, of the State Department's efforts to establish the
validity of the JCA-USA request for additional planes and
parts--already two of the C-97s had been temporarily canni-
balized for spare parts to keep the others flying.   Ferguson
was very concerned that the air supply routes were the new
target of FMG efforts to end the civil war.   "He was also
concerned with the safety of the relief personnel--both air
crews and staff in Biafra--and the increasing problems
because of the fall of the Umuahia."[5] Gene Dewey then gave
the conference members a brief review of the military situation and he pointed out that even though Umuahia had fallen,
the Biafrans, in spite of their decreased territory and
famine, were very much in control of the area in which they
were living.   Karl Western, M.D., of the Public Health Service was next to point out that the war survivors in the
Nigerian territory were receiving approximately 600 calories
of food per day; obviously inadequate for these already malnourished people.   An early copy of Dr. Hughes's article,
"Malnutrition in the Field: Nigerian Civil War, 1968-9,[6] was
passed around the meeting to support Western's presentation.
The meeting adjourned after Ferguson assigned Dewey to look
into the possibility of obtaining more planes for the relief
effort.

As if to emphasize Ferguson's valid concerns, on the
following evening (May 7-8) the JCA-USA lost a C-97 belly
landing at the Uli airstrip after it was accidentally hit by
anti-aircraft fire.   But if the FMG attacks stymied the Biafran relief air bridge, it served as a spur to pro-Biafran
lobbyists in America.   Senator William Proxmire (D-WI)
stated that the only way to end the conflict was for the
U.S. to sign the U.N. Human Rights Treaty, especially the
Genocide Treaty. Needless to say, the international observer
teams that were in Nigeria and Biafra dispelled the genocide
concept in 1968 for the State Department officials, but not
to the satisfaction of journalists and some humanitarian
groups.   Proxmire tried to use these two groups (media and
the public) to create interest in the U.N. Human Rights
Treaty, which the U.S. government had not yet ratified.
There were 22 occasions in 1969 when Proxmire used the civil
war in Nigeria to bring attention to the Genocide Treaty
issue.[7]   One of the more striking of the Proximre's statements was presented on Tuesday, May 27, 1969, when he said;
"Because of Senate failure to ratify the Human Rights Conventions, the professed American commitment to human rights
may appear to be an empty pledge."[8]   Ten days earlier, a
more serious statement had been made on the Senate floor
when Eugene McCarthy (D-MN) asked the Senators to recognize
the state of Biafra: "It is time to reexamine our policy of
One Nigeria which resulted in our acceptance of the death of
millions as the price for preserving a nation that never
existed....Our goal should be the recognition of Biafra
which has demonstrated that it represents the interests of

its people. We should seek to de-escalate great power involvement. We should seek massive relief."[9]

The State Department decided that McCarthy's call for Biafran recognition could not go unanswered. Taking the latest U.S. Embassy report from Lagos, several rebuttals were advanced by the State Department for a coordinated attack on those who supported the recognition of Biafra. The pragmatic arguments asked the pro-Biafran supporter to first determine the area to which Biafra would have title. Where would they fix the boundaries? Would the Mid-Western Region be included? What groups would be allowed to have the final say? The diplomatic arguments then asked the Biafran lobbyists to offer real suggestions on how to impose peace if the Biafrans did not concede to the boundary terms, or Nigeria for that matter? To what lengths would the issue be carried to impose an external settlement? In an Orwellian reversal of concepts, the State Department also tried to argue that the pro-Biafran groups were in support of U.S. activity, i.e., support for effective relief.

A major reason for the unsuccessful jockeying by the pro-Biafran advocates for more power to change, adjust or moderate the existing American relief policy was the result of their former success in the appointment of Ferguson to an ambassadorial-level coordinator and his special relief team for Biafra. Therefore, rather than openly attack Senator McCarthy or the aggressive relief lobbyists, the State Department cooperated with Congressman Diggs to undercut any and all of the public lobbyists in support of Biafra.

Without a doubt, it fell to Elliot Richardson, Under Secretary of State, to exercise the leadership of the U.S. foreign policy toward the Nigerian conflict. His link with the humanitarian relief was made possible by his position as chairman of the ARC Board of Governors,[10] and his political role was augmented by Kissinger's appointment of Richardson to be the NSC chairman of the Nigerian issue. Because of this later position, Richardson was aware of the Central Intelligence Agency's (CIA) report of May 29 along with several other classified reports on the Nigerian conflict. The 1969 CIA report reviewed the first two years of the secessionist war. It confirmed the possibility that Biafra, under the leadership of Odumegwu Ojukwu, might win its 1967-1969 war of secession against the FMG. The report judged the Biafrans could continue fighting, even if Ojukwu were to leave the scene.

The CIA concluded that it was French assistance that enabled the Biafrans to continue fighting the war, and that the Biafrans' technical ingenuity helped them continue the war despite Biafra's faltering economy.[11] Efforts to mediate and bring about a truce between Nigeria and Biafra, the CIA report stated, would continue to falter because Biafrans balked at negotiating on the basis of One Nigeria. Instead, Biafra would continue the war with the aid of military supplies airlifted in from France, Portugal, and South African sources. If French aid to Biafra could be terminated, the report continued, then the FMG could eventually win a conventional war against Biafra within three months. However, given the French aid to Biafra, if they remained at the current level of 150 tons per week, then the prospects were that Nigerian FMG would slowly chip away at Biafra in a war of attrition.[12]

There had been a quickening pace of FMG activity in Nigeria looking beyond the strife and conflict toward reconstruction and development. Nigeria's Ibaden Conference on National Reconstruction and Development (March 24-29) was an impressive effort to determine future policy decisions. But the burgeoning tax riots in Western Nigeria and the rumors of another potential military coup against Yakubu Gowon's administration had a negative effect on the international perspective of the FMG's finances and its military control over the Nigerian system. However, it was clear that the Nigerians were intent on controlling their own destiny and the conduct of the civil war and relief.

In May, Gowon transferred three front-line army commanders in an attempt to avert accusations of a military stalemate. A similar stalemate attitude existed in the Nigerian Air Force with regard to the Biafran airlift, but now Gowon gave standing orders to shoot down any unauthorized flights. Spurred by the fear of an impending international incident, Washington informed Edward Kinney that the United States had decided, based on Ferguson's report, to replace the JCA-USA destroyed C-97, but that no publicity would be allowed on this replacement.[13] Kinney was glad to inform his colleagues in JCA-USA that the new aircraft would be leaving for São Tomé on June 3. The State Department also requested that the embassy military attache James Langley ask Col. Shiltu Alao, the commander of Nigeria's Air Force, not to shoot down any innocent planes.

When the Swedish Red Cross relief DC-7B plane, with a crew of four and piloted by Michael Brown (an American), was shot down by an FMG MiG-17 on June 5, 1969, Nigeria braced itself for a battering by world opinion. Enraged international outcries, however, were curiously muted. In a State Department statement the following day, spokesman Robert McCloskey went only as far as to say that the United States "must deplore this attack." Although it was known that arms flights flew late, rather than early in the evening with the relief flights, McCloskey went "on background" to say, "Arms flights and relief flights are intermingled. Both utilize the same major Biafran airstrip, both use similar flight patterns over Nigerian territory to reach it, and both operate only at night. Thus, there is danger of confusion between the relief flights and arms airlift....Any Nigerian attempt to intercept an arms flight runs that risk of hitting the relief planes."[14] This background comment was inserted by the African Bureau staff rather than by the interagency group that had been given responsibility for drafting U.S. formal responses to relief questions. These comments were vague and inaccurate, but accurately reflected State Department's attitude more than reality. Following this tragic shootdown, general uncertainty and rumors of a new Nigerian night-fighter capability brought the Biafran relief air bridge to a virtual standstill.

In spite of Kinney's efforts to keep the JCA-USA air bridge functioning, the FTR staff on São Tomé were inclined to blame Kinney for their inabilities rather than be aggressively inventive. Shortage of spare parts continued to

plague the JCA-USA operation, and among the most difficult
of these to obtain were the replacement engines. So serious
had the situation become that between June 13 and June 25
the JCA-USA operation made only two flights.

World attention was also directed toward the political
role of the ICRC and the American efforts to improve relief
shipments during June.   On Wednesday, June 18, Ferguson
announced a Nigerian and Biafran agreement in principle on
the Cross River Project proposal. The <u>Dona Mercedes</u>, with a
900-ton capacity, arrived in Lagos the next day. It was to
make one test run for an empirical exploration of the operation's feasibility, with the expectation of further trips
by the <u>Dona Maria</u>, which arrived in Lagos the following day.
But this arranged project was quickly dashed by the actions
and statements of hard-liners in the FMG.

Suddenly, on June 19, Lindt was arrested and declared
<u>persona</u> <u>non</u> <u>grata</u> by the Lagos government.   The ouster of
the ICRC Director from Nigeria was a setback for the whole
relief organizational structure and the U.S. government. It
was especially a major setback after months of U.S. planning
to have the ICRC Director respond adequately to the needs of
the suffering. Eleven days later Anthony Enharo, a leading
Nigerian hawk, announced the "Nigerianization" of all existing ICRC relief programs, saying that aid to Biafra would
continue but only with inspection and approval by FMG officials. Furthermore, Enharo declared that all supplies would
be restricted to basic essentials and would not include fuel
or spare parts to maintain the distribution network inside
Biafra.[15] The one-shot test run by the <u>Dona Mercedes</u> up the
Cross River was' also ruled out. That action, coming on the
heels of the confused status of the ICRC and the FMG statements that were made in Lagos indicating that the hawks were
coming out of the woodwork and exerting a very strong influence in Lagos, removed any doubt there might have been about
a real possibility of the Nigerians coming to any agreement
on relief for the millions starving in and around the war
zone.

If the American influence was limited by the De Gaullist
attitude toward the arms supplies to Biafra and by the U.K.
and Soviet attitude toward the arms supplies to Nigeria, it
was also a self-limiting influence in the relief system.
The United States had been preserving its neutrality at all
levels of government by working under the auspices of the
ICRC.[16] This indirect influence faced a real problem when
the FMG decided that the NRC would take over all aspects of
the ICRC relief activity on June 30.

The African Bureau and U.S.A.I.D. were immediately
instructed by Richardson to devise new approaches to the
relief problem in Nigeria and Biafra. Even as options were
being worked out, the department's dilemma was brought,
albeit briefly and with little notice, to public view.
Almost caricaturing the department's confused position,
which sought to maintain good diplomatic relations with the
FMG versus humanitarian considerations for Biafra, Secretary
William Rogers publicly deplored Nigeria's use of starvation
as a weapon of war during a midday news conference on July
2, only to issue a revised statement later the same day
asserting that relief shipments could increase only if

blockaders and victims reached agreement.[17]   At about the same time, Morris and other senior administration officials were publicly saying that U.S. policy on Nigeria was under review and that there might be a major shift.[18]   The so-called shift resulted in part from the letters which Nixon sent to ICRC President Marcell A. Navill, Bishop Swanstrom of JCA-USA, President Felix Houphouet-Boigny of the Ivory Coast, Canadian Prime Minister Pierre Trudeau, and General Gowon urging all the parties to "work out ways to open up the supply lines."[19]   Reacting to these public options, Ferguson and his staff met over the July 4 weekend to draft a special memo for Richardson to accompany their comprehensive study on "Emergency Relief in Nigerian and the Biafran Enclave,"[20] which pointed out the inadequacy of the presidential option.   Ferguson emphasized the need for Nigeria and Biafra to become independent of either the British or the French, and the necessity of getting Gowon's government to seriously negotiate on the Cross River Project.

These Cross River negotiations, which had yet to begin in earnest for Ferguson, became the focus of considerable U.S. attention during July because it was the only viable plan the United States had left.   In early July it appeared that neither Nigeria nor Biafra would accept the river corridor proposed by Ferguson.   The Lagos regime, suspecting Ferguson of secret pro-Biafran sympathies, claimed the food brought in would go to soldiers instead of civilians.   The Biafran leaders, who saw the Special Coordinator as captive of a pro-Federal State Department, again feared a military violations of the access route.   Ferguson's staff then proposed "Operation Black Bishop" as an attempt to break the existing impasse. Ferguson and Jean Mayer, Nixon's Nutrition Adviser, met the President at San Clemente on July 15 to give this new plan the stamp of presidential approval. After the meeting, Ferguson flew to Rome to meet with the Pope to arrange for a Black African Bishop to be sent to Biafra while emissaries of Ethiopia approached the FMG.   The idea was to flush minimum bargaining positions from the two sides.   Nixon wrote to Gowon and appealed on humanitarian grounds to permit resumption of ICRC relief flights into Biafra and to accept the Cross River Project, adding that the United States expects humane statesmanship.   To backstop the gambit and convince the FMG to negotiate on the Cross River Project, Richardson met on July 14 with Ambassador Lucet of France and British Ambassador Freeman to emphasize U.S. concern.

Richardson's testimony before Senator Edward Kennedy's Subcommittee on Refugees the following day (July 15) becomes all the more important for a better understanding of the American attitude toward the Biafran relief problem.   His statement is the clearest picture of U.S. foreign policy on this issue.[21]   Using the most recent State Department report of early July, Richardson dealt with the relief program first.   He pointed out that the United States was at the forefront of relief contributions and relief supplies.   The latest figures that were available to Richardson showed that the United States contributed 49 percent of the grand total (25 percent of the private sector and 60 percent of the public sector) as of July 1, 1969.

The tragedy of this civil war, according to Richardson, was how to convince the combatants to enlarge the relief supply routes. The obstacles to any agreement were on both sides:

> On the Federal side: First, a concern that international relief has aided the Biafran war effort. For example, the Federal Military Government charges that the relief effort generates foreign exchange which the Biafrans use for the purchase of arms, that the night time airlift provides a cover for arms flights, and that food and medicine intended for civilians, are allocated to Biafran troops.
>
> Second, a belief that starvation in the enclave is exaggerated by Biafran propaganda to enlist international sympathy and political support.
>
> Third, popular pressures on the Federal Military Government, as the war dragged on, to exercise the most stringent controls over international relief, regardless of the consequences.
>
> On the Biafran side: First, a fear that Federal control over relief shipments would enable the Federal Military Government to regulate the flow and contents to serve its own political or military purposes.
>
> Second, a professed fear that food passing through Federal territory might be poisoned.
>
> Third, a belief that Biafran military security, would be jeopardized by relief corridors, including daylight flights, that were not guaranteed by third parties.[22]

Richardson stressed during the Senate Subcommittee Hearing that the focus of all U.S. efforts was relief, even if all relief questions are inextricably bound to the political and military issues of the civil war.

The month of July is important, therefore, because it witnessed an end to the ambiguous and vacillating policy. Not only did Richardson give public testimony of a return to the original U.S. support for the FMG, but it was the first time that the U.S.A.I.D. disaster memos were referred to as the U.S.A.I.D. "Nigeria Relief/Rehabilitation Operations." It was also the last month of hastily published monthly reports on U.S. contributions to Nigerian relief and the last recorded U.S. contribution of $75.3 million in private and public pledged assistance (see Table 7.1). What is striking is the final U.S. relief contribution figure of $72.3 million in actual relief assistance recorded at the end of the civil war.

Table 7.1. Contributions to Nigeria/Biafra Relief,
            July 1969

Country	Private	Public	Total
West Germany	$13.5	$ 10.0	$ 23.5
Norway	3.8	9.5	13.3
Netherlands	4.4	5.3	9.7
United Kingdom	2.5	5.0	7.5
Switzerland	2.7	4.6	7.3
Sweden	4.1	1.7	5.8
Canada	.9	2.8	3.7
Denmark	.7	1.2	1.9
Ireland	1.4	.3	1.7
Subtotal	33.9	40.4	74.3
All Others	2.5	1.3	3.8
Subtotal	36.4	41.7	78.1
United States	12.1	63.2	75.3
Grand Total	**$48.5**	**$104.9**	**$153.4**

Source: U.S.A.I.D., "Contributions to Nigeria Relief," Nigeria Relief Rehabilitation Operations, July 1, 1969 update, Annex I, II.

Table 7.2. U.S. Contributions to Nigeria/Biafra Relief,
            July 1969

Monthly Period	Contribution	Percent
To June 24, 1968	$ 3,457,531	5
June-July 24	3,688,615	5
July-August 19	2,301,312	3
August-November 25[a]	11,599,862	15
November-February 25, 1969[a]	11,212,442	15
February-March 25	7,189,338	9
March-April 15	17,799,500	24
April-June 1	12,537,517	17
June-July 1	5,459,051	7
Total	**$75,245,168**	**100**

[a]This period can be divided only in approximate thirds of 5
    percent each month.

Source: This table is reduced from U.S.A.I.D. disaster memo tables.

Only before Ferguson's appointment in February 1969 did the U.S. government have such a low 7 percent contribution to relief. If the sum total of actual and committed contributions in July 1969 were officially recorded as $75,245,168 (see Table 7.2) and the final total American contribution recorded for the entire Nigerian Civil War as $72.3 million, it would be assumed that someone, somewhere, decided to withhold the $2,945,168 of relief authorization until the existing funds were expended.[23] The time for anyone to stand up for such a policy would have been June-July 1969.

During the hearing, Senator Kennedy prodded Richardson with these questions: "Is our relief policy hostage to some deeper political commitment to the unity of Nigeria? And in the same vein, is United States' recognition of an independent Biafra the answer to our dilemma?" Richardson rejected the recognition of Biafra out of hand, it would be done only "at the risk of rising Soviet influence in Federal Nigeria."[24] It was then that Kennedy asked the Under Secretary "How many refugees are there?" This was the most fundamental question that, until Kennedy's inquiry, no one had thought to scrutinize. Since it was the policy of the United States to accept British reports as the core perception of the Nigerian problem, the State Department did not attempt to verify for themselves the relief population of Biafra or Nigeria. It was a political hot potato. Not until Senator Kennedy's examination in July was Richardson challenged to discover the actual relief population.

Richardson was not the only official motivated to reexamine American policy toward Nigeria and Biafra. Impressed by a full-page appeal in the July 14 issue of The New York Times,[25] Nixon had instructed Kissinger to provide new approaches to the Nigerian problem. The NSC staff, following Kissinger's instructions, outlined these four options for a settlement: (1) Four-Power talks (United States, U.K., Soviet Union, and France), (2) an American-Canadian attempt, (3) a U.S.-Ethiopian venture, and (4) a solo attempt with America's good offices. Four-power talks were judged as usefully going to the heart of the arms problem, but it would very likely arouse African ire for bypassing African institutions and parties. The U.S.-Canadian approach was of doubtful value due to the extremely difficult position of Canada vis-à-vis both Britain and France. And while Haile Selassie was one of those most interested in a peaceful solution, a joint venture with Ethiopia was ruled out because the Biafrans distrusted Haile Selassie, feeling he was hopelessly pro-Federal. The prospect for U.S. good offices was at once the most promising and yet the most hazardous because of high exposure and blame for failure.

One week after Nixon ordered Kissinger to produce a new mediation plan, The New York Times reporter Peter Grose wrote that the White House "has apparently chosen to follow the same course"[26] as the Johnson administration on Nigeria. Grose cited Richardson's testimony before the Senate Subcommittee on Refugees that the administration had considered and rejected extending official recognition to Biafra. Seeing this, Nixon shot off a quick note to Kissinger disagreeing with the State Department's emphasis and requested an immediate change in policy. But, delay tactics were now to be an advantage for the State Department.

Richardson let State Department officials know that it would be a tough job to keep the White House from recognizing Biafra. Whereas the White House had a split camp on this issue of recognition, the State Department was in a stronger policy position because its few Biafran supporters could be controlled. A further step to control the policy was taken with the appointment of David Newsom as the new Assistant Secretary of State for African Affairs in July 1969 to replace Palmer.[27] Newsom's special interest in the Nigerian conflict were along the lines of his former training developed during his assignment in the North Africa and Arab oil economy states.[28]

This strengthening of a northern-controlled One Nigeria policy in Washington was complimented by the appointment of William Trueheart as the third U.S. Ambassador to Nigeria. Trueheart had been assigned to London as a political officer (his official title) during the same two years (1960-1961) that Newsom was stationed in the U.S. Embassy in London.[29] The difference in Trueheart's training was the emphasis on intelligence collection and covert operations. Trueheart had been assigned in 1961 to Saigon as the U.S. Defense Council Minister, reassigned in 1964 to be Deputy Director of the Office of South East Asian Affairs, and then in 1967 he was made Deputy Director for Coordination of the Bureau of Intelligence and Research (INR). Trueheart admitted that his work was actually interrupted by the appointment as ambassador to Nigeria in 1969.[30] Richardson had convinced him to accept the position because there was an urgent need to improve embassy reporting from Lagos. The unquestionable tenet was that embassy communications could not allow any American pro-Biafran supporter the opportunity to call for the recognition of Biafra as a state. Trueheart's position as ambassador in the embassy ensured that all informational exchanges would be placed in the context of supporting a One Nigeria policy. Besides, Trueheart's ability to control sensitive intelligence communications would complement Newsom's affinity for the Moslem FMG leadership of the oil economy of Nigeria.

Before venturing out to Nigeria as Ambassador Trueheart paid a visit to several oil companies to discuss their economic problems created by the Nigerian conflict. This action caused quite a stir among those in the Ripon Forum society.

> Before going out to Lagos, Ambassador-designate Trueheart was wined and dined by the U.S. oil companies with interests in Nigeria, including round-trip transport to a corporate headquarters in one company's executive jet. In one semi-public appearance shortly before his departure Trueheart's remarks made it plain that he had been more thoroughly briefed on the financial stakes of the oil companies than on the life-saving activities of the relief agencies.[31]

Trueheart's responses to these accusations was straight forward, he needed as much information as possible to evaluate the Nigerian situation. He had the distinct impression, which was eventually verified in the field, that the oil companies had a better rapport with the FMG than the embassy staff. In his estimation the oil companies' good relations with the Nigerian government could be used to allow the United States to develop better relations with the FMG. This in turn would lead to a better position to negotiate some relief agreements from the combatants. Trueheart was also given the difficult assignment of creating a better working atmosphere within the American embassy.

The mediation concept and the concern over the State Department's pro-Federal bias eventually led Nixon to authorize Kissinger to direct a secret probe into the possibility of some future negotiating potential. This probe was kept separate and secret from the State Department. Immediately following his session before Kennedy's Senate Subcommittee on Refugees, Ferguson was sent by Morris to see the President at San Clemente. Unable to get past Nixon's "palace guards," Ferguson went instead to Geneva to convene talks on the Cross River Project. Elbert Mathews, who was about to end his tour in Nigeria, tried as one of his last ambassadorial acts in Nigeria to persuaded Gowon to send a delegate to Geneva. The Nigerian delegation, however, consisted of low-ranking officials who were attached to their Berne Embassy and who, contrary to Ferguson's requests, lacked a mandate for settlement. The Nigerians, therefore, had to refer everything back to Lagos and, quite naturally, never received any replies. In contrast Ojukwu, who had on July 17 written Nixon that the "proposal by Dr. Ferguson for a surface relief corridor, making use of the river...is acceptable," sent one of his cabinet members, Sylvanius Cookey, with, according to Biafran sources, a full mandate to reach a conclusion.[32] This decision by Ojukwu was in line with his public comments. "America is the only country that can halt or neutralize the other two powers [Great Britain and Russia] on the side of Lagos. The key to Africa falls upon the United States, whichever way she jumps--and until she jumps, we won't really know where Africa will jump."[33]

As the first Cross River Project meeting ended with no progress, Ferguson told Biafran officials he would press the State Department to influence the FMG to negotiate seriously during the next round of meetings, slated for August 25. From Ferguson's pledge grew "Operation Nettle," which combined ICRC and Cross River Project negotiations as well as peacemaking probes in an effort to break the deadlock which gripped each area. To spur accord with the ICRC, Newsom was to fly to Lagos to assuage concern there over a long-standing but oft-postponed American commitment to supply JCA-USA with two more C-97s. At the same time, Newsom was to tell Gowon that the United States would hold up release of the planes for a few weeks while attempts were made to revive bargaining with the ICRC.

The most important aspect of Operation Nettle, though, was the proposed talks with Gowon in which Newsom was to speak with Nixon's personal authorization and in extreme privacy on a possible U.S. mediation role. He was to ask the FMG if the United States could act as an honest broker. Supporting Newsom's flight to Lagos, Ferguson was to reopen the Cross River Project talks in preparation to expand the political discussion. Should Gowon respond favorably, then Newsom and Ferguson planned to meet with French Foreign Minister Schumann to enlist French aid in the initiative. Britain would be informed of U.S. intentions as Newsom journeyed to Lagos, and informed of results on the return from Paris.

Operation Nettle was never implemented. When the news of this proposal reached Rogers who was then at San Clemente, he personally vetoed it. The Secretary made it perfectly clear that there was no role for the United States in Nigeria. Rogers later upbraided a senior U.S. diplomat over the Nigerian peace and relief initiatives, saying he would have been forced to repudiate a U.S. relief initiative had Biafra accepted. But Ferguson went again to Geneva seeking some breakthrough on the Cross River Project. There negotiations continued their futile course.

Unlike the Cross River Project, hopes were not high for agreement on reentry of the ICRC into Nigerian relief. By late summer 1969, it was evident that the Nigerians were not going to negotiate. Finally on September 5, the FMG agreed to ICRC relief fights direct from Cotonou, Dahomey, into Biafra, reserving the right to call down any plane for a spot check at Lagos.[34] The FMG "tacitly" accepted the notion that any plane called down could be refused landing at Uli. In effect, there would have been two kinds of flights; those coming unchallenged, never touched by the FMG, and those called down at Lagos and then refused at Uli. The substance of the agreement had been whittled down to meet the Nigerian requirements to provide for flights only during the day, from 9 a.m. to 5 p.m., from the Cotonou airfield where just six planes were parked. Moreover, the accord allowed for such flights for only three weeks. In part, Lagos's approval was known to be in response to a very tough Nixon letter. But it also stemmed from the actions of ICRC President Navill who presented one agreement to Biafra, which Ojukwu accepted, yet signed quite a different agreement with the FMG. The ICRC-FMG agreement had no assurances against a sneak attack on Uli. Consequently, on September 14, Biafra rejected the day flights agreement. Refusal was ostensibly based on the "call down" provisions of the pact, but at about the same time the Biafran officials repeated earlier demands for a third party to guarantee the inviolability of a dayflight agreement. Two days later the FMG rejected Biafran calls for such a guarantee.[35]

Anxious to keep channels open for agreement, Nixon had approved Morris's proposal to make a presidential statement. On September 20 Nixon made a statement warning both sides of the perils of intractability, but praising Nigerian motives of "humane statesmanship." It was coupled with a quiet offer of help to the ICRC in implementing an inviolable relief airlift. At the same time, in furtherance of political mediation probes, Nixon authorized a proposal for secret meetings with Biafran representatives in New York City.

During the course of the war several American private groups sought to advance these peace and relief initiatives. There were so many plans that the Nigerians were often on the verge of just throwing up their hands in disgust at such interference. For example, at the beginning of June, the Committee for Nigeria-Biafra Relief pushed a plan calling for the use of a helicopter carrier to ferry goods into the Biafran enclave. The scheme was presented verbally and by letter to Kissinger, Rogers, and Richardson. In early July 1969, Ferguson asked the committee to hold off so as not to endanger the ICRC talks taking place at that time. The plan, however, had already reached Biafra and Ojukwu had informed the State Department on July 22 that relief borne from off-shore was acceptable; adding that they would accept in principle that inspectors at the point of origin could include Nigerians. Work continued on this proposal and in an August 20 meeting with State Department officials the committee's Executive Director Dan Jacobs and Gen. William Tunner (USAF-retired), who had commanded the Berlin Airlift, were told that the idea was workable but that the United States would do nothing because the State Department felt that the FMG would not agree to any proposal. Still, by early October the concept had garnered enough interest and support that it was jointly announced by former Vice President Hubert Humphrey, Coretta Scott King, and Tunner. In a subsequent meeting with American officials, Jacobs was informed that since the announcement of the proposal it was not being taken seriously enough by some inside the government decision-making structure. Jacobs was told, therefore, that they could continue to negotiate agreements on their own initiative, but that the United States would take no immediate action on it. Eventually it also became a victim of politics. JCA-USA also played messenger to Biafran and Nigerian representatives in opposite wings of a Swiss hotel in the fall of 1969, but neither combatant was really interested.

Perhaps the most promising private effort, which grew into a secret NSC probe, was that taken by Norman Cousins during the fall of 1969. Returning from a tour of Nigeria and Biafra in late August, after meeting with leaders on both sides, Cousins advised the White House that both Gowon and Ojukwu were prepared to hold immediate talks without preconditions. Moreover, both sides expressed an interest in having a respected third party take the initiative or facilitate talks. Cousins was seen as a possible go-between until Nixon decided when and if a follow-up would be a success. On September 2, Kissinger discussed the proposal with the President. Nixon wanted the Cousins venture to be unofficial and disavowable unless a positive response was forthcoming, in which case Nixon wanted the possible American role as an honest broker in advancing negotiations. When Cousins approached the Biafrans, however, the President wanted him to be more specific on some necessary preconditions for negotiation. While supposedly asking on his own, Cousins was to add that he had reason to believe that U.S. action would be forthcoming if there were a positive, public response from Ojukwu.

Perhaps signaling an inclination toward some greater flexibility Ojukwu proposed a new peace plan on September 9 to the British Committee for Peace in Nigeria that, unlike previous announcements, did not call for a cease-fire before negotiations. The next day Gowon, on his return from the OAU Conference in Addis Ababa, also called for negotiations without prior conditions. Two days later Biafra accepted and asked Gowon to name a third country to facilitate their discussions. But in a telling insight into the politics of the FMG, Enharo, on September 13, asserted that such a parley could occur only in the context of One Nigeria.

Meanwhile, Cousins had approached the Biafrans, meeting Foreign Minister Godwin Onyegbula in Paris on September 10. From the conversations it became clear that Biafra wanted to negotiate, eventually in the context of a reunited Nigeria. Onyegbula, according to official sources, wanted to come to Washington to talk to Kissinger to pin down exactly how Biafra would wish to relate negotiations to the OAU, what they expected of an American role, and what concessions were necessary. Instead, Nixon and Kissinger authorized Morris to meet quietly with Onyegbula in Cousins New York apartment.

This meeting was held on September 25. Accompanying Morris was White House Fellow and noted political scientist, Charles Hermann. In addition to Onyegbula, Biafra was represented by its delegates to Britain and America. Morris opened the discussion by stating that his presence implied no U.S. commitment of any kind but that he was there mainly to ask and listen. Their talk quickly moved to the subject of preconditions to negotiation. Onyegbula agreed that preliminary meetings could be held without a cease-fire, which would enhance Lagos' position, leaving them holding a substantial portion of Biafra. Biafra proposed no preconditions and would not accept FMG insistence on One Nigeria prior to a settlement. Onyegbula then asked if America's relations with Britain precluded a mediating role. Stating that the United States would attempt to be scrupulously impartial, Morris then asked what Biafra expected of a mediator. A mediator could play a useful role in shuttling between sides before face-to-face meetings began, replied Onyegbula; but he cautioned that there were definite limits to what that could achieve. A respected third party could get both parties to the bargaining table and act as the formal mediator in the talks. While it was not necessary for the United States to fill both roles, Onyegbula thought it highly desirable. Any talks, the Biafran added, required strict secrecy.

When the role of the OAU was raised Onyegbula said the OAU was acceptable if it were represented by countries friendly to both sides. Noting that the OAU Consultative Committee was totally pro-FMG, the Biafran Foreign Minister wondered aloud why the United States had so often promoted the role of the OAU. Replying to another inquiry, Onyegbula expressed distrust of any Soviet role, saying they would try to sabotage negotiations, but Britain was seen as absolutely essential to bring around the FMG. Then Morris asked what practical arrangements could lead to reconciliation. Phased cooperation in the areas of economic activity, leading eventually to a common market arrangement, and some shared oil

revenues and trading relations were seen as possibilities.
It is unthinkable to exist apart from Nigeria--economically,
Onyegbula added.   Biafra was ready to have serious discussions with the FMG on precise arrangements envisioned in the
FMG's concept on One Nigeria, but Biafra had not fought a
long war simply to return to status quo ante.   And while
Biafra welcomed a U.S. mediation role, negotiation was not
to be a form of surrender. Biafrans were prepared to fight
to the death rather than give in to a one-sided settlement.

The Biafran position left some room for maneuver but the
FMG became increasingly rigid as pressure grew in Nigeria
for a quick military victory. Press accounts of strife in
Nigeria and conflicting statements by the FMG leaders gave
rise to uncertainty over the future of Gowon's regime.   An
October 1969 CIA report estimated that the frustrations of
the inconclusive civil war and its concomitant famine had
sharpened fundamental tensions in Federal Nigeria and once
again gave rise to reports of impending coups.   Hopes for
negotiations between Nigeria and Biafra received a serious
setback, however, as the FMG hawks publicly reneged on
Gowon's conciliatory remarks. At one point Gowon had even
accepted the ICRC day flight agreement by personal fiat even
though it was known that an actual vote in the Executive
Council would have gone heavily against him.

Conventional diplomacy too had its spurt of activity
during the fall of 1969, made possible largely by the infu-
sion of the new leadership by Newsom, Trueheart, and the
Country Director for Nigeria William Brubeck.[36] Under its
new directors, the African Bureau again began working toward
the goal of political negotiations between the belligerents.
But the American role in any negotiations was to present no
specific plans that might run the risk of premature attack.
Instead, the State Department concentrated on advancing
ideas and exploring the views and activities of the parties
concerned. The African Bureau recommended over and over
that the stated objective should be a solution within the
framework of a One Nigeria. Whereas the U.S. government's
public position continued to be very circumspect and low
key, their private efforts were a good deal more focused and
specific.

By mid-October, Richardson received a commitment from
the Nigerian Foreign Ministry on the inviolability of the
proposed daylight airlift. This FMG decision was in reaction
to their successful shooting down of the American JCA-USA
Stratofreighter N52676 on September 26, killing its FTR crew
of five and two Biafrans. Uli was closed temporarily until
Ojukwu visited his troops in the area and rallied them to
again make Uli secure for relief supply deliveries.   After
this, Uli was never again threatened by the FMG until the
end of the war.

Following the necessary consultation among Washington
officialdom on this issue, Ferguson was dispatched to Gabon
to meet with Sir Louis Mbanefo, Biafra's Chief Justice. The
Libreville proposal stated that Gowon had "assured" the
United States that during the specified daylight hours of
ICRC relief operations, no hostile actions would be taken
against the ICRC relief airlift.   These assurances were
referred to Ojukwu and his Foreign Minister, including the

New York-based representatives. The Foreign Minister, backed
by the New York Mission, argued for acceptance. But according to a former Biafran official, the Biafran military's
recommendations were such as to make it clear that any
infringement by Nigeria would be fatal to Ibos and Biafra.
Weighing in with the military was, what the same official
termed, the real test of what might be regarded as international opinion, and that was the shooting down of the Red
Cross and JCA-USA planes.
      Finally, on October 14, 1969, Mbanefo formally rejected
the American assurances. The proposal, according to Mbanefo,
fell short of the necessary assurances requested; insisting
that any agreement on specifics would have to include a
statement of what actions the United States would take if
Nigeria broke the pact.   Biafran officials also noted the
proposal barred only daylight attacks on the relief airlift
but not on the airfield, which was Biafra's main link with
the world.
      The African Bureau imputed other motives to Biafra's
rejection, especially since the staff believed that the FMG
could attack Uli by day any time they chose or dared to, as
well as at night. That the FMG certainly knew where Uli was
and often found it by night with flares was proof enough for
the African Bureau staff. They also believed that the Biafrans had other airstrips in use and, therefore, used an Uli
"sneak attack" possibility as international propaganda. The
opinion of the State Department was that the U.S. priority
was relief; the Biafran priority was winning the war--and
using the relief issue was one of their weapons. Palmer and
the African Bureau decided that the Biafran "third party
guarantee" ploy was part of a long-standing and perfectly
sensible effort to get the United States or some other third
party directly involved in the war. Both the FMG and the
Biafrans were playing a double game and trying to avoid a
relief agreement.
      In the wake of the rejected Libreville proposal, the
State Department pushed for a presidential statement condemning Biafra for refusing the plan. They wanted a strong
denunciation to protect U.S. standing with the FMG, which
claimed the United States gave it no credit when it did do
something constructive concerning the issue of famine and
the United States did not scorn Biafra's refusals. Such a
public rebuke would imply that the United States meant business. The State Department drafted and sent to the White
House a proposed statement, reporting "a serious setback" on
relief, a key section of which read, "We believe that the
ICRC proposal is realistic and reasonable. We consider that
the Federal Government of Nigeria, in agreeing to the ICRC
proposal, acted in full accord with its humanitarian responsibilities. We believe that the integrity of the ICRC
relief program, and the assurances of the United States Government should adequately satisfy the legitimate security
concerns of the Biafran authorities." Morris had the White
House turn down this statement. Although Secretary Rogers
had himself opposed a condemnation by Nixon, feeling it
undesirable to have the president publicly admit failure,
and that such a statement was unnecessary in light of low
domestic concern, Rogers made virtually the same statement

on November 12, saying, in part, "We believe that the ICRC proposal is...a realistic and reasonable scheme. We consider that the Federal Military Government, in agreeing to the ICRC proposal, has acted constructively and in accordance with its humanitarian responsibilities. We also believe that the proposed arrangements for daylight flights meet in a reasonable manner the legitimate security of the Biafran authorities."[37]

By late fall, a respected nongovernmental intermediary was enlisted to begin discussions with both sides on postwar reconstruction, a subject not directly linked to peace negotiations. The idea was that someone must start with a modest proposal, find something that Nigeria and Biafra would talk about, with someone they would talk through, and try to lead them gradually into negotiations without spooking either of the parties involved. These efforts, though, came to an abrupt halt in mid-December when Rogers vetoed all steps necessary to set private peace probes in motion.

Shortly after assuming his post, Brubeck embarked on a tour of European and African capitals in what was described as an information-gathering mission. The purpose of the tour seems to have been basically to explore the possibility of discrete cooperation among several countries to get a negotiation going over the Nigerian Civil War. The United States was looking to Haile Selassie and Houphouet as possible sponsors, and to the French, British, and other Europeans to lend support. Another purpose of this junket, however, was not diplomatic. It was also to read the riot act to the U.S. Embassy staff in Lagos, and thereby, making it very clear that there was a presidential policy and that they were going to carry it out whether they liked it or not. Official sources also reported that Brubeck made it clear to Gowon that U.S. interest and involvement in the issue was to bring about a settlement of the fighting, and not in a settlement in favor of either side. Cabling U.S. Embassies on the itinerary, Newsom advised that the purpose of Brubeck's junket was to exchange views and learn current attitudes and interests of governments concerned, adding that while desiring broad and thorough discussions the State Department wanted it understood that the visit reflected a continuing American concern and was not a new U.S. initiative or new political role in peacemaking.

Following in the footsteps of the Brubeck Mission was an African tour by Secretary Rogers, who seemingly carried the latest word on American policy. Rogers told African leaders the United States was hesitant to express political views on the Nigeria-Biafra issue inasmuch as the United States could become involved in negotiations as an intermediary. Rogers also carried such messages to countries which had abstained from a recent OAU resolution, which endorsed the Nigerian position. The policy of "indirect exhortation" had its consequences, for in the wake of the OAU's September meeting there was a flurry of African initiatives. However, with the United States on the sidelines, there was no chance of success. At the same time, Nixon instructed Kissinger to have the NSC staff make a secret probe for additional direct U.S. mediation. The African Bureau was also instructed to explore mediation prospects. State Department officials

were somewhat bewildered and disillusioned by the apparent
inaction of all parties. It seems to have been a policy of
bankruptcy.

This State Department caution also affected the mechani-
cal aspects of Biafran relief. Concerned with the political
impact of the disposition of C-97s the African Bureau sent a
memorandum to Secretary Rogers, which pointed out that the
possibility existed that, in the next two weeks, the ICRC
relief effort might break down because neither side agreed
to conditions for daylight flights. The question bound to
be raised concerned the disposition of four C-97s sold to
the ICRC. Noting the pending deliveries to JCA-USA, the
African Bureau advised Rogers that if these planes were
delivered to JCA, this would certainly increase the strain
between the U.S. government and FMG. In the eventuality that
the ICRC negotiations would collapse, the African Bureau
suggested forestalling ICRC action on the other C-97s for as
long as possible. This approach went to the source of the
problem in trying to soften the damage that would inevitably
result from the additional C-97 transactions and the potential breakdown of the ICRC programs.

Within the State Department there were other inhibitions
to action. Ferguson's office often worked to keep its projects under wraps because they believed that there were some
officials in the State Department who would have told the
Nigerians of their negotiations in an attempt to get them to
fail. Some items of exceptional sensitivity were held with a
high degree of control. Even in their normal dealings with
the U.S. Embassy in Lagos, there were continued problems for
Ferguson and his staff. A few embassy staffers reported that
Washington's cabled instructions were often resisted.

But as the Cross River Project talks, ICRC negotiations,
and indirect exhortation failed, Richardson prepared to move
ahead on the NSC's authorized probe. He planned to begin
with an approach to the British and French at an early
November NATO Sub-Ministerial Conference. While in London,
Richardson was scheduled to meet secretly with Onyegbula,
marking a new diplomatic episode. The meeting, however, was
canceled by the State Department despite a joint NSC-State
Department directive of September 9, 1969 requiring White
House clearance on all Nigeria-Biafra related cables.
Instructions to the Under Secretary lacked such concurrence.

By mid-November the U.S. initiatives seemed largely
spent. Cross River talks had failed, the two LSMs were
pulled out of Nigeria, and even the river conspired to
thwart a breakthrough with its seasonal drop in the water
level, which would last through February. ICRC negotiations
were futile because the Biafran skepticism toward the Red
Cross was high, aggravated by an earlier ICRC accord with
the FMG that differed substantially from an agreement with
Biafra. Various officials believed that the whole Red Cross
episode really was not to save Biafra but to save the Red
Cross and to demonstrate that the Red Cross was flying in
some relief. Ambivalence overtook American political ploys
as the NSC moved for direct mediation, Rogers eschewed
direct involvement of any kind, and the African Bureau--
finally motivated to try to carry out presidential wishes
for greater activism--found itself caught between the two.

Obscured U.S. intentions led to bitter criticism by Ojukwu
who declared, "The entire confusion over relief has been to
a large extent due to the maneuverings of the United States
[that]...made many proposals on relief, but somehow again
and again it has fallen in line with the Lagos viewpoint."[38]
    There were to be more hopeful signs, more possible nego-
tiations, more attempts to increase the relief flow during
the winter of 1969-1970, but all would be snarled in the
demand for One Nigeria despite the level of famine the conflict caused in Biafra. It is internationally argued that
starvation as a means of warfare is permissible only when it
causes capitulation or is reasonably calculated to do so.[39]
Given that starvation was about to produce the surrender of
Biafra in two months, the idea and image of starvation as a
political weapon of war seemed acceptable to many government
officials.[40]

Notes

1. U.S.A.I.D., The Nigerian Relief Problem, Mar. 25, 1969, p. 1.
2. National American Red Cross, General Records, Mar. 12, 1969, p. 2.
3. U.S. Congress. House Committee on Foreign Affairs, Report of the Special Coordinator For
Nigerian Relief: Hearing before the Subcommittee on Africa, Apr. 24, 1969, p. 16.
4. Ibid., 22.
5. National American Red Cross, General Records, May 7, 1969. The FMG had captured the
Umuahia airstrip on April 23, 1969.
6. S.P.F. Hughes, "Malnutrition in the Field: Nigerian Civil War, 1968-9," British Medical
Journal, 2 (May 17, 1969): 395-460. Hughes was the medical officer of Save the Children Fund.
7. Congressional Record, 91st Cong., 1st sess., Vol. 115,March 24, 26, 27, April 1, 3, 14, 15,
18, 22, May 1, 5, 14, 16, 20, 23, 27, June 9, 12, 16, 17, 18, 19, 1969.
8. Ibid., May 27, 1969, 115:13967.
9. Ibid., "Biafra," May 16, 1969, 115:12796,115:12798. See also Kirk-Greene, Crisis and Conflict in Nigeria, 2:405-408.
10. The Board of Governors of the National American Red Cross also included Robert Finch (Secretary of H.E.W.), George Shultz (Secretary of Labor), Paul Volcker (Under Secretary of Treasury
for Monetary Affairs), David Packard (Deputy Secretary of Defense), and Roger Kelley (Assistant
Secretary of Defense, Manpower and Reserve Affairs).
11. "1969 Reports Concluded Biafra Survival Keyed to Flow of French Aid," Fourth Quarterly
Collection of the 1975 Declassified Documents Reference System, p. 2. Material from the
Nigeria/Biafra Clearing House papers, Swarthmore College Peace Collection, Swarthmore, Penn.
12. Colwell, "Biafra," 17.
13. JCA-USA appealed to U.S.A.I.D. in May 1969 to increase the reimbursement figure for C-97s
on the grounds that $2500 for each successful flight could adequately cover the actual cost of that
flight; and on May 21 a new reimbursement figure of $3500 a landing was approved.
14. U.S. State Department, News briefing (transcript of press, radio and television), June 6,
1969.
15. "Relief Take-Over Upsets Agencies," Baltimore Sun, July 1, 1969.
16. Johnson, Statements of the United States Government, no. 1. It was President Johnson's
message to Haile Selassie on August 5, 1968, that stated that "the International Committee of the
Red Cross, supported by many voluntary agencies and governments, including our own, stands ready to
mount a major relief effort in the affected areas" (p. 9); and Secretary of State Rogers in his
press conference on July 30, "Although the political impasses which prevents free movement of
relief supplies into the secessionist area has not yet been fully overcome, a major relief effort
by the International Committee of the Red Cross is underway. That effort has the full cooperation
and support of the United States Government" (p. 11); and Assistant Secretary of State for African
Affairs Palmer, in a July 23 statement before the Subcommittee on Africa of the House Foreign
Affairs Committee, "We recognize that the implementation of an effective relief program in Nigeria
is an enormous enterprise. The ICRC is expanding its organization to carry out such a program and
has just named Mr. Auguste Lindt, the Swiss Ambassador to Moscow and formerly UN High Commissioner
for Refugees, as the High Commissioner of Nigerian relief operations" (p. 13).
17. "Biafra: The Cost of Bureaucracy," Ripon Forum, 6, no. 3, Mar. 1970, p. 3.
18. Jim Hoagland, "Biafran Relief Pressures Building Up," Washington Post, July 7, 1969, p.
23A.
19. "Nixon Appeals to All Parties to End Impasse on Biafran Aid," The New York Times, July 19,
1969, p. 4.
20. U.S.A.I.D., Emergency Relief in Nigeria and the Biafran Enclave, July 1967 through June
30, 1969, Foreign Disaster Relief Report Reprint, 1 - 84.
21. U.S. Congress. Senate Judiciary Committee, Testimony of the Honorable Elliot L. Richardson, Under Secretary of State: Hearing before the Subcommittee on Refugees, July 15, 1969 (herein-
after cited as Kennedy's Hearing). Richardson could have sent several competent officials,

especially his special aid William Brubeck, but he decided instead to testify personally so as to put an end to the endless talk and leaderless policy.

22.   Ibid., 6.

23.   U.S.A.I.D., "Nigeria Relief Assistance A-1082," dated May 12, 1970. On January 15, 1970, A.I.D. distributed through the Office of Nigeria Relief/Rehabilitation Operations a document that stated, "The U.S. Government contribution to benefit war victims now totals $64 million.   Private American donations are estimated at $14 million, bringing the full account to $78 million" (p. 1). This would give the impression that the U.S. government had contributed in actual and anticipated relief funds the amount of $5.7 million between July 1969 and January 1970. Such an amount, based on the grand total of $78 million, would be 7 percent of the grand total; or a 1 percent increase per month!   To balance the records, it must be remembered that the United States was the single largest contributor to the Nigerian relief for starvation.

24.   Kennedy's Hearing, 13.

25.   "Imperatives for Biafran Relief" (editorial), The New York Times, July 14, 1969, p. 34. .

26.   Peter Grose, "Change on Nigeria Ruled Out by U.S.," The New York Times, July 21, 1969, p. 19.

27.   Palmer, interview with author, Chevy Chase, Maryland, July 23, 1975. Palmer felt this change allowed him to become more personally involved in the Nigerian crisis and time to work on possible solutions to the political-humanitarian dilemma.

28.   U.S. State Department, Biographic Record 1972, "Newsom, David." Newsom's first contact with Africa was a Deputy Director Officer of North African Affairs, followed by his position as Deputy Officer in charge of Arab Peninsular and Iraq Affairs. After 10 years, Newsom was appointed in July 1965 as Ambassador to the Arab oil state of Libya. Newsom's success in these areas that required "de rigueler" diplomatic sympathy for Moslem aspirations was rewarded by the appointment as Assistant Secretary of State for African Affairs.

29.   U.S. State Department, Biographic Record 1972, "Trueheart, William." Trueheart and Newsom (both born in 1918) were also in the U.S. Navy before joining the State Department.

30.   Ambassador William Trueheart, interview with author, Washington, D.C., June 26, 1975. It is clear that the increased demand for a higher level of intelligence reports, information control and analysis were the major factors behind Trueheart's appointment.

31.   "Biafra," Ripon Forum, p. 18.

32.   This personal letter from Ojukwu to Nixon, July 17, 1969, is mentioned in Richard Mauzy, "Bureaucracy and Linkage Politics: The United States and the Tragedy of Biafra" (Masters of Arts thesis at Arizona State University (Aug. 1978). Mauzy worked with Morris after Morris moved from the National Security Council to project director in the Humanitarian Policy Studies, the Carnegie Endowment for International Peace.

33.   Colwell, "Biafra," 5.

34.   "Lagos Said to Approve Flight Plan," Washington Post, Sept. 6, 1969, p. 14D

35.   Jim Hoagland, "Nigeria Rejects Biafran Request for Relief Flight Assurances," Washington Post, Sept. 17, 1969, p. 28A

36.   U.S. State Department, Biographic Record 1972, "Brubeck, William. Brubeck was a senior staff member of the NSC from July 1963 until his transfer to London as the Political Officer in November 1964. He was in this position only four months before being promoted to Consul General in London. Washington recalled Brubeck in August 1968 and appointed him Country Director for Nigeria in October 1969. He worked very closely with Richardson during this period.

37.   U.S. State Department, Press release, Nov. 12, 1969, pp. 3-4.

38.   Colwell, "Biafra," 14-15.

39.   George Mudge, "Starvation as a Means of Warfare," International Lawyer 4, no. 2 (1970): 265-268. Also Esbjorn Rosenblad, "Starvation as a Method of Warfare," International Lawyer 7, no. 2 (1974): pp. 253-270.

35.   Michael Stewart, British Foreign Secretary, before the House of Commons on July 7, 1969, Hansard 786, no. 143, c. 953.

8

Relief Assistance or Political Intervention?

Two specific events that became public during November 1969 highlighted the political problem of U.S. involvement in the Nigerian and Biafran relief assistance. The first was the building of a FMG road by Americans alongside the Nigerian battlefront and the second was the official report of the U.S. Relief Survey Mission on the famine areas of Biafra.

The Nigerian road project from Calabar to Ikom was first authorized in 1963 by U.S.A.I.D., and construction of the road began in early 1967.[1] Work on the road was interrupted that July when civil war erupted. After the FMG recaptured the territory the construction work was resumed. By August 1968 the road was cleared and graded according to a slightly altered design route as calculated by the new FMG administration. Allegations began to surface in the fall of 1969 that these changes in the direction of the Calabar-Ikom Road and its military use--although the road was not completely finished--was proof that the United States was actively involved in the conflict on the side of the FMG. Because the road was being redirected to within seven miles of the front line of battle, it would be of tremendous assistance to the FMG in their movements to and from the conflict area.

Robert Smith informed the necessary State Department officials with his internal classified memorandum (dated October 28, 1969) of the impending public exposure of this road project. He also presented what he believed was the best manner in which to refute charges that the U.S. construction was to support the FMG military.

C. CONCLUSIONS
Our conclusions relative to the allegations are:

1. The recent changes in the project were requested for economic/political reasons, not military. They reflect changes in Nigerian economic and political priorities as a result of the establishment of the South East State.

> 2. The road is still in the very early stages
> of construction and will not be open for gen-
> eral traffic until 1972.   Some military and
> commercial vehicles have been reported using
> some of the roughly graded sections of the
> road.[2]

Although a heavily drawn personal "arrow" was penned on the
memo pointing to this last sentence, Smith did not bring to
the attention of his superiors the road's potential for a
serious incident or confrontation. Since the A.I.D. construction on the edge of the military battlefield was being
handled by an American contractor, American workers would
likely be on the scene. As a practical matter, any American
working or supervising this road construction so close to
the war could be targets themselves for a Biafran attack--if
only to dramatize the Biafran cause.

Such an attack was not merely a hypothetical possibility.
The Biafrans had attacked a comparable road project in similar circumstances in May 1969.[3] In that incident, a European
oil company had begun to open up roads on the Federal side
(west) of the Niger River, which was the dividing line
between the FMG and Biafran forces. The Biafrans began to
send some of their military units across the Niger River to
disrupt the company's operations by attacking the workers.
In one attack on a group of Italian workers several were
killed and another 29 of the oil men were captured and taken
to the town of Orlu, in Biafra. Sentenced to death for aid-
ing the FMG troops, the Italians were rescued from execution
only by concerted diplomatic efforts, including those by the
Vatican.[4]

This same concern for American workers on the Calabar-
Ikom Road was expressed by an independent consultant hired
by the State Department's INR to analyze this sensitive project. Recommended by Roger Morris to INR for the job, C. W.
Beal conducted a thorough analysis of the case and concluded
his report by stating that "A.I.D. should suspend its assistance for the road project until the war is over." This
needed to be done, he said, because

> A.I.D.'s approval of the project earlier this
> year may have rested on two assumptions which
> could have separated the road from the civil
> war. One assumption was that the war would end
> in a federal military victory within the pre-
> sent fiscal year, FY 1970. This assumption was
> repeatedly expressed in testimony to the House
> Committee on Foreign Affairs last June. A sec-
> ond assumption could have been that the road
> would not be useful militarily until its com-
> pletion, anticipated in mid-1972. Events have
> overthrown both possible assumptions.[5]

But Joseph Palmer refused to accept that there needed to be
a change in this project. Although the African Bureau
attempted to delay, if not completely prevent the public
exposure of the road project, Rowland Evans and Robert
Novak used the "leaked" Calabar-Ikom Road Project in their

<u>Washington Post</u> article of December 12, 1969.[6]
The same day this article appeared, Senator Charles
Goodell brought up the Nigerian road issue within the context of the Senate consideration of the House Resolution
14580 dealing with the Foreign Assistance Act of 1969. During its Senate floor debate, Goodell proposed an amendment
to prohibit "the use of American AID funds for the improvement, development, or construction of the road between Calabar and Ikom in Nigeria."[7] His concern for a coherent and
humanitarian U.S. foreign policy in Nigeria was expressed in
the dilemma, which the State Department refused to face.
"For AID to cut funds for immediately needed food and medical relief, while increasing funds for a long-range development project like the Calabar-Ikom Road, is difficult for me
to understand,"[8] said Goodell. The Assistant Secretary of
State for Congressional Relations tried unsuccessfully to
convince Goodell that this project was following a neutral
policy. Therefore, to salvage similar projects involved in
the Foreign Assistance Act of 1969, Richardson made the
decision to cease all American involvement in the road until
after the war.
Back in late October, Elliot Richardson had also reacted
to a NSC memo that commented on the pessimistic interpretive
report from ICRC officials on Biafra. Morris, following in
the footsteps of Senator Edward Kennedy's inquiry on the
actual number of refugees, suggested that the African Bureau
gain a firsthand verification of the ICRC report, and he
added in his classified memo,

> My own reaction to the Red Cross report is con-
> cern about relief rather than negotiating a
> Nigerian victory. If we do take the Red Cross
> impressions seriously, and proceed to verify
> them, we would then face some immediate choices
> not of our own making:
>
> --How to respond to a "revolutionary humanitar-
> ian airlift" if the Red Cross or other
> respected voices call for one.
>
> --What to do about strengthening JCA and other
> functioning relief agencies to avert mass human
> disaster that will not wait on the casual
> mechanics of a peace probe. If we truly dis-
> cover that Biafra is about to die, we certainly
> know by now that the irrationality of its own
> leadership, the indifference of the FMG, and
> the inertia of the great powers offer no first-
> aid remedy in diplomacy.
>
> Most of us have recognized that if the food
> situation got bad enough we could encounter a
> rather severe moment of truth: At the point of
> collapse--while the political deal is being
> made--someone with the means and the conscience
> will have to stage the real rescue operation
> that had been the victim of civil war politics
> and great power calculus up to that point.

> Without that, the Feds would probably find
> themselves reunified with a grave-yard.

Spurred into action by the NSC, Richardson ordered Clyde
Ferguson to organize a special relief survey team to be sent
into Biafra. The members of the team were Gene Dewey, who
had become Ferguson's Chief Logistics Management Adviser,
George Thomas, the Administrative Assistant, "Pat" Flaherty,
a logistician on loan from the Defense Department, and Karl
Western, an epidemiologist from the U.S. Public Health Service. Dewey was appointed head of the team because he was a
combat-tested officer who enjoyed a high reputation. It also
went without saying that he would be collecting very sensitive strategic and security information during the course of
the survey in Biafra.[9]

To add to the pressure on the State Department while
Ferguson's special relief survey team was in Biafra, there
was an increase in congressional requests as to the validity
of The New York Times stories about the snafu on handling of
food for Nigerian and Biafran refugees in liberated territories. Richardson sent Helen Wilson to talk to Samuel Krakow
on November 4, 1969, to see if it would be possible for the
State Department to transfer $100,000 through ARC to the NRC
without going through the officially required contract. As
Krakow reported to Ramone Easton, "AID most anxious to help,
but wants some control over funds. There is great reluctance to turn over cash to Nigerian Red Cross."[10]

When the survey was completed, the Dewey team flew to
Geneva to draft their reports. At the same time in Washington, Krakow met with three A.I.D. officials involved with
the Nigerian relief (Ed Marks, Wilson, and Beverly Carl) and
with Bighinatti of the Disaster Services of State. Marks,
who had just returned from a trip to Nigeria, recommended
"that we [National American Red Cross] make a contribution
directly to the Nigerian Red Cross; this can be token contribution but will give the Nigerian Red Cross some status
in the eyes of the Rehabilitation Commission and will give
some evidence that the Nigerian Red Cross is really a window
to the outside world."[11] Therefore, a way had been found to
channel funds for relief. But the lingering question of control remained. "The U.S. Government is anxious to support
the Nigerian Red Cross for several reasons: this will keep
it out of politics; it is good to encourage voluntary support in Nigeria; and also, the society can maintain a good
contact with the outside world. There is considerable controversy as to who should control relief--the National Rehabilitation Commission or the individual states; thus, the
danger of the handling of relief becoming a serous political
issue."[12] Another handling of relief that would also become
a serious political issue occurred when Ferguson accepted
and agreed with Dewey's November 17 preliminary report.
While unpolished, the report gave clear and strong indica-
tions that a potential crisis was imminent.

In his drafted political-military section of the report,
Dewey noted the very real possibility of Biafra's collapse
within 60 to 90 days. His grasp of the combatants' viability
was the product of several months involvement in the Nigeria
and Biafra scene; including an earlier visit in May and June

1969 to the Biafran enclave. Those tours had provided an impressive picture of a determined Biafran people, but this October-November survey presented a drastically different picture whereby the Biafran leaders seemed more hardened and willing to amortize their people whose morale had plunged. Dewey attributed this change to severe hunger--coming after two years of war and starvation. The serious shortage of food off the main supply routes was resulting in a dehumanizing struggle to survive.

The breakdown of Biafran military discipline, which Dewey saw as an "alarming trend," contributed to the gloomy picture. Increasingly it was reported that Biafran soldiers commandeered vehicles, including relief trucks, and appropriated food crops by threats and force. More and more the troops--whose uniforms now consisted of maybe a cap or tattered shirt with an insignia--began to appear in the relief feeding lines. "The stark reality of the situation," Dewey stated, "was that soldiers were poorly fed and becoming increasingly hungry."[13]

Just how hungry the Biafran population had become was the survey work of Western. A 28 year old epidemiologist employed at the Communicable Disease Center in Atlanta, Georgia, Western's previous experience with famine situations in Nigerian-held territory had called him to Dewey's attention. In terms of experience and knowledge Western was well qualified, even if he was Dewey's third choice for the job. The two originally requested physicians had turned down the offer because they said that they held on-going program responsibilities. Besides, any doctor selected for this team knew that he would never be allowed reentry into Nigeria once the inevitable negative report on the level of starvation was made public. Western, young, tested, and with no program obligations, was considered expendable.

Unlike many observers and experts who made headlines with findings based on secondhand information, impressions, and conversations, Western based his conclusions on the hard data of the war's effects on the noncombatants. "Slow, creeping starvation of almost the entire population is the key impression today in Biafra, as distinguished from earlier days of more spectacular `epidemics' of classical Kwashiorkor and mass deaths due to severe nutritional depravation," wrote Western in his classified report. Western's judgment was that the acceleration in the deterioration of the nutritional reserve status of almost the entire population was acute. Using a composite of cluster sampling methods developed and tested in Nigeria and by examining 2,676 children and adults (more people than are interviewed for a Gallup Poll), Western estimated the population of Biafra (thought to be from 8 to 10 million) at 3.25 million, and of these people over 1 million (31.4 percent) had famine edema. Famine edema, or severe malnutrition, is a manifestation of chronic deficiency of protein which results in the patient's death in a matter of weeks. It is the last stage of starvation in which the body's cells begin to consume themselves, producing extra fluid in the body. Western's survey also found that the Biafran people were suffering from the highest rate of famine ever recorded in history; for "almost one third of the population had edema, a proportion three times higher than in the worst sieges of World War II, including those of Leningrad and the Western Netherlands," he wrote in his report.

Virtually every segment of the Biafran population was affected, adults over 45 and children 4 years of age and under were hit the hardest, with edema rates of 52.1 percent and 42.2 percent respectively. Based on his survey, Western estimated 400,000 people received daily feeding in Biafra and 1,700,000 needed three rations weekly. To arrest further nutritional decline, he recommended a selective feeding system providing a 630-calorie diet. Food imports of 262 tons daily of balanced amounts of cereal, corn/soy meal, stockfish, and dry milk would be required. Such rations could easily have been accommodated within the existing airlift, although it did require some changes in cargo mix.

Adding to this deadly nutritional crisis, increased mortality was threatened by ever-present disease. Among the important goals of Western's survey was an assessment of the measles program, because if anything was going to kill the children after their advanced protein-calorie malnutrition it would be an outbreak of measles. The measles epidemic season was December to March and, noted Western, the susceptible population was under-immunized, particularly in recently disturbed-areas. Serious threats were also noted from tuberculosis, whooping cough, hepatitis, and yaws. This analysis of the Biafran situation was obviously important given its clear warning of an impending crisis.

The third component of the survey report concerned logistics. Flaherty, Dewey's hand-picked expert who died shortly after the team ended its mission from a disease contracted while in Biafra, had conducted a thorough review of supply factors, which included road conditions, power facilities, and communications. He concluded that the unusually severe and long rainy season had made surface communications inside Biafra an impassable mudhole. This normally major problem was compounded by near depletion of petroleum and gasoline supplies. In spite of the bad roads and their deteriorating effect on the vehicles, Flaherty found no evidence of cracked frames in the trucks, and the tires were in surprisingly good condition. He even projected that Biafran lorries were "usable for three more years." But the trucks were falling apart in terms of spare parts that under normal conditions would have been in stock. The fleet of trucks were quite literally being held together with some wires and bravado; for they were the essential food link between the airfields and the distribution centers.

Another tragic shortcoming of the Biafran relief scene was the breakdown of the food distribution network. Some 70 percent of those requiring feeding were being covered by both Catholic and Protestant relief teams, while the remaining 30 percent received little or nothing at all. Instead of coordinating their efforts inside the beleaguered area, the Catholic organizations doled out food through their church parish system while the Protestant relief organizations distributed on their provincial basis. Those who were most in need were deteriorating outside these redundant religious distribution centers.

The picture was grim with the Biafran army inching toward disintegration, low popular morale, a starved populace, and an irrational relief distribution system on the verge of collapse. There was little reserve left, either in the material wherewithal to wage war or in the realm of the fighting spirit to survive what Biafra had experienced in the spring. Should the enclave suddenly fall as projected, and the food distribution flow be interrupted, then time would become the mortal enemy. Ferguson informed a mid-December meeting of relief executives that a delay in food distribution in Biafra of 20 to 30 days would be near catastrophic--the present state of malnutrition would bring about mortality on a colossal scale.

On his way back to Washington, Ferguson gave a confidential briefing to Maurice Foley, Under Secretary of Britain's Foreign Ministry, in London on November 21. This first briefing, which covered the entire intelligence report on military and health conditions, was given to the FMG's strongest ally and not to any U.S. official. This is indicative of the continuing American habit to instinctively inform the colonizer of their colonial affairs.

Five days later, with the final draft of Dewey's military and logistics report and Western's medical report in hand, Ferguson presented the survey conclusions to the State Department. This briefing, however, was the occasion of a most serious and tragic communication failure. The American officials understood the implications of Dewey's prediction of a potential 60 to 90 day collapse of the conflict, and Flaherty's detailed description of logistical conditions. But it seems uncanny that every official claims that he or she missed the clear indication of Western's report that over 1 million human beings were about to die in Biafra.

On November 29, Ferguson's staff drafted a memorandum to Richard Nixon which pointed out that the possibility of negotiating ICRC daylight flights were presently remote. It was also very doubtful that the Cross River Project would ever materialize, despite the fact that the present relief into Biafra was wholly inadequate. This memo was later incorporated into an implementation memo from Richardson and forwarded to Nixon on December 4. Richardson paid only passing notice to Western's findings and failed to point out Dewey's predictions. The main purpose of Richardson's memo was to develop a future course of action along the lines of reconstruction and development.

Richardson considered four basic options in this memo: (1) U.S. withdrawal from relief programs with a published justification, (2) maintenance of the existing U.S. relief support, (3) use of American political influence short of guarantees to break the relief supply impasse, and (4) increased U.S. support for the relief organizations already flying supplies into Biafra and the possible extension of support for new and better airlifts. The first was a strawman option, or as one official quipped, "The U.S. could ill afford to lose those humanitarian brownie points." The second and third options were irrelevant inasmuch as Nixon's request for action presumed that the United States did not want to maintain the existing level of commitment, nor had the meager U.S. influence in Nigeria expanded since their support for Biafran relief. The fourth option was selected so as to fit in with the growing strength of the White House over the traditional foreign policymaking by the State Department; although such a policy was expected to further strain U.S.-Nigerian relations.

To support this new policy stance, Henry Kissinger agreed to the transfer of ICRC's four C-97s to JCA-USA and an increase of JCA-USA supply tonnage by phasing out five low-capacity DC-6s and replacing them with the C-97s. This plan also called for the expansion of the airfield facilities at São Tomé to accommodate more aircraft. Together, these actions were expected to increase the air bridge nightly relief support by 85 percent, bring food and medical deliveries at Uli to about 300 tons nightly. A note of caution was expressed by Richardson to Kissinger whereby this policy was committing the United States to a possible collision course with the FMG.

In late November, Richardson made the decision to shift the major U.S. relief assistance work away from Ferguson's group back to William Brubeck's special staff. Richardson requested that the African Bureau begin to base future relief to Nigeria on a postwar supply system, rather than on the existing on-going conflict supply system to Nigeria and Biafra. They also began to look for a contingency plan in which the United States would be dependent on (a victorious FMG) Nigerian cooperation. This course of action would not be possible if Ferguson were still in charge of U.S. relief to the devastated areas. Based on Dewey's prediction of an immanent Biafran collapse, the State Department assumed that none of the agencies that ran "illegal" relief into the enclave would be allowed to continue their operations. Because the NRC and other international agencies handling relief in FMG-controlled territory were regarded by the African Bureau planners as manifestly incompetent, they believed the major problem was to find a competent group that the FMG would accept. The League of Red Cross Societies was ultimately considered the least compromised of the mercy organizations in Nigeria; and so the State Department set out to carve a postwar relief niche for this group.

Despite the varying personal accounts of the scope of Ferguson's oral report to the State Department, he clearly discussed Western's survey.[14] That meeting, some State Department officials felt, was called to inform and not to decide and, therefore, it would be incorrect to describe the briefing as anything outside the normal standard meeting. There were memos sent to several officials with a "need to know," and one was sent to the White House on December 10. This memo to the NSC was quite similar in content to the briefing later provided to relief groups, only shorter. However, the memo to the White House did not mention the anticipated collapse of Biafra within 60 to 90 days, nor did it mention the degree of famine edema except in passing that it was a fatal condition. The memos and meetings, after the initial rush to inform the British, seemed to lack any sense of urgency. The State Department's (after-the-fact) explanation was that they failed to grasp or understand that the Western survey was not the usual approximation but had scientific substance. The entire survey with its dire log-

istical findings coupled with the documented slow, creeping
starvation that buttressed the prediction of collapse was
never sent to Morris at the White House for obvious reasons
--his predictable reaction and action.

A real concern over possible violence by the FMG troops
moving into Biafra after a collapse of the secession led the
State Department to look seriously into the possibility of
an international observer to moderate the victor's conduct.
To gear up for the impending Biafran collapse, Palmer and
Ferguson made special arrangements, in mid-December, with
the British Ambassador for mutually identifying and organiz-
ing logistical resources for a "crash" relief effort. In
addition to international efforts, the State Department
began to examine the manner of a U.S. response to Biafra's
capitulation.

The first contingency plan for postwar American action
was submitted by Ferguson to Richardson on December 10. It
recommended that Balair Ltd. (operators of the ICRC and JCA-
USA airlifts) receive U.S. financial support to acquire four
freight versions of the DC-7 to fly more food into the
devastated areas at the war's end.

Meanwhile, Western took it on himself back in late
November to speak at several conferences concerning his survey conclusions. The involved relief group pushed him for
additional information on the classified findings and they
were always referred to the State Department for the medical
report.   However, because the medical report was only one
part of the larger sensitive military and political evaluation of the humanitarian crisis, the State Department did
not release the findings. The African Bureau later explained
that the delay as due to a problem of when the properly
informed executives would be available, and when Ferguson
and Dewey would be available as well for official comments.

The first meeting that alerted the relief agencies that
something important in the report was being overlooked came
on December 15 in Washington, D.C.; almost three weeks after
Ferguson had received the final draft of the medical report.
Western's briefing covered the situation inside Biafra,
omitting any mention of population estimates or projected
collapse for security reasons. He referred to edema as a
measure of advanced protein deprivation, and called attention to the unconscionable distribution system in Biafra.
Having received and issued official gloomy forecasts all
along, the independent relief agencies thought that the U.S.
government had finally caught up with them.   But these
agencies quickly realized that the U.S. responses were not
reflecting their official perception--the real message was
that the government had missed its own message.

Richardson reacted to these public disclosures by approv-
ing Ferguson's suggestion to fund Balair relief activities.
Then, on December 23, Ferguson began arranging for an Ice-
landic airline, which was supported by the Order of Malta
with only thinly veiled U.S. financial backing, to fly four
DC-6s twice nightly into Uli from Libreville. This would
send an extra 2,100 tons of emergency rations a month into
the conflict areas.

Contingency planners worked against the clock to augment the relief flow. Another plan was drawn up, specifically in light of the conditions portrayed in the October survey, calling for cargo helicopters to ferry relief after the war had ended. Helicopters were considered especially useful in the immediate aftermath of any war when roads were clogged with refugees and military equipment. The plan, however, was never cleared out of the State Department, nor was it ever formally suggested. The reason for this plan's rejection lay in its high visibility and the prediction of FMG sensitivity to visible foreign assistance. Helicopters did not have the potential for solving the political problems involved, which was the main barrier to sufficient relief supplies.

In Nigeria, the FMG forces were scoring advances in their final assault on the Biafran heartland. Operations in the Onitsha area and southwest of Owerri were stalled, but around Aba and Ikot Ekpene the FMG forces reported gains. Then, on Christmas Day, the Third Marine Commando Division lopped off the eastern sector of Biafra, meeting the First Division in Umuahia. About a week later the Federal Defense Ministry announced that Nigerian forces had cut Biafra into three parts. The long-awaited end of Biafra's secession was at hand.

Supporting the relief-oriented efforts preparing for an international as well as a U.S. response to the inevitable Biafran collapse was a continuing negotiations strategy for the State Department. In part, the negotiating effort was an acknowledgment of Biafran resilience. After months of planning, maneuvering, and coordination, the African Bureau was still pinning its hopes on upcoming Nigerian-Biafran talks under Haile Selassie's mediation and the possible expansion or, in the event the talks bogged down, continuation of talks under a respected third party enlisted by the State Department. The basic approach was for the United States to play a more active but still indirect role. They continued to believe that the only way to resolve the war was the insertion of a mediator and expansion to issues more appropriate to outsiders such as development of an international observer force or a rehabilitation consortium. There were problems on all sides, though. Haile Selassie was willing to try once again, but he walked a very delicate course between both Nigerian and Biafran sensitivities and their polemics. Problems in the U.S. position further complicated matters. One American official, writing at this time to Morris about the situation, commented,

> It all remains...very iffy and we continue to operate under the Secretary's constraints about not getting out in front, while continuing to feel White House pressure to "do something." Like you, we are not sanguine about achieving much with all this, but we are under an injunction to keep trying and even slim chances seem worth trying if the alternative is a protracted war. My guess is that it would take a considerable swing back in the balance, e.g., failure of the Federal military initiative and relative

recuperation of Biafran strength, to create anything like a negotiating climate, and that doesn't seem the likeliest prospect at the moment.[15]

Death drew nearer still for uncounted thousands who, in desperate nutritional condition, continued to deteriorate. A grim appreciation of the situation was voiced in a meeting of church relief groups in Stuttgart, Germany, over the January 10-11 weekend (as Odumegwu Ojukwu secretly fed Biafra) when it was stated that millions might not survive even a temporary interruption of relief. JCA-USA, however, offered some encouragement with the news that their relief supply deliveries had improved when FTR was replaced by the Balair group of Switzerland. Balair had doubled the number of relief flights for JCA-USA in the first month alone when they were hired on November 2 (see Table 8.1). When these increased relief activities were presented to the State Department, however, a JCA-USA officer remembered Richardson as saying it was true, but the only lasting solution to the relief problem was an end to the war.

Nonetheless, as Biafra disintegrated into its worst period of famine, American agencies converged to manage the U.S. response. On Saturday, January 10, 1970, JCA-USA issued emergency instructions to Balair to ground all their C-97s after that evening's flights. On the two return flights to São Tomé, JCA-USA aircraft evacuated 90 Biafran relief workers. Their internal relief distribution network had finally collapsed.

Table 8.1.   Relief Airlifts to Uli, Biafra

	Nord-Church-Aid	JCA-USA	Canai-Relief	Daily Average Flights	Metric Tons of Cargo	
					Monthly Average	Daily Average
January	290	6	13	10.0	2,819	91
February	153	43	15	7.5	2,104	75
March	244	153	56	14.6	5,123	165
April	187	107	29	10.7	3,658	122
May	191	99	57	11.2	4,013	130
June	51	32	37	4.0	1,515	51
July	162	119	41	10.4	3,920	126
August	181	125	31	10.9	4,110	133
September	213	115	76	13.5	5,136	171
October	218	62	85	11.8	4,507	145
November	211	122	90	14.1	5,399	180
December	276	156	113	17.6	7,104	229

Source: Joint Church Aid-U.S.A., Annual Report 1969, Jan. 12, 1970, p. 8.

President Nixon ordered the Special Action Group, chaired by Kissinger, to devise a plan action to meet this emergency. At the same time, the State Department's Inter-Agency Working Group and the Inter-Departmental Operations Group began to review and coordinate their activities in Nigeria. The following day the White House told the media that Nixon had ordered C-130 transport planes, as well as helicopters that were at Pope Air Force Base, North Carolina, placed on special alert for possible use in Nigeria. Nixon had also discussed the developing situation by telephone with British Prime Minister Harold Wilson. After the White House's unilateral announcement, Palmer phoned Richardson and the NSC complaining that the public notice of the U.S. alert was irresponsible and ruinous to relations with Nigeria. Then,

> The end of the war came like a flash of tropical lightning, momentarily illuminating a half-remembered landscape, and reimposing itself on the consciousness of a world which had already pigeonholed the conflict, along with Vietnam and the Middle East, as 'insoluble.' It took everyone by surprise, including the victorious Nigerian armies as they raced across great tracts of Biafran territory long denied to them.[16]

Viewing the confusion that followed Biafra's January 12 surrender, Nixon was concerned that the United States should do all it could to aid the emergency relief effort. Toward that end he authorized an additional $10 million for urgent relief, conferred again with Wilson, and exchanged cablegrams with Yakubu Gowon informing him of the latest U.S. offer of relief assistance, as well as American readiness to provide aircraft and helicopters for food distribution. Nixon also told Gowon that Ferguson's reports on conditions in the area "would be made available to the government of Nigeria so that they could be totally aware of the situation from the relief standpoint."

To underscore presidential concern, David Newsom was ordered to convey Nixon's offer personally to Gowon and to raise the question of increased relief and international observers. The African Bureau's concern over Nigerian sensitivities translated into a brief instruction cable message drafted for Newsom's visit to Lagos that contained only two points: that the C-130's were on standby and $10 million was offered only because the British suggested it. Morris challenged these instructions as inadequate and redrafted the message to detail presidential concern and offers of help, including Ferguson's files. Although Morris eliminated the apologetic tone, he did advise Newsom "not to press" the issue of relief.[17]

Newsom met Gowon on January 13 and delivered Nixon's message. Gowon responded strongly to the visit, saying Nigeria had won the war without help and didn't need it now. Nigeria was fully prepared for reconciliation with the Eastern Region, which they would handle along with relief in their own way. But the formal response to the President was

properly diplomatic, cabling Nixon that Gowon appreciated
the President's candor and would respond to the offer
shortly. Western's report and its grim implications were not
specifically presented because Newsom said that he did not
know what the Western Report really implied until after he
returned to Washington. Newsom was not alone in this igno-
rance, by now all too many of the key officials in the State
Department and the White House were numbed by the numbers
game of the Vietnam "headcounts." All the Western Report
told laymen was that under wartime conditions, 1800 tons of
relief food a week was the minimum hold-the-line need
against massive starvation.

Although a general summary of Western's findings had
been sent to Newsom on December 9 and to Richardson the following day, the report's actual relevance to planning and
postwar relief in Nigeria remained largely undetected until
a member of Ferguson's staff worried aloud to Morris on January 13 that the African Bureau and U.S.A.I.D. officials
were ignoring its implications in planning relief, as would
Newsom. The full report, a bulky document replete with
statistical tables and charts, had never been sent to the
White House. The NSC immediately called Ferguson's office to
angrily demand the entire report. Kissinger was immediately
informed of these developments and he called Richardson to
suggest that the entire Western Report be given to the FMG,
and that the American transport planes near Nigeria be read-
ied for airlift operations.

The following day, Morris delivered a memo to Richardson
pointing out that among the implications of the survey was
the clear possibility of 1 to 1.5 million deaths within the
next three weeks. Morris also recommended an immediate high-
level approach to Gowon specifically on the report, definite
increased shipments and production of food, an offer of more
trucks and helicopters, transfer of cargo aircraft to Nigeria for internal airlift, and other emergency measures. He
then sent six copies of the Western Report air pouched to
the U.S. Embassy in Lagos with instructions that it be immediately delivered to the appropriate Nigerian officials.
(The reports arrived two days later.) Morris also contacted
Western at the Communicable Disease Center in Atlanta, asking for a projection of food requirements. Western's memo,
received at the White House on January 14 noted, "In terms
of what is going to be needed to meet this situation, the
relief agency is going to have to supply the 250 tons of
high quality protein food that the airlift was flying in,
plus the local food that won't be available because of
social disruption, plus the amount of food that is needed to
arrest the deterioration that was occurring within the
enclave at the time it fell." This meant that feeding only
those with pronounced edema a minimum of 3,500 tons weekly
would be needed, and to feed an estimated 1 million edema
victims and provide the remaining population with a 600-cal-
orie daily intake would require about 6,000 tons per week.
Taking into account the ravages of the conflict over the two
intervening months between his original report and this
recent White House request, Western estimated that to feed
3.2 million starving people a 2,000-calorie diet would call
for 10,500 tons weekly, and an additional purchase of local

food (except yams); which set a total goal of 20,000 tons. At the time Western made these projections based on his report, A.I.D. was shipping 2,000 tons of food imports plus 1,000 tons local purchase weekly--some 500 tons under Western's first bottom-line figure and much less than his latest minimal estimate.

U.S.A.I.D. planning called for 2,000 relief tons per week, just shy of Nigeria's target of 2,225 tons and considerably less than the 10,000 tons urged by the NSC staff. Lacking on-the-spot reports of inadequate supplies and without the insights of Western's latest estimates, the State Department was unwilling to suddenly overstep the FMG's food distribution goals. Moreover, the United States was capable of maintaining a continuous supply of relief food that could be airlifted into Nigeria up to 10,000 tons a week. But there was no policy on how to get these supplies to those in most need. The problem was not seen by the logistical mind of the African Bureau as one of getting the wherewithal of relief--trucks, planes, and relief workers--into Nigeria and into action, but rather one of how to persuade the FMG to accept outside help. Although no decision was made to increase immediate deliveries, stockpile programming for São Tomé and Fernando Po did begin.

But one of the first acts of the FMG occupying army, after the Biafran surrender, was to shut down and eventually destroy the Uli airstrip, thereby closing the quickest relief route into the stricken area. When JCA-USA offered all its food and medical stores and aircraft, which included the ICRC's C-97s, to the FMG, Gowon refused. Yet, citing recent U.S. talks with Britain on truck availability for relief shipments and relying on the known availability of short-term food stockpiles, State Department officials had told the press on January 12 that the Nigerian relief situation was in pretty good shape. Despite Dewey's report that had portrayed dismal road conditions and few usable arteries because the existing roads were congested with military vehicles and refugees, the State Department stated that they did not even know if the need will develop for an internal food airlift. There were some concerns expressed at the press meeting, however, by Robert McCloskey: "My honest judgment is that one cannot write off the prospect that there might be some uncontrolled violence by Federal troops. One cannot write off the prospect that there will be inefficiencies in the relief effort, such that you have some substantial starvation. But these would not be matters of policy, and I would hope that with all the efforts going into it maybe they will be held to a minimum."[18]

Although the U.S. Embassy did not have people in the field until January 19, journalists attending the noon briefing on January 14 heard spokesman McCloskey assert, "There is a relatively large-scale effort under way now, and apparently is showing some, or having some impact."[19]   In Lagos for his meeting with Gowon, Newsom told newsmen that the existing evidence did not suggest a large-scale famine in Nigeria. Richardson also assuaged a concerned American public by suggesting that normalcy returned rather rapidly because that was what was reported by one fringe combat-town's experience. In the wake of Nigeria's victory,

Richardson added to his remarks, "We have had to recognize that too conspicuous an initiative by the United States might be counterproductive, so we have followed the course of encouraging initiative by others. We feel that, from the point of view of the United States, this was a successful course."[20]

A good example of the State Department continually using fronts in international affairs is their relationship with UNICEF. Acting on information that UNICEF was interested in a helicopter program, Brubeck had phoned UNICEF's Deputy Director on January 14 to make such an offer. Learning that UNICEF had no plans or capability to undertake a helicopter airlift program, Richardson secured Rogers's authority to approve a $2 million credit line to be opened to support whatever projects could be worked out between UNICEF and the FMG. After the meeting, Brubeck called UNICEF to say that the United States could not offer helicopters now because of their political high visibility, but would airlift UNICEF trucks to Nigeria if the need arose.

The tone and direction of U.S. policy had become vague with the sudden end of the conflict, which is why Richardson decided to have a thorough review of postwar relief. He called a meeting of the State Department Inter-Agency Group on January 15. At this meeting, the NSC argued--on the basis of Western's most recent extrapolation of starvation need-- that relief planning should proceed on the basis of 10,000 tons. Morris suggested the relief planning should be accel- erated, relief shipments should include high-protein foods, and to expedite its delivery helicopters should be offered to UNICEF, which had good relations with the FMG. But most important, Morris stressed that the Western Report and its implications should be presented immediately to Nigerian officials at the highest possible levels with an emphasis on urgency. To calm the fears expressed by Palmer and other African Bureau FSOs that too conspicuous an action by the United States would damage relations with Nigeria, the NSC staff reasoned that, should conditions be as bad as Western suggested and the FMG continued to minimize the situation, Nigeria would appear to the world as callous, incompetent, and possibly vengeful, thus obliging the United States to take even more conspicuous steps--particularly considering domestic interest.

Following the January 15 Inter-Agency meeting, portents of disaster began reaching Washington officialdom. The only information the State Department or the White House had after the Biafran surrender was secondhand, i.e., from the FMG or from U.S. officials reporting from fringe areas. But famine is a particularly silent and difficult disease to observe. Thus the reports that emanated from the collapsed enclave were coming largely from untrained observers and may not have accurately reflected conditions as they existed. These official optimistic reports were seized on by the African Bureau as evidence that U.S. policy was working. Nonetheless, reports persisted about the pessimistic condi- tion of food and medical relief in the former Biafran area. Radio intercepts recorded a British missionary doctor's broadcast from Orlu that the situation there was "very bad." He was reporting calamitous road transport with impassable

highways and downed bridges, and he was pleading for immediate food shipments "to save thousands of lives." A host of
relief workers, recently returned from Biafra, journeyed the
corridors of Congress and the State Department carrying new
messages of alarm.

Seeking firsthand observations, Kissinger had sent a
team into the troubled area on January 19. The team was
headed once again by Dewey, and included three U.S. Public
Health Service physicians. They spent two days touring the
region, discovering negligible food distribution and definite widespread malnutrition. A sample survey by Dr. Matthew
S. Lowenstein revealed that 40 percent of the children were
in serious nutritional condition.

Also on Monday, January 19, Western and Dr. William
Foege were summoned to Washington for consultations with the
National Institutes of Health. A special briefing for Kissinger and the NSC staff with Western and Foege was arranged
to discuss the implications of the October survey as it
might relate to postwar relief. Western and Foege told
those at the meeting that 20,000 to 40,000 tons of food were
needed per month in the area to avert massive starvation, as
well as to feed people in other areas of need. Nigerian Red
Cross planning had called for 9,000 tons monthly, but its
distribution was dismal.

Suddenly Kissinger said he understood fully that the
people in the former Biafra territory were in the midst of a
catastrophe. After the NSC briefing the two medical doctors
were sent to brief Newsom, Ferguson, and Brubeck at the
State Department. They were also to discuss the implications of the medical survey and explain how the new tonnage
figures were derived from previous data. It was the first
time State Department officials had an oral briefing on
Western's figures and it clarified most of the questions
they had on the report. Later that same day, the White
House noted that President Nixon expressed his belief that
everything was being done to deal with the relief problem
and that the problem was not understated.

However, Dewey cabled from Lagos that a disaster of
major proportions appeared to be developing in the former
secessionist area. The team also reported that pervasive
military lack of discipline made relief distribution academic, as soldiers looted and commandeered trucks. Hospitals
were also crippled as young nurses failed to report to work,
fearing rape by marauding troops. Relief was demonstrably
inadequate and the team reported that the trucks inbound to
the relief area were far too little and too late to handle
400 to 500 tons daily, which the effort required. The only
visible alternative to using commercial trucks immediately
available was to effectively increase the numbers of trucks
being operated by the NRC, which would then move the food
being airlifted directly into the center of the relief area.

The FMG, in an attempt to dismiss rumors of starvation
which the Dewey team had reported to Washington, escorted a
group of foreign journalists through the fallen enclave on
January 21. Although there were no massacres in evidence,
it was clear that relief to the area was woefully inadequate. Reports emanating up to that date from the enclave
area had generally seriously underrepresented the dimensions

of the problem. It was particularly explosive because the press had seen just enough during their escorted visit to realize how inadequate the relief effort was in the wartorn area. These press accounts increased the immediate humanitarian alarm being voiced in America.

The morning after the NSC team's new report had reached the State Department, Newsom and Ferguson, who by now were fully aware of the Western Report, were telling Kennedy's Senate Subcommittee Hearing on Refugees that the situation in Nigeria, although serious, was under control. The secret and classified messages of the entire week, however, had been leaked to the Senator. Kennedy proceeded to put these officials through an embarrassing session, exacting a full admission that conditions were worse than anticipated. Shockwaves of these explosive reports reached beyond the damage of public and congressional relations with the State Department.

The African Bureau fired off an immediate terse query to its Lagos Embassy: "First press ticker reports from newsmen who visited enclave (Reuters and AP) are lurid and depict widespread violence and chaos and starvation. We anticipate very strong press reaction here and demands for great disparity between situation as we have been depicting on basis observer reports and accounts now being filed by reporters. We need urgently new evidence and explanation that can be supplied to put situation in better perspective."[21]

Spurred by the reports of Dewey and Western and a copy of the verbatim congressional hearing, Nixon personally demanded that a special meeting be held in his office to find out what the State Department officials were actually doing in Nigerian foreign policy.[22] For all Nixon's apparent interest in the starving Nigerians, which was expressed in campaign statements, the Ferguson appointment, and secret mediation probes, the President's one and only meeting with State Department officials on Nigeria-Biafra was not held until January 20, 1970. At that meeting, Secretary Rogers, Ferguson, and Newsom offered Nixon optimistic outlooks for U.S.-Nigerian policy. As David Robinson recalled: "Before and after that meeting, the President was ranting and raving about the Department of State, they've let all those people die and they just (don't) care. But confronting the bureaucrats in his Executive Office Building hideaway, there was no fierce grilling by an outraged chief executive. Instead, Nixon was perfunctory and almost distracted, though he knew he was being misled.[23]

The White House was fighting to increase relief assistance because of the political and moral points it hoped to gain from the public; the State Department was fighting to limit further political intervention in Nigeria's domestic relief system because of diplomacy and pragmatic points in international affairs. The President, caught between these two powerful agencies and their conflicting policies, left it to others to convey to these in-fighting bureaucrats (State Department officials and the White House officials) his weakened concern for the starving in Nigeria.

Notes

1. U.S. State Department, A.I.D., "Country Field Submission FY 1969: Nigeria," p. 1 B.
2.   Robert S. Smith, Acting Administrator, U.S. State Department African Bureau, "Calabar-Ikom Road," Oct. 28, 1969, p. 3.
3. Daily Telegraph, May 15, 1969.
4. Peter Nichols, "The Pope Given Credit for Oilmen's Release," The (London) Times, July 9, 1969, p. 4.
5. C. W. Beal, "The Calabar-Ikom Road, An A.I.D. Project in Nigeria with Serious Military Implication," Nov. 21, 1969, p. 3. It is important to note that his report begins with this statement: "Whatever positions we may hold on the Vietnam war, we are all agreed that the United States should be especially careful in the future to avoid progressive entanglement in local conflicts which do not directly affect our national interest."
6. Roland Evans and Robert Novak, "AID Bureaucrats Going Full Speed against U.S. Neutrality on Nigeria," The Washington Post, Dec. 12, 1969.
7. Dec. 12, 1969, Congressional Record, 91st Cong., 1st sess., 115:38723.
8. Ibid.
9. Colonel Arthur Dewey, interview with author, New York City, New York, June 8, 1976.
10. National American Red Cross, General Records, Nov. 4, 1969. After checking their files, ARC did find that around 1963 the ARC participated in a transaction of a $100,000 U.S. donation to the Algerian Red Crescent without signing a contract.
11. Ibid., Nov. 17, 1969.
12. Ibid.
13. Dewey, interview with author.
14. Ferguson, like so many participants, has yet to fulfill his promise to publish his memoirs on the Nigerian/Biafran relief question.
15. Mauzy, "Bureaucracy and Linkage Politics," p. 150.
16. St. Jorre, The Brothers' War, 393.
17. Elizabeth Drew, "Reports: Washington," The Atlantic (June 1970): 26.
18. U.S. State Department, Transcript of Press and Radio News Briefing, Jan. 12, 1970.
19. Ibid., Jan. 14, 1970.
20.   U.S. State Department, "Remarks by the honorable Elliot L. Richardson, Undersecretary of State, to the Foreign Policy Conference for Editors and Broadcasters," Jan. 15, 1970.
21. Deptel 2365 to Lagos, Jan. 23, 1970.
22. As a matter of interest, during the entire 30 months of the Nigerian Civil War, the Nigerian Ambassador, despite his repeated requests, was never once received by the President of the United States. The Nixons were said to be very personally involved with the relief and yet they never once brought the Nigerian Ambassador, or any Biafran for that matter, into the public picture.
23. Mauzy, "Bureaucracy and Linkage Politics," p. 161.

9

Shroud of Silence

There were immediate State Department reactions to the presidential meeting. On January 21, Clyde Ferguson, who said
he had gained a new political and personal understanding of
both the Dewey and Western Reports of impending starvation
and death after seeing the President, without permission
usurped JCA-USA private property.[1]   He ordered the Chief of
the U.S. Air Force, via the U.S. Embassy in Geneva, to
direct Balair officials to fly as quickly as possible the
four JCA-USA C-97s from São Tomé to Cotonou, Dahomey. This
airfield in Dahomey was the base from which Balair had been
flying ICRC relief into Biafra. Balair officials, believing
that the American government completely controlled JCA-USA,[2]
accepted the Air Force instructions to move the C-97 planes.
Balair also gave instructions to the Israel Aircraft Indus-
tries to ready the C-97 completing service at Lod Airport in
Israel for its flight to Dahomey; presumably to carry additional relief supplies into eastern Nigeria. This was a
grandiose show of a potential U.S. relief operation to
appease those who might demand immediate action to ward off
impending famine disaster.
      JCA-USA officials exploded over the usurpation of their
property in peacetime by the military, but were unable to
change the <u>fait</u> <u>accompli</u>. However, the end of the war and
its air bridge turned these frustrations into a financial
silver lining. Kinney was able to cancel the JCA-USA contract with Balair Ltd. without impunity, inform Ferguson's
office that the disposition and removal of all C-97s from
Cotonou was now a U.S. expense and problem, and turn the
JCA-USA attention to the minor inconvenience of cleaning up
the Salazar Airport on São Tomé so that there would be absolutely no criticism from the Portuguese authorities. By May
1970, having returned all C-97 parts, engines, and scrap
from overseas to their point of origin in Georgia, Texas and
Arizona, JCA-USA slipped quietly into history.
      Although private groups could slip into silence, it was
not that easy for the government. David Newsom had reacted
to the President's meeting by cabling the U.S. Embassy in
Lagos to revise the tonnage estimates, with instructions to
bring Western's figures to the immediate attention of the

FMG. Noting that the new tonnage figures were at variance with Nigerian estimates, the State Department telegram emphasized that the Nigerian authorities may need to be persuaded to increase the relief food supply amounts. In a separate telegram message to Ambassador Edward Trueheart, Newsom expressed doubt that Yakubu Gowon realized the real gravity of the famine situation. Newsom cited Western's medical report and said a crash feeding program was needed to avoid massive death by starvation. He suggested that the existing FMG food plans were inadequate, as was truck transport, and that a major relief airlift was needed. Newsom also asked Trueheart to obtain a personal briefing with Gowon on the situation and to relay that information, as soon as possible, to other Nigerian officials.

Another State Department working group chaired by Elliot Richardson determined on the same evening of January 21 that the embassy staff should also approach the FMG ministers on the security and relief situation. The following day, acting on Roger Morris's recommendations of January 14, Richardson ordered the embassy to offer increased airlift assistance to the FMG, and increased emergency foods to the NRC. Still not trusting the U.S. Embassy reports from Lagos, Richardson --on the basis of the working group's proposal--decided on January 23 to send a member of his staff to consult with Trueheart in Lagos.

The volatile press accounts of Wednesday (January 21), plus Dewey's public comments, gave the public the last news flair of urgency to avert massive starvation. Journalists, debriefed by the U.S. Embassy staff, also called for more relief by testifying to the absence of relief food and medical teams in the stricken area as well as signs of great hunger. From the stricken area came still more reports of starvation and jammed roads. Dr. Lyle Conrad estimated on January 22 that 1 million people in Owerri required full feeding, recommending an immediate airlift somehow to the nonexistent Uli airstrip as the only way to save hundreds, thousands of lives. Although still extremely sensitive to outside criticism and maintaining the situation had been greatly distorted by irresponsible journalists, the FMG began to display some willingness to accept external aid.

Dewey, Trueheart, and U.S.A.I.D. officials Michael Adler and Edward Marks met with Nigeria's Minister of Economic Development and Rehabilitation, Allison Ayida, on January 22 to discuss U.S. assistance. The Americans outlined the U.S. willingness to support relief efforts to the greatest extent possible. Ayida discussed current needs and vigorously focused on elements considered top priorities. Later that same day Adler and Dewey, along with the ICRC's delegate to Lagos, met again with the Minister who said he wanted to use the entire ICRC fleet at Cotonou for an internal airlift from Lagos to Enugu and Port Harcourt, flying with NRC markings. He also told his visitors that he could use the two DC-6s the State Department had previously located in Iceland to begin flights immediately, adding that on the way down from Iceland the planes could bring in some high-protein stockfish. Ayida, however, noted that Nigeria had turned down a previous military airlift sponsored by Britain due to the clumsiness of announcement. While he was not optimistic

that the FMG's official position would change due to political and psychological problems, Ayida said such problems
could be minimized if the ICRC, JCA-USA and military markings on the aircraft were painted over and civilian, not
military flight plans were filed. Trueheart considered this
a major breakthrough, and cabled his optimistic belief to
Washington after the meeting.

The American response was quick.   Presidential Press
Secretary Ron Ziegler announced U.S. agreement at the White
House noon briefing and the State Department began arranging
for a charter operator, including those formally of JCA-USA
in Cotonou for backup and possible movement into Nigeria.
Over the expressed distaste of the U.S. Air Force, the C-97s
were painted a neutral color (although their shape continued
to be distinctive).   But the State Department again fell
into false optimism and told newsmen the following day that
two U.S.-supplied C-97s had begun operating in the internal
relief airlift, when in fact the empty planes had only been
testing the runways at Enugu and Port Harcourt and concluded
the airstrips could not handle fully laden Stratofreighters.

For almost two weeks after Biafra's fall, FMG authorities
were not fully appraised of the gruesome implications of the
only scientific survey of conditions inside the enclave.   On
the same day that Ferguson told the American public of the
magnitude of the problem, the Western Report was finally
carried to Nigerian officials in the Ministry of Health. Two
U.S. Public Health Service physicians, David J. Miller and
Stanley Foster, met with the Nigerian Chief Medical Adviser
to discuss the actual level of feeding needed versus political expectations. They stressed the necessity of imported
food per week; while NRC estimates called for 2,000 tons in
food imports with 1,000 to 2,000 tons of local purchases,
the a U.S. projection was for 5,000 to 10,000 tons weekly.
Although advised of the data, Trueheart reported that the
FMG could not be expected to change its estimates in favor
of Western's estimates, at least in part because Miller,
then Chief Medical Adviser to the NRC, supported NRC targets
and could not be expected to persuade NRC to accept the
estimates of Western.   Trueheart indicated to Washington
that he was opposed to pressing the FMG on the use of the
hoped-for airlift. However, the Nigerians upped their distribution target from 3,000 to 4,000 tons weekly (although
the target was never met), increasing threefold to fourfold
that week.

A special State Department official was sent to Lagos on
January 25 to brief Trueheart and his staff on the Western
Report and tonnage estimates. Trueheart accepted the implications, and when embassy staff began to argue statistical
validity he dismissed their arguments outright on the basis
that the report implications were just too clear-cut. As a
consequence of this meeting Trueheart was persuaded of the
importance of bringing Gowon and his FMG Ministers to understand Western's implications as soon as possible. Trueheart
took Western's report that day to Ayida.   Yet, despite
repeated efforts throughout the rest of the month, Trueheart
was unable to see Gowon.   Certain Nigerians, knowing he
wanted to argue the Western Report and the magnitude of the
relief problem, were determined he should not see Gowon.

Gowon finally circulated an announcement to all embassies on
February 2--obviously aimed at Trueheart--saying that for
the indefinite future he would be too busy to see diplomats.
Nigeria was simply not prepared to admit, on the basis of
evidence available to them, that the problem was anything
like the magnitude or urgency Western's report suggested. On
January 29 Trueheart reported completion of his briefings to
Nigerian officials--except Gowon--and that their reaction
was one of skepticism.

Arriving at Ikeja Airport the day Trueheart briefed Ayida
on Western's report was Claus Ruser, Richardson's assistant,
charged to "consult" with the U.S. Embassy.   Accompanying
Ruser was Col. Richard Kennedy from the NSC staff, and William Mithoefer of the State Department's INR Bureau.   Ruser
and Kennedy remained in Lagos one week (January 26 to February 1), sizing up the attitude of the U.S. Embassy staff and
the Nigerians toward the relief scene.   They reported that
one of the first impediments to the U.S. relief effort was
British High Commissioner Glass.   In an hour-long meeting
with Glass shortly after their arrival, Ruser and Kennedy
were subjected to a spirited defense of the view that food
requirements were not greater than before.   Glass also told
the Americans that he personally would not support a U.S.
demarche to Gowon.

Following this session, Ruser and Kennedy advised Washington that it was essential that maximum pressure be
brought to bear on the British, noting that the High Commissioner's general posture was at cross purposes with American
relief policy.   Glass successfully and substantially diminished whatever chances Trueheart's efforts might have had to
improve relief to the starving in Nigeria.   The British
position was seen as particularly vulnerable, as were the
FMG and Washington, due to more evidence of the grotesque
tragedy unfolding in former Biafra.   Conditions were bad all
over the former Biafran area and not confined to the Owerri
area (which was bad enough with the NRC reporting an 85 percent edema rate and increasing roadside death) as deliveries
to the zone fell "substantially short" of even the low NRC
estimates.

Ruser and Kennedy reported another major problem was the
American embassy staff, where the attitude seemed to be
"diplomatic business as usual."   The principal concern of
the embassy FSOs centered on improving relations with the
FMG, and they were reluctant to press their hosts on famine
numbers or relief needs.   Ruser and Kennedy suggested that
there was middle ground on which the embassy, using technical channels and discrete contacts, could bring the facts
before the Nigerians meaningfully and without involving
political pressures.   But given the basic inclination of the
embassy staffers, they would not to do anything that might
rub the Lagos regime the wrong way.   Trueheart and his staff
considered it essential for some time that the most urgent
need was to improve the information system of the relief
problem.

Everyone agreed by now that a new medical survey was
desirable: the FMG wanted their own legitimate information
and Trueheart weighed in for a new survey.   Arriving during
the last week of January was the U.S. contingent of the

joint American-Nigerian survey team. From the U.S. Public
Health Service came doctors Conrad, Philip Hopewell, and
Stanley Foster. The non-Public Health Service participants
included Dr. Michael Latham, who flew in from the Philip-
pines at the request of the White House, Dr. Davida Taylor,
who had been in Biafra the previous summer and was asked to
join the survey team by Richardson, and heading the group
was Dr. George Lythcott, a Columbia University nutritionist
and medical consultant to Ferguson.   On their arrival, the
team members were rushed through customs by the U.S.A.I.D.
staff, taken to a hotel, and told they would probably want
to rest a few days before going out. The physicians did not
want to tarry and immediately huddled to plot survey
strategy.   At a subsequent meeting with the U.S. Embassy
staff, repeated suggestions were made that the group relax
and enjoy Lagos for a few days and go out after the weekend.
Finally Kennedy rose and told the gathering that President
Nixon and Kissinger were waiting for this survey and they
should get it, quickly. There were no more suggestions of
delay from the embassy.
      Before leaving for the disaster area the doctors met
with three embassy officers who had toured the area and had
reported on the conditions they saw to Washington, saying
there were no great flocks of vultures or piles of bodies to
be seen and the children were nice and fat. After questioning the officers at length an urgent cable was fired off by
the survey team to Washington to counter the report that was
filed by these embassy officials. The survey team's cable
stated that the previous official report had no medical sig-
nificance and should not be used therefore as basis for
assessing condition of population, food needs, or tonnages
of relief supplies required.
      Just before the team was to enter the field, Miller, who
was not chosen to be part of the survey team, said he felt
compelled to protect the U.S. Public Health Service organization from possible Nigerian wrath, and so he informed the
FMG that Taylor had worked in secessionist Biafra.   Trueheart was reportedly furious with Miller's disclosure. When
Trueheart was told by the FMG on Friday, January 30, that
Taylor was an unacceptable team member, there was no choice
but to drive her to Ikeja for a plane out of Nigeria.
      The survey went forward, though, coming out with about
the same results as Western's October survey. Using similar
methods and measuring a different population, the study
found more than 1 million people suffering from edema, of
which about 700,000 were children. As a result, the NRC
announced that it was reversing its relief tonnages downward
from 4,200 tons weekly for 3.1 million victims to 3,640 tons
for an estimated 2.2 million in need. Although the shocked
American team regarded these estimates as too low they did
not press the FMG for an upward revision, fearing to endanger acceptance of other valid portions of the report.   A
shroud of silence was once again thrown over a human
tragedy.
      Jim Hoagland prophetically wrote in the Washington Post
that "the Nigerian relief program continues to be crippled
by politics, bureaucracy, and complacency."[3]   By early
February relief food and medicines began to appear in

increasing quantities in the heart of what once had been
Biafra. But it was not enough. Even Ferguson, in a CBS
interview, admitted that compared to other major famines
--the Netherlands in 1945 or Leningrad--this was about three
times as large as ever faced by any government anywhere.

In a series of meeting on April 8, 1970, Ferguson, John
Foley, and James Pope met separately with CRS-USCC (representing the defunct JCA-USA) and Balair officials to iron
out any final difficulties.[4] After sorting out technical
and financial matters, Captain Herzog of Balair was willing
to go on record when he told Ferguson, "I will keep in close
contact with you. There might be an airlift between Uganda
and a certain part of Sudan."[5] When Jean Chenard of CRS-
USCC was broached with the future possibility of another
joint venture in Africa, he let it be known that CRS was not
involved in present efforts to aid Southern Sudanese refugees. The Verona Fathers, formerly based in Southern Sudan,
were "pretty well in control" of relief in the Sudan.   He
went on to say that CRS-USCC would look into the question of
relief airlift to the area. The experience of the relief
feeding programs in Nigeria and Biafra were to link several
humanitarian groups to Africa's future famine.

Meanwhile, feeding the famine-ridden population in the
recently won area and in territory long-captured by the FMG
failed to reach the goals set by the United States for April
1970, with an average of only 50 percent of those estimated
in need receiving but 49 percent of planned rations.   Meanwhile, the FMG shifted its emphasis from emergency relief to
long-term rehabilitation, prompting Richardson to cable
Trueheart in Lagos in early April to express high-level concern over dangerously low stockpiles. It was estimated that
without additional food shipments, relief stockpiles would
be depleted by May.

The former FMG stiffness, which outright refused foreign
assistance in the aftermath of victory, eventually loosen up
and relief-laden American and British planes and trucks were
allowed to enter into Nigeria without fanfare, although they
did not reach their targets easily.   Planes were assessed
normal landing fees in excess of $400, and the trucks they
carried often sat for weeks on the Lagos docks while the
bureaucrats went through standard paperwork, especially the
bills for the standard licensing fees. At the same time,
Nigerian businesspeople rented their trucks to the relief
effort for a profit. Information from the devastated areas
became very scarce. Without independent sources of relief
information, humanitarian groups could not continue their
pressure on the U.S. government or Nigeria.

The State Department prepared an updated breakdown of
financial commitments to the Nigerian relief effort on May
12, 1970. This rare five-page (now declassified) document,
signed by Secretary William Rogers, shows how important the
U.S. resources had been to the relief effort.[6] The worldwide relief contributions during and after the conflict was
a grand total of $251 million, of which the U.S. public and
private donations amounted to $112 million (44.6 percent).
However, even this justifiably proud record was buried away
from the public domain of information for fear it might disrupt U.S.-Nigeria relations.[7]

Only the U.S. government had the resources on the scale
necessary to combat the magnitude of the suffering and starvation in Nigeria and Biafra (see Table 9.1). Based on the
U.S. relief contributions of $72.3 million during the war,
the private sector gave 21 percent of the total donations.
Although this relief contribution was only 9 percent of the
worldwide contributions, if the American humanitarian groups
had not become involved and had not insisted that the American government ignore the premise that politics and relief
were inseparable, the United States would have never felt
that such relief actions should have been undertaken.   The
certain and inevitable increased starvation in Nigeria and
Biafra would have staggered the human mind.

In August, seven months after the fighting stopped, a
U.S. Public Health Service doctor reported that there was a
continuing requirement to feed 850,000 persons in the East
Central State. This was because the relief distribution in
July had been less than one-third the amount required. There
was a continuing occurrence of new malnutrition cases and
unresolved distribution problems of necessary food to the
starving population.

Taken singularly, the curtailment of the American relief
effort in the Nigerian civil war seemed at the time minimal
and all to quickly forgotten by the public. But the recent
civil wars in Africa, combined with the drought, form a pattern of neglect and inertia--a policy of man-made calamities
which inevitably take a high toll in human lives.

Table 9.1. Total Contributions to Nigeria/Biafra Relief,
            May 1970

Source	Contribution	Percent	Aid per Person[a]
U.S. Public	$ 57.3	34	0.287
U.S. Private	15.0	9	0.075
Subtotal	72.3	43	0.363
Other Nations[b]	94.0	57	0.546
Total	**$166.3**	**100**	**0.448**

[a]Population in millions: United States = 199; other nations
   = 172.2.
[b]West Germany, Norway, Sweden, Netherlands, England, Canada,
   Switzerland, Denmark, Ireland. The Netherlands and
   Canadian governments reneged on a portion of their
   pledges to relief groups after the war.

Source: U.S. State Department, Nigeria Relief Assistance A-1082, May 12, 1970, pp. 1-5.

Notes

1. Joint Church Aid-USA, Report to the Trustee-Directors, Mar. 30, 1971, p. 3 confirms this fact: "Time and time again it was emphasized that, having appropriated the aircraft illegally, the responsibility for their return Stateside was that of OACNR/Balair. Since no bills covering such costs were ever received by JCA-USA, and since JCA-USA secured a release from all authorities concerned, it is obvious that the point was made."

2. Because JCA-USA exercised far more control over their relief activity than ICRC, which had been forced to delegated authority to the American approved Balair Ltd., and because Balair had only been under contract with JCA-USA since November 2, 1969, it was inevitable in the pressure situation which the end of the Nigerian civil war presented to Balair officials that they revert to their past experience with the ICRC wherein the United States did contribute and control most of the relief supply operations.

3. Jim Hoagland, "Nigerian Red Tape Slowing Food Lift," Washington Post, Jan. 31, 1970.

4. James Pope, interview with author, Washington, D.C., April 6, 1976. Pope was the Public Relations officer for Ferguson's U/CF team.

5. U.S. State Department, U/CF, "Memorandum of Conversation," Apr. 8, 1970, p. 1.

6. It has been next to impossible to obtain records, documents, or interviews for this time period, as testified to by the scarcity of notes in the last two chapters. A case in point: no State Department record on this period was ever sent to Central Files. Instead, the records were kept in a specially sealed filing cabinet in the African Bureau office. The same can be said of the White House files. Were it not for the partial courage of several individuals who requested confidentiality, even this brief recounting of the ending the American involvement in the Nigerian tragedy would not have been possible.

7. U.S.A.I.D., "Country Field Submission FY 1972-Nigeria," July 1970, pp. 4-5. "Despite continuing resentment over U.S. refusal of outright support during the civil war and over our initial actions in the relief area after the war, we believe that the outlook or U.S./Nigerian relations is basically good."

Epilogue

The Biafran famine elicited an unusually profound humanitarian crisis in America. The two complicating dimensions of this crisis were the argument that Biafra's right to self-determination was an humanitarian one, and the argument that the FMG was perpetrating genocide on the Ibos through the blockage of relief. Relief operations for Biafra, largely in violation of Nigerian airspace and its blockade, were undertaken and justified in the name of humanitarianism. Because the issue was complex it was possible to argue on moral grounds rather than on legal grounds--sovereignty was overridden when human life was at sake. Yet, despite these assertions, the relief was at the core of the political controversy, especially those of the JCA-USA.

All governments, however, will resist humanitarian intervention if that involvement is seen to jeopardize the government's political interest or survival. Similarly, if the government finds the humanitarian involvement converging with its political concerns, then the intervention will receive greater support. For humanitarian activity to succeed, therefore, they must find convergence between their needs and the government's political needs. As so often happens in reality, it is difficult to assess the motivational mix behind each and every action; but acts may be humanitarian even if politically motivated.

JCA-USA was able to meet the political needs of the White House and Congress, but not those of the Defense or State departments. At the root of these political and bureaucratic struggles were the different conceptions about the requisites for international peace and security on the one hand, and international justice on the other hand. Yet it would be an oversimplification (and wrong) to say that the departments preferred stability over justice, while the White House and Congress responded to the public's preference for the reverse. It might be more accurate to say that the former considers stability through technological mechanics (e.g., logistics and statistics) as a requisite for humanitarian activity, while the later considers the humanitarian process to be a requisite for peace and security. Needless to say, it is not yet possible to provide a set of objective and generally agreed on criteria against which to judge this or any human case of alleged humanitarian intervention. But some judgment, however subjective, is necessary to eventually establish principles that will lead humankind to a stable and just society.

Lessons learned from American policy toward the Biafran famine have not been implemented in recent African disasters caused by civil war. Photographs of emaciated Biafrans, Nigerians, Ethiopians, Sudanese—and most likely other peoples in the future—lead many to conclude that the cause of the starvation is lack of food. The real culprit is most often the civil war raging between the existing government and rebel forces; both seeking international legitimacy to control the political, economic, religious, and cultural way of life within arbitrarily drawn boundaries.[1] The humanitarian challenge in each crisis is to bring the combatants and other governments to examine the following: "A moral question: How can children, women and men be allowed to starve, as in the Sudan today, when food is available in the country and there is no drought? The answer is sovereignty. Food is being used as a weapon by both sides in a devastating civil war."[2] Unfortunately, because explanations must be left to another day, contemporary African famine has yet to stir American humanitarian involvement to the same degree as that of the Nigerian Civil War.

This book has presented a unique human story where the political and humanitarian needs converged at certain points but at others they did not. The humanitarian response to the Biafran famine, however, demonstrates that America and Americans can be moved to action through the generation of a moral issue.

Notes

1. After the Nigerian civil war, Gowon wrote a confidential letter to President Yahy Khan of Pakistan warning him to on no account allow the voluntary relief agencies into East Pakistan if the leader wished to keep control over the conflict. Morris Davis, Civil Wars and the Politics of International Relief: Africa, South Asia, and the Caribbean (N.Y.: Praeger, 1975), 85.
2. Peter Davies, "Paradox of Humanitarian Assistance: When Food Is a Weapon, Those in Need Will Starve," Los Angeles Times, Nov. 9, 1988, p. 11.

Bibliographic Essay

Primary Sources

The Republic of Biafra publications came from their (Enugu) Ministry of Information, in particular <u>January 15: Before and After</u>, Vol. 7 (1967); <u>Meeting of the Nigerian Military Leaders Held in Aburi, Ghana</u> (1967); <u>Nigerian Crisis 1966</u>, Vols. 1-7 (1967); <u>Republic of Biafra: Vital Facts</u> (1968); <u>Ahiara Declaration: Principles of the Biafran Revolution, June 1, 1969</u> (1969); and their highly controversial official statements in the <u>Markpress</u> editions of <u>Press Actions</u>, Vols. 1-3 (February 2, 1968-December 31, 1969).

The Federal Military Government of Nigeria published their views through the Lagos National Ministry of Information, in particular <u>Nigeria 1966</u> (1966); <u>Nigeria: Guide to the National Military Government</u> (1966); <u>Meeting of the Nigerian Military Leaders, Held at Dedause Lodge, Aburi, Ghana</u> (1967); <u>Framework for Settlement: The Federal Case in Kampala</u> (1968); <u>The Secessionist Regime and the Non-Ibo "Minorities" in the East of Nigeria</u> (1968); <u>I Believe in One Nigeria-Zik</u> (1969); <u>Ibos in a United Nigeria</u> (1969); and <u>Our Aim-Rehabilitation, Reconstruction, Reconciliation</u> (1969).

The official record of the British House of Parliament are found in <u>Hansard</u>, 1966-1970. Speeches at the United Nations are found in <u>Verbatim Records</u>. Special interest should be given the <u>Interim Reports by the Representatives of the Secretary-General of the United Nations</u>, First (October 9, 1968), Second (October 30, 1968), Third (December 10, 1968), Fourth (January 17, 1969), Fifth (May 16, 1969), and Final (February 14, 1970); and the periodic U.N. <u>Reports on Activities</u> signed by representatives of Canada, Britain, Sweden, and Poland.

The U.S. <u>Congressional Record</u>, Vols. 113-116 (1967-1970) present the officially accepted version of statements by Senators and Congressmen on the Nigerian Civil War. Several original verbatim <u>Congressional Record</u> statements, which were later expunged from the final official version, may be found among Nigeria/Biafra Clearing House Papers, Swarthmore College Peace Collection, Swarthmore, Pennsylvania. Other relevant congressional information may be found in committee and subcommittee records, such as the <u>Report of Special</u>

<u>Fact-Finding Mission to Nigeria</u> (February 7-20, 1969) submitted by Congressmen Charles Diggs and Herbert Burke, and the <u>Report of the Biafra Study Mission</u> (September 25, 1969) by Senator Charles Goodell. Testimonies by other government officials, involved groups and individuals are found in <u>Congressional Committee Hearings</u>, for example, <u>Testimony of the Honorable Elliot L. Richardson Under Secretary of State: Hearing before the Subcommittee on Refugees of the Senate Judiciary Committee</u> (July 15, 1969), and <u>Testimony of the Honorable C. Clyde Ferguson, Jr., Special Coordinator on Nigerian Relief: Hearing before the Subcommittee on Refugees of the Senate Judiciary Committee</u> (January 21, 1970).

The U.S. State Department <u>Biographical Record</u>, <u>Bulletin</u>, <u>News Letter</u>, and <u>Statements of the United States Government on the Problem of Nigeria</u>, give the public domain a vague and often misleading description of their record in the Nigerian crisis between 1966 and 1970. Other sources of general policy analysis for this case study are found in the U.S. Agency for International Development (U.S.A.I.D.) Foreign Disaster Relief Report Reprint <u>Emergency Relief in Nigeria and the Biafran Enclave, July 1967 through June 30, 1969</u>; <u>Nigeria Relief Problem</u> series (December 13, 1968-January 15, 1970); <u>Nigeria-Disaster Emergency Relief Report</u> series from the Office of Private Resources/Voluntary Agencies Division, and their <u>Post-War Nigeria Relief: Food Stocks/Distribution</u> (February 25, 1970); the improvised data in the 1968 <u>Disaster Memos: Nigeria-Civil Strife</u>, Number One (June 24), Number Two (July 24), Number Three (August 7), Number Four (August 12), Number Five (August 19), Number Six (September 3), Number Seven (September 8), Number Eight (September 30), Number Nine (October 29), and Number Ten (November 25); and individual statements by State Department officials such as the "Address by the Honorable Nicholas De B. Katzenbach Under Secretary of State at Brown University," Providence, Rhode Island (December 3, 1968) and the "Remarks by the Honorable C. Clyde Ferguson, Jr., Special Coordinator on Relief to Civilian Victims of the Nigerian Civil War, Lagos" (March 25, 1969).

Government records that give more policy formation detail are to be found in the declassified U.S. Embassy documents (especially from Lagos) sent to Washington as annual "Country Field Submission FY 1966-Nigeria," "FY 1967," "FY 1968," "FY 1969," "FY 1970," "FY 1971," and "FY 1972"; the periodic documents from the field such as the <u>Politico-Economic Relations with Communist Countries-Nigeria</u>, Parts I, II (A-693 May 14, 1965 and A-708 May 21, 1965), and "Nigeria Relief Assistance" (A-1082 May 12, 1970). Additional description of policy decisions and their concomitant action are found in the declassified U.S. airgrams and telegrams between the State Department and the involved U.S. Embassies; as the "Memorandum of Telephone Conversation with AID's General Council's Office on August 9, 1968" sent to Howard Kresge, PRR/PRDS/VAD (August 15, 1968), the "Summary of Meeting on Contingency Planning on Nigeria Relief" presented by Clyde Ferguson in Washington on Wednesday (May 7, 1969), the "Nigerian Relief Assistance, Airgram A-1082" (May 12, 1970), and the undated "Calabar-Ikom Road Memo" authored by Robert Smith, Acting AA/AFR.

Personal and unofficial assessment of policy by American bureaucrats were useful as a backup check for interviews and confidential information.   For example, one of the central actors in the relief efforts was Robert Smith, State Department Officer-In-Charge of Nigerian Affairs, whose article, "U.S. Policy Toward the Nigerian Civil War," expressed very important personal opinions. Another important unofficial source was Richard Mauzy's M.A. thesis, "Bureaucracy and Linkage Politics: the United States and the Tragedy of Biafra" (1978) because he worked closely with Roger Morris at the Carnegie Endowment for International Peace. Morris took many of the relevant classified documents with him when he left his National Security Council post (this was during the Watergate period), and shared them with Mauzy.   Other personal assessments are by the State Department Country Director for West Africa, Roy Melbourne, in "The American Response to the Nigerian Conflict, 1968," <u>African Studies Association, Issue 2</u> 3, no. 2 (Summer 1973): 33-42, and Senator Charles Goodell's "Biafra and the American Conscience," <u>Saturday Review</u> 52 (April 12, 1969): 24-27.

Another important source of policy decision documentation between 1968 and 1970 is found in the private, public, and international relief organizations archives and in the Nigeria/Biafra Clearing House Papers, Swarthmore College Peace Collection.   These files hold records relating to the American Committee to Keep Biafra Alive press releases in New York City; Africa Concern and Joint Biafra Famine Appeal press releases in Dublin, Ireland; the American Jewish Committee press releases in New York City; American National Red Cross <u>General Records, Nigerian Civil War</u> in Washington, D.C.; Catholic Relief Services-USCC news releases and <u>Quarterly Information Bulletin</u> in New York City; Church World Service press releases in New York City; International Committee of the Red Cross "Annual Report," <u>Handbook</u>, press releases, and their <u>International Review of the Red Cross</u>, nos. 82-141 in Geneva, Switzerland; Peat, Marwich, Mitchell and Co., <u>International Committee of the Red Cross: Report on Relief Operations in Nigeria</u> (Geneva: ICRC, July 1, 1970); Joint Church Aid, International, "Summary of the Conclusions, Recommendations and Actions Taken at the Meeting of the JCA Executive Working Group, August 12/14, 1969," and press releases in Geneva; Joint Church Aid-USA "Annual Report," <u>Progress Reports and Financial Statements</u>, <u>Report to the Trustee-Directors</u> (March 30, 1971) in New York City, and the confidential <u>History of Joint Church Aid</u>, Vols. 1-3, by John A Daly, C.S.Sp. and Anthony G. Saville; Leagues of Red Cross Societies "Annual Report" in Geneva; the United Nations press releases and High Commissioner for Refugees <u>Bulletin</u> in New York City; and the World Council of Churches press releases in Geneva.

Those who allowed their interviews to be recorded for public documentation are listed here with gratitude, Holy Rosary Sister Holly Cherney (member of the Clearing House for Nigeria/Biafra Information), Colonel Arthur Dewey, Holy Ghost Father Dermot Doran, Ambassador C. Clyde Ferguson, CRS-USCC Executive Director Edward Kinney, National American Red Cross Director Robert Martin, Ambassador Elbert Mathews, Ambassador Thomas Melady, National Security Council African

Specialist Roger Morris, Bishop Godfrey Okoye, C.S.Sp., of
Port Harcourt, Ambassador Joseph Palmer, II, Special Coordi-
nator for Nigeria and Biafra Relief Public Relations Officer
James Pope, African-American Director Ronald Springwater,
Ambassador Edward Trueheart, and State Department Nigerian
Desk Officer John Wilson.

Secondary Sources

Two historical books covering this case study merit special
mention: Suzanne Cronjé, The World and Nigeria: The Diplomatic History of the Biafran War 1967-1970 (London: Sidgwick
and Jackson, 1972); and John de St. Jorre, The Brothers'
War: Biafra and Nigeria (Boston: Houghton Mifflin, 1972).
     Several important bibliographical references for the
Nigerian conflict are George Affia, Nigerian Crisis, 1966-
1970: A Preliminary Bibliography (Lagos: University of
Lagos, 1970); Carolyn K. Colwell, Biafra: A Chronology of
Developments Attending the Secession of the Eastern Region
of Nigeria, January 15, 1966-January 12, 1970 (Washington,
DC: Library of Congress Legislative Reference Service,
1970); A.H.M. Kirk-Greene, Crisis and Conflict in Nigeria: A
Documentary Source Book, 1966-1970, 2 vols. (London: Oxford
University Press, 1971); and the extensive "Footnotes to the
Text" and "Bibliography" (pp. 612-788) in Laurie Wiseberg's
Ph.D. thesis, The International Politics of Relief: A Case
Study of the Relief Operations Mounted During the Nigerian
Civil War (1967-1970) (Ann Arbor, Mich.: Xerox University
Microfilms, 1975).
     Some general sources that give an excellent background on
Nigeria: Okoi Arikpo, Development of Modern Nigeria (Balti-
more, Md.: Penguin Books, 1967); Obafemi Awolowo, Thoughts
on the Nigerian Constitution (London: Oxford University
Press, 1966); E. A. Ayandele, The Missionary Impact on Mod-
ern Nigeria, 1842-1914 (New York: Humanities Press, 1967);
Sir A. T. Balewa Nigeria Speaks: Speeches Made Between 1957-
1964 (Ikeja: Longmans, 1964); H. L. Bretton, Power and
Stability in Nigeria (New York: Praeger, 1962); James Cole-
man, Nigeria: Background to Nationalism (Berkeley, Calif.:
University of California Press, 1958); Thomas Hodgkin, Nige-
rian Perspectives (London: Oxford University Press, 1960);
Claude S. Phillips, Jr., The Development of Nigerian Foreign
Policy (Evanston, Ill.: Northwestern University Press,
1964); Frederick Schwarz, Jr., Nigeria: The Tribes, the
Nation and the Race: The Politics of Independence (Cambridge, Mass.: M.I.T. Press, 1965); Richard Sklar, Nigerian
Political Parties (Princeton, N. J.: Princeton University
Press, 1963); and C. S. Whitaker, Jr., The Politics of Tradition: Continuity and Change in Northern Nigeria (Princeton, N.J.: Princeton University Press, 1970).
     More relevant analysis of the Nigerian crisis is found
in the works of: Nietyong Akpan, The Struggle for Secession,
1966-1970 (London: Frank Cass, 1971); Nnamdi Azikiwe, "Les
origines de la guerre civile au Nigeria," Revue Française
d'études politiques Africaines no. 49 (January 1970): 44-55;
Ross Baker, "The Emergence of Biafra: Balkanization or

Nation-Building," Orbis 12, no. 2 (Summer 1968): 518-533; Ola Balogum, "La question de l'auto-determination et la guerre civile au Nigeria," Revue Française d'études politiques Africaines no. 49 (January 1970): 40-43; Lindsay Barrett, "The Nigerian Crisis: An Arena for Africa's Struggle for Self-Determination," Negro Digest 1 (October 1969): 11-15, 65-67; Zdenek Cervenka, The Nigerian War, 1967-1970 (Frankfurt am Main: Bernard & Graefe Verian Fur Wehrwesen, 1971); Robin Cohen, A Greater South: Or What Might Have Happened in the Nigerian Civil War (Birmingham, U.K.: University of Birmingham, 1971); Stanley Diamond, Nigeria: Model of a Colonial Failure (New York: American Committee on Africa, 1967); Frederick Forsyth, The Biafra Story (Baltimore, Md.: Penguin Books, 1969); John Hatch, Nigeria: Seeds of Disaster (London: Henry Regnery, 1970); Thierry Hentsch, Face au blocs: La Croix-Rouge Internationale dans le Nigeria en guerre (1967-1970) (Geneva: Institute Universitaire de Hautes Études Internationales, 1973); Jean Herskovits, "Nigeria: Africa's New Power," Foreign Affairs 53, no.2 (January 1975): 314-333; George Knapp, Aspects of the Biafran Affair: A Study of British Attitudes and Policy Towards the Nigerian-Biafran Conflict (London: Britain-Biafra Association, 1968); S. G. Ikoku, "La sucession Biafraise: mythes et realities," Revue Française d'études politiques Africaines no. 49 (January 1970): 56-64; Hugh Lloyd, Mona Mollerup, and Carl Bratved, The Nordchurchaid Airlift to Biafra, 1968-1970 (Copenhagen: Folkenkirkens Nodhjaelp, 1972); Robin Luckham, The Nigerian Military: A Sociological Analysis of Authority and Revolt, 1960-1967 (London: Cambridge University Press, 1971); Joseph Okpaku, Nigeria: Dilemma of Nationhood: An African Analysis of the Biafran Conflict (New York: The Third Press, 1972); Alain Murcier, "Petrole et guerre an Nigeria," Revue Française d'études politiques Africaines no. 47 (November 1969): 51-60; Sir Cecil Rex Niven, The War of Nigerian Unity, 1967-1970 (Totowa, N.J.: Rowan and Littlefield, 1971); Arthur Nwankwo and Samuel Ifejika, Biafra: The Making of a Nation (New York: Praeger, 1969); Julius Nyerere, "Why Tanzania Recognized Biafra," Africa Report 13, no. 6 (June 6, 1968): 27; Odumegwa Ojukwu, Biafra: Selected Speeches and Random Thoughts (New York: Harper & Row, 1969); Joseph Okpaku, Nigeria: Dilemma of Nationhood: An African Analysis of the Biafran Conflict (New York: The Third Press, 1972); George Orick, "Nigeria: A Study of Hypocrisy," The New Leader (January 1, 1968): 7-11; John Oyinbo, Nigeria: Crisis and Beyond (London: Charles Knight & Co., Ltd, 1971); S. K. Panter-Brick, ed., Nigerian Political and Military Rule: Prelude to Civil War (London: Athlone Press, 1970); Scott Pearson, Petroleum and the Nigerian Economy (Stanford, Calif.: Stanford University Press, 1970); Sayre Schatz, "A Look At the Balance Sheet: Petroleum Smooths the Way for the Economy's Recovery from the Effects of the War, But What About the Future?" Africa Report (January 1970): 18-21; L. H. Schatzl, Petroleum in Nigeria (Ibadan: Oxford University Press, 1969); Ralph Uwechue, Reflections on the Nigerian Civil War: Facing the Future (New York: Africana Publishing Corp., 1971); and Auberon Waugh and Suzanne Cronjé, Biafra: Britain's Shame (London: Michael Joseph, 1969).

Admittedly highly selective, the American policy forma-
tion perspective is presented in the following references:
Graham T. Allison, <u>Essence of Decision: Explaining the Cuban
Missile Crisis</u> (Boston: Little, Brown, 1971); Lee Auspitz,
"Anatomy of a Bloody Mess: Biafra and the Bureaucrats,"
<u>Ripon Forum</u> 5, no. 2 (February 1969):5-11; Christopher Beal,
"How the State Department Watched Biafra Starve, <u>Ripon Forum</u>
6, no. 3 (March 1970): 8-12, 17-19; Beverly May Carl, "Amer-
ican Assistance to Victims of the Nigeria-Biafra War:Defects
in the Prescriptions on Foreign Disaster Relief," <u>Harvard
International Law Journal</u> 12, no. 2 (Spring 1971): 191-259;
Edward Chester, <u>Clash of Titans: Africa and United States
Foreign Policy</u> (New York: Orbis Books, 1973); David Howard
Davis, <u>How the Bureaucracy Makes Foreign Policy: An Exchange
Analysis</u> (Toronto: Lexington Books, 1972); John A. Davis,
"Black Americans and United States Policy Toward Africa,"
<u>International Affairs</u> 23, no. 2 (1969): 236-249; Morris
Davis, "Audits of International Relief in the Nigerian Civil
War: Some Political Perspectives," <u>International Organiza-
tion</u> 29, no. 2 (Spring 1975): 501-512, and "The Structuring
of International Communications About the Nigeria-Biafra
War," <u>Peace Research Society, Papers 18</u> (London: The London
Conference, 1971), 61-72; I. M. Destler, <u>Presidents, Bureau-
crats, and Foreign Policy: The Politics of Organizational
Reform</u> (Princeton, N.J.: Princeton University Press, 1972);
John H. Esterline and Robert B. Black, <u>Inside Foreign Policy: The Department of State Political System and Its Sub-
systems</u> (Calif.: Mayfield, 1975); Melvin Gurtov, <u>The United
States against the Third World: Antinationalism and Inter-
vention</u> (New York: Praeger, 1974); Theresa Hayter, <u>Aid as
Imperialism</u> (London: Penguin Books, 1971); Samuel Hunting-
ton, "Foreign Aid for What and for Whom?" <u>Foreign Policy</u> 1,
no. 1 (Winter 1970): 161-189; Richard Lillich, "Intervention
to Protect Human Rights," <u>McGill Law Journal</u> 15, no. 2 (June
1969): 205-219; Roger Morris and Hal Sheets, <u>Disaster in the
Desert: Failures of International Relief in the West African
Drought</u> (Washington, D.C.: Humanitarian Policy Studies,
1974); George Mudge, "Starvation as a Means of Warfare,"
<u>International Lawyer</u> 4, no. 2 (1970): 232-272; Harold Nel-
son, James McLaughlin, Barbara Marvin, Philip Moeller, and
Donald Whitaker, <u>Area Handbook for Nigeria</u> (Washington,D.C.:
U.S. Government Printing Office, 1972); Berkeley Rice, "The
Cold-War College Think Tanks," <u>Washington Monthly</u> (June
1969): 22-34; William Rogers, "A Post-Mortem on Biafra,"
<u>Ripon Forum</u> 6, no. 5 (May 1970): 3-11; Esbjoin Rosenblad,
"Starvation as a Method of Warfare," <u>International Lawyer</u> 7,
no. 2 (1974): 253-270; Karen Rothmyer, "What Really Happened
in Biafra?" <u>Columbia Journalism Review</u> 9, no. 3 (Fall 1970):
43-47; Francis Russell, "Formulating Foreign Policy," <u>Orbis</u>
17, no. 4 (Winter 1974): 1344-1353; Richard Sklar, "The
United States and the Biafran War," <u>Africa Report</u> 14, no. 8
(November 1969): 22-23; Audrey Smock, "The Politics of
Relief," <u>Africa Report</u> 15, no. 1 (January 1970): 24-26;
Richard Snyder, H. W. Bruck, and B. Sapin, <u>Foreign Policy
Decision-Making</u> (New York: The Free Press, 1962); Karl
Vasak, "National, Regional and Universal Institutions for
the Promotion and Protection of Human Rights," <u>Human Rights
Journal</u> 1, no. 2 (1968): 179; Immanuel Wallerstein, "From

Nixon to Nixon: Is America's Outmoded Policy Towards a Changing Africa about to Cross a New Frontier?" <u>Africa Report</u> (November 1969): 28-30; Ronald Walters, <u>The Formulation of United States Foreign Policy Toward Africa, 1958-1963</u> (Ann Arbor, Mich.: Xerox University Microfilms, 1971); and Stephen Weissman, <u>American Foreign Policy in the Congo, 1960-1964</u> (Ithaca, N.Y.: Cornell University Press, 1974).

Finally, extensive use was also made of the following newspapers, magazines and journals issued between 1966 and 1970; <u>Christian Science Monitor</u>, <u>Daily Telegraph</u>, <u>The Economist</u>, <u>Evening Herald</u>, <u>Guardian</u>, (Dublin) <u>Irish Press</u>, <u>Independent</u>, <u>Jeune Afrique</u>, <u>The (London) Times</u>, <u>Le Monde</u>, <u>The New York Post</u>, <u>The New York Times</u>, <u>Observer</u>, <u>West Africa</u>, and the <u>Washington Post</u>.

Index

About the Author

JOSEPH E. THOMPSON is Associate Professor of Political Science at Villanova University. He has been a contributor to many books, among them *Northern Ireland: Living with the Crisis* (Praeger Publishers, 1983), and *Irish American Voluntary Organizations* (Greenwood Press). He was involved in a research trip to Nigeria in 1977 and is a former Scholar-Diplomat in the State Department African Program on the Nigeria Desk, 1975 and 1977.